The
Small Business
Legal Advisor

Other McGraw-Hill Titles for the Small Business Audience

Stephen C. Harper
THE McGRAW-HILL GUIDE TO STARTING YOUR OWN BUSINESS

Jeffrey L. Seglin
FINANCING YOUR SMALL BUSINESS

J. K. Lasser Tax Institute
HOW TO RUN A SMALL BUSINESS

The Small Business Legal Advisor

William A. Hancock

Second Edition

McGraw-Hill, Inc.
New York   St. Louis   San Francisco   Auckland   Bogotá
Caracas   Lisbon   London   Madrid   Mexico   Milan
Montreal   New Delhi   Paris   San Juan   São Paulo
Singapore   Sydney   Tokyo   Toronto

Library of Congress Cataloging-in-Publication Data

Hancock, William A.
    The small business legal advisor / William A. Hancock. — 2nd ed.
        p.   cm.
    Includes index.
    ISBN 0-07-026003-6 :   — ISBN 0-07-026002-8 (pbk.) :
    1. Small business—Law and legislation—United States. I. Title.
KF1659.H36   1992
346.73'0652—dc20
[347.306652]   91-25193
                                                        CIP

1 2 3 4 5 6 7 8 9 0   DOC/DOC   9 7 6 5 4 3 2 1

ISBN   0-07-026003-6   {HC}
ISBN   0-07-026002-8   {PBK}

The sponsoring editor for this book was James H. Bessent, Jr., the editing supervisor was Fred Dahl, and the production supervisor was Suzanne W. Babeuf. It was set in Baskerville by McGraw-Hill's Professional Book Group composition unit.

Printed and bound by R. R. Donnelley & Sons Company.

Contents

Preface

Although there are substantial changes in this second edition of *Small Business Legal Advisor*, the overall intent has not changed. It is to provide businesspeople with a convenient and inexpensive way to have a "conversation" with a lawyer about some important legal aspects of starting and running a small business. It's designed to be an informal chat and definitely not a substitute for specific legal advice.

To start, let me say a little about my credentials. After graduating from law school in 1966, I spent four years with a small corporate law firm, during which time I assisted in providing legal advice to a wide spectrum of small businesses. In 1970 I left private practice to join TRW Inc. as a member of their legal staff. After ten years at TRW, I left to devote full time to my writing and publishing activities. I formed a small company called Business Laws, Inc. We publish legal newsletters and reference books for corporate lawyers.

It is on the basis of this experience that I offer my perspectives on how to avoid some of the legal difficulties I have seen others encounter. As a businessman, I am well aware that the last thing you want to spend your time on is legal matters. We would all like to run our businesses free of disputes or interference from the government. On the other hand, we all know that this is impossible.

The basic premise of this book is that in the long run, you *can* run your business with less legal hassle if you spend a small amount of time in the beginning to understand the relevant laws, and what you must do, should do, and don't have to do. The theory is much like the tag line of a popular oil filter commercial on television a few years ago: "You can pay me now, or you can pay me later."

We all know that legal time is expensive. This informal chat is inexpensive—and you won't be subject to any sales pitch from the lawyer. Remember, lawyering is a business just like any other. Most lawyers will give you their honest opinion on what you need, but there are three things you must be aware of:

1. *Lawyers must be conservative.* If there's even a slight possibility that you need something, they almost have to recommend that you get it. Put yourself in your lawyer's position. You ask if you need good terms and conditions on your purchase order and sales forms, or a review of your employment practices for Equal Employment Opportunity purposes, or any of the other things mentioned in this book. Your lawyer, realizing that your risk is small (though there is no such thing as zero risk), and trying to save you money, says no. The next day you get sued. A lawyer just can't run that risk. He or she must recommend the most conservative approach.

2. *Lawyers all have a very high opinion of themselves and their abilities.* The idea that you might be able to get a fairly good set of terms and conditions from a book is heresy to most lawyers. The concept of asking the government for help is even worse.

3. *Lawyers need to earn a living.* There is a surplus of lawyers right now, and there is a strong economic incentive for them to do a good job for any clients they have already—which means charging appropriately.

This book is not intended to take the place of your lawyer, but rather to help you get the most value for your dollar from him or her.

There are a number of ways that "the law" can directly save you money. Most of these involve taxes in one way or another. This book is not a tax planning book per se, but I will spend some time on that subject because of its overriding importance. I will also spell out the clear things so you can get the benefit of obvious tax advantages. There are some things, however, which are just too complicated for a book like this. For them, I will give you a brief explanation and recommend legal counsel. Pension and profit sharing plans are prime examples.

Regarding this new edition of the *Small Business Legal Advisor*, it updates the previous book and reflects developments since its publication in 1982. Here is a brief run-down of some of the more important things covered in this second edition.

While I will attempt to touch all the bases that I know about in this book, *The Small Business Legal Advisor* should be supplemented with similar advice on your taxes, insurance, and general financial matters.

Every small business owner should have access to professional help on all these subjects. The very first chapter of this book is "How to Find and Use a Good Lawyer," and the principles I talk about in that chapter would be applicable to other professionals too.

Workplace issues have become more important than ever. We have seen the development of the concept of "unjust dismissal," which basically changes the focus of the employer-employee relationship from one of "at-will employment" to one in which employers need some very clear justifications to fire someone. We have also seen the emergence of legal issues in the workplace relating to smoking, substance abuse, and AIDS. Then there was the enactment of the Americans with Disabilities legislation, which greatly increased workplace protection for the handicapped. And we have seen a host of new rules on toxic substances in the workplace.

Environmental issues have also greatly increased in importance. Practically all commercial transactions now need to be examined by an environmental lawyer. The exposures are very high. It is not at all unusual to have the possibility of environmental liability that exceeds—sometimes by several orders of magnitude—the value of real estate holdings or even businesses that you may want to buy or sell.

There is an entirely new chapter in international buying and selling because the world is increasingly becoming one large integrated marketplace.

Tax rates have changed dramatically. We now, for the first time in almost anyone's memory, have rates which are actually lower for individuals than for companies. There was also a relatively minor change in the rules on calculating tax on the sale of a business, but that minor change has had the dramatic effect of making it very difficult for small business owners to sell assets. There is now a substantial tax penalty for selling assets which will force many transactions into a sale of stock in the company instead.

William A. Hancock

The
Small Business
Legal Advisor

1

How to Find and Use a Good Lawyer

The first chapter is devoted to finding and using a good lawyer because I want to make it very clear that this book is not intended as a substitute for legal advice. I do not recommend that you attempt to be your own lawyer or to use the advice contained in this book without discussing it with your counsel. I do, however, recommend that you think about these subjects yourself, try to understand them, and use your lawyer as an advisor to help you anticipate and solve your business-legal problems. If you do this, you will be able to handle these matters much better and more cost-effectively. If you do not, one of the following things *will* occur.

1. The subject will cause you a legal problem and you will have to call your lawyer to get you out of it. In that case, the *best* that your lawyer can do is to get you out of the problem without too much liability. At worst, you will have both the liability and the attorneys' fees. Typically, attorneys' fees in problem situations are higher than in planning situations, simply because more time is involved.

2. If you do not think about the subject yourself and do not do your own homework, but still realize you need legal help, your legal fees will be much larger than necessary because of the time your lawyer spends doing things you could do yourself.

3. Most likely, you will simply drift along without knowing if you have any risk or are missing any opportunities. No one will sue you, and

1

the government will not cause you any problem. This may seem like a fairly good alternative except for that big factor, *The Unknown*. What you do not know *can* hurt you. You can operate your business for years without any product liability suits, employment discrimination problems, or labor law problems. Perhaps you can even operate indefinitely that way. In my judgment, however, that is gambling. If you want to do it, just be sure you know what you are doing and what your risks are. I think you will find the risks are too serious to justify the small savings in legal fees that ignoring these potential areas of difficulty entails.

How Do You Find a Lawyer?

Finding a good lawyer is a little difficult to address in the abstract. A lot depends on where you are coming from. One person might never have used a business lawyer before and now wants to start or buy a business and needs legal counsel for the first time. Another person might know a lawyer but has some doubts as to whether that lawyer is experienced enough in business law to be helpful. Therefore this section of the chapter is merely a list of some ideas and concepts that you can consider.

Preparing an Invitation

One way to find a good lawyer is to shop for one. You prepare an "invitation" to lawyers to tell you what they can do for companies such as yours, and how they charge for those services. The invitation should describe your business, at least briefly. You then interview the lawyers and make your decision.

Law is a competitive field. You will find that lawyers, at least those in larger communities, are used to receiving invitations. Many even have relatively standard presentations.

To whom do you send the invitations? A referral from a satisfied client should be sent an invitation. However, it has to be the right kind of referral. It must be from a fellow businessperson, ideally with roughly the same size and kind of business. Specifically:

The fact that a lawyer handled a divorce or accident very well means practically nothing. You need a business lawyer.

The fact that a lawyer did a good job on estate planning for someone is important for you; small business owners need good estate planning advice. However, it is not relevant to what we are discussing in this book—business law. If you know of a good estate planning lawyer who is with a fairly large firm, my suggestion would be to simply call that person and ask if the estate planning lawyer could put you in contact with one of the firm's corporate partners.

Check your local newspapers for lawyers who make presentations to chamber of commerce groups. The presentations may be on tax, employment law, environmental, or any other business subject. Those lawyers, or their firms, would be on your invitation list.

Your banker or insurance advisor may want to suggest lawyers for your invitation list.

Cull the invitation list down to at most a dozen or so names, and ask for a brief written proposal. You may not get it, but I suggest you ask anyway. Those on your list will probably want to talk with you. My suggestion is to take a two-stage approach. First get preliminary information about prospective lawyers, then decide on three or four lawyers to talk with in more detail. There is no reason to be secretive or bashful about your process. In fact, the best thing to do is to explain to all lawyers you talk with exactly what you are doing.

The first step is to get a list of lawyers who appear to have the basic qualifications you need. What are the basic qualifications?

1. Some other business clients—the closer they are to you in size and industry the better.
2. Expertise and experience in at least most of the subjects discussed in this book.
3. Other lawyers in the firm with more detailed experience in specific subjects.

The first letter should say something like the this:

Dear Lawyer:

I have a small business [or am going to be buying a small business] and I am looking for legal counsel. Your name has come to my attention, and I would like to ask if you would be willing to describe your practice to me. This will help me in deciding which lawyer to retain.

Let me give you a little background about my business. This should help you decide if you would be interested in representing us, and also to tell us what experience and qualifications you and/or your firm have that may be relevant to our needs.

The Name of my company is _____.
   We are located at _____.

Our business is _____.
We have _____ employees.
Our annual sales are _____.

Some of the things I would be interested in are:

A description of your firm and its capabilities
A description of the experience you may have in our industry, with
  companies our size
Any other information which might be useful to both of us in deciding if a lawyer/client relationship would be mutually beneficial

The Interview

The letter should get some response, which allows you to see if the lawyer meets the basic requirements. With those who do, you would then
take to the next step, which is a more detailed interview. (Try to visit the
lawyer's office rather than meeting in your office or in a restaurant. A
careful look around a lawyer's office can tell you a lot.) Here are some
things you may want to explore in the interview.

*Are there other clients whose circumstances are roughly the same as
yours?* A lawyer who represents a number of businesses is going to have
a much better base to work from and will be able to provide you with
much more constructive advice than one who has only a few business
clients. The law on the subjects covered in this book is developing rapidly, and there are many publications to read and seminars to attend. If
your lawyer has a good client base over which to spread these professional expenses, he or she is more likely to engage in them.

Does the law firm provide client seminars? Many firms offer client
seminars. The subjects are usually items of current interest such as employment law, tax changes, or environmental laws. Firm clients are invited to a briefing, usually without charge. Client seminars are a very
positive indication of a top-quality firm. The reverse is not necessarily
true. The fact that the firm does not give client seminars does not mean
it is not a good one.

*Does the firm have a Washington office or a firm in Washington with
which it has a steady relationship?* (The same question is appropriate for
your state capital.) The federal and state governments are so pervasive
in today's business regulatory climate that many problems simply cannot be solved without going to Washington or your state capital. Further, advance information on key developments is usually easier to obtain from Washington or the state capital than elsewhere. Having a

Washington or state capital office is an almost sure indication of a good business firm. Again, however, the reverse is not true. Do not eliminate any firm just because they have only one office in your town.

Does the firm send out client bulletins on recent developments? Many firms periodically send out client bulletins about matters they know the clients are interested in. These may be printed, but are often simply typed letters informing the clients of recent developments. Since they are not personalized, and since the same letter is sent to many clients, the cost is relatively small. Most of the time it is simply absorbed in the firm's overhead, though of course, the clients pay the bill for that too. Client newsletters or bulletins are a mark of a good firm.

How does the firm charge? You should be told how the firm charges, and I prefer the hourly billing arrangement to a retainer. In some cases, for simple projects, a fixed fee may also be possible. You should be told what the firm's hourly rates are and whether they submit itemized bills. I believe you should always insist on itemized bills. You should not accept one-line invoices like "For services rendered during the period...$$$$$$$." You should also know exactly who in the firm worked on your projects. That should be disclosed on the invoices.

Does the firm use paralegals? This is a very important development in law practice. The basic idea is simply efficiency. Most corporate law firms bill out their lawyers—even fairly junior ones—at rates in excess of $100 per hour. This hourly rate is caused, at least in part, by the rapid increase in starting salaries paid to lawyers graduating from law school. Since lawyers are just as much concerned about pricing themselves out of the market as clients are about paying large legal fees, lawyers are always looking for ways to provide the same top-quality service to their clients, but at a lower rate. One answer is the paralegal, which is a cross between a lawyer and secretary. A paralegal generally has some specific training in an area of law, and will be able to handle routine tasks under the general supervision of the lawyer. If your law firm has no paralegals, that is a bad sign.

What is the firm's automation situation? One reason to visit your lawyer's office is to check out the equipment people are using. Personal computers on most of the desks, modern duplicating machines, faxes, and dictation equipment are all pluses. If you see a room full of secretaries typing on standard typewriters, you need to ask some questions.

Can your lawyer offer you estimates of cost for the following things? While we feel that hourly rates are the fairest, we also feel that experienced corporate counsel should be able to tell you, within a range, what certain relatively standard services cost. If not, this is probably a sign that the lawyer or the firm does not do that kind of work regularly enough to have developed figures on the cost. You might want to ask for cost estimates for these relatively standard projects:

Standard set of purchase order terms and conditions

Standard set of sales terms and conditions

Employment agreement (no special problems)

Buy/sell agreement (between shareholders so that one can buy the other one out in the event of death or disability)

Standard profit sharing or defined contribution pension plan (Although these vary widely, they are important and you want a lawyer who has done them.)

Relatively standard partnership agreement

Relatively standard incorporation

The idea of the interview is not to shop for the lowest price. It is instead to test whether the lawyer has sufficient experience and the willingness to answer these questions. The lawyer will probably want to qualify the answers to these questions by saying that each situation is unique, which is true. However, in my view, you are entitled to a relatively straight answer to a question on how much these standard things should cost.

The only unacceptable answer is one to the effect that the firm will take the time necessary to do a good job, and whatever that costs you will pay.

Does the firm have experience with preventative law techniques such as auditing your employment practices in advance of a problem to see if they are acceptable? You may or may not want the firm to do this for you. We are, however, trying to see if the firm is progressive, and preventative law programs are one sign of that. Also, if you do want the firm to help you on preventative law matters, the fact that they have done it for others will make it easier, and therefore less expensive, for them to do it for you.

What are the firm's views on arbitration and other alternative dispute resolution techniques? If they are unfamiliar with anything but arbitration, that would be a bad sign. (See Chap. 10 for a listing of some of the alternative dispute resolution techniques firms should be considering today.)

Last but not least, remember the basic idea: We hire lawyers not firms. Make that clear, and be sure that the individual lawyer you are interviewing understands that you will be looking to him or her for *everything*. It is your lawyer's responsibility to get tax help from the tax partner, estate planning from the estate planner, and so on. If one of the qualifications you want in your lawyer is access to other specialists, you should meet those other specialists just to be sure your lawyer is not the only person in the firm you can get along with. You should also understand how the lawyer you are going to hire fits within the power structure of the firm. You should have a partner in charge of your business, and it should be a senior enough partner so that, when additional resources are required, the partner can get them.

You get the idea: Ask the kinds of questions that are important to your business. You are not trying to get too specific information, just a feel for whether the lawyer is experienced in the areas of law that may affect your business.

Key Point. The law is not mysterious or mystical. It is a business. Lawyers sell legal advice, and you are the buyer. You approach buying legal advice just like buying accounting advice/services or anything else. (The approach I outlined here works equally as well for hiring your accounting firm.)

Can you show the lawyer this book, highlight this chapter, and ask for a comment? Certainly.

Selecting the Lawyer

You then make a selection on the basis of your interviews. (Keep your notes, however; if it does not work out, you may want to go back to your second choice.)

Personal chemistry and your ability to work with the lawyer are, I believe, just as important as the objective qualifications of the lawyer. Of course, it is a personal thing. You should, however, build into the interview process some questions that answer the question "Can I work effectively with this person?" For example, when we used a procedure something like that just described to hire an accounting firm, one of the most qualified firms was eliminated on this point. Their abilities, energy, qualifications, and experience were among the highest on our list, but they were just too pushy for us. You should do your best to find out in advance whether or not there will be a chemistry problem with your lawyer. In my experience, most lawyer/client relationships that do not work out run aground on those shoals, not because the lawyer lacks ability.

Here are some other things to ascertain:

The fees question is first. The exact numbers or procedures are not as important as whether the lawyer gives you the feeling that they will work with you to make the most efficient use of legal time and keep fees down, or whether they will do what is required, take the necessary time, and hand you the bill.

Does your lawyer speak and write plain English? This will be hard to address during an interview. The problem comes with the preparation of legal documents. In my view, documents should be, at least in large part, understandable by nonlawyers. If they are not, they promote dispute rather than prevent it. You might want to ask your lawyer a direct question on this and see if there is agreement.

The lack of timeliness is one of the biggest raps against lawyers—and often a justified one. They seem to take forever and a day to do anything. Again, it is going to be hard to get at this during an interview, but you might try. "What is the average length of time it takes you to return a phone call?... If you go out of town, do you have someone in your office to return phone calls?...What is the average length of time it would take you to review a three- or four-page letter or similar document that I may want your thoughts on?"

Conclusions.   I think you can see from this discussion that there are many parallels between hiring a lawyer and hiring any other employee. The interviewing process is less than perfect. There are no guarantees. However, some careful thought and planning, combined with a conscientious and common sense approach, give you your best shot at getting a good lawyer.

Large Firm or Small Firm

There is quite a debate as to whether a small business owner is better off with a large firm or a small one. *Large* and *small* are, of course, relative terms. In most major cities a large firm might have several hundred lawyers, medium firms 50 or even a hundred or so, and firms under 25 would be considered small. In a smaller town, a firm of a dozen lawyers may be the largest. In my view, there is no one answer to this question.

I would, however, like to share some thoughts with you.

1. The hourly rates charged by larger firms are generally not much different from those charged by the smaller firms in the same city.

2. The hourly rates charged by larger firms in big cities are generally substantially higher than the hourly rates charged in smaller towns.

3. In today's complex legal world, it is very hard to see how a firm of less than a dozen or so lawyers could provide you with an adequate spectrum of advice and service. This is particularly true if your business is growing.

4. The legal business is a lot more competitive today than in years past. If a firm wants to grow, it needs to get more clients, and that means adding small businesses. It is very difficult to get a substantial business to switch firms. If a law firm wants to grow, it needs to add small business clients, and then grow with those clients.

5. We recommend you not to hire firms, but to hire lawyers instead. Even if your lawyer is in a firm of hundreds of other lawyers, you should be looking to your lawyer to provide the services required. This would tend to indicate that a lawyer in a large firm with many other specialists would have an advantage over a counterpart in a smaller firm. Note, however, that the reverse could be true. The large firm lawyer would want to use only experts within the firm, and would be reluctant to refer you to an outside specialist. The smaller firm lawyer might be less reluctant to do this.

6. Law firms, like any business, are likely to give most of their attention and their best service to their best clients. If your firm has annual billings of millions of dollars, and you pay only a few thousand, you will not be a valued customer. Again, however, you should be hiring lawyers not firms. That means that the comparison is not the annual firm billings, but the billings of this partner. You can be a very important client to a single lawyer within the firm even if you do not spend a lot of money on legal fees as compared with the firm's total billings.

7. Some feel that the power and prestige of a large firm is helpful. To some extent, we are known by the company we keep.

As you can see, there are considerations going both ways on the large-firm/small-firm question. No generalization is valid, and the question is usually best resolved by focusing on the best individual lawyer for you, with the size of that lawyer's firm being secondary.

How to Use Your Lawyer

Once you find a lawyer, you should be very careful how you use legal services. My advice is to be completely open and make sure that the lawyer understands exactly what you want and that you understand exactly what the lawyer is going to do and how much it will cost. You should not simply treat your lawyer as a scrivener to draw up papers based upon something your friends have done or something that you read in this book. That is much too expensive. Your lawyer gets paid to provide you advice and only incidentally to embody it in proper legal documents.

On the other hand, there is no reason to give a lawyer a blank check to go ahead and provide all kinds of legal advice and services which may be beneficial to you but which you may not want. For example, your first visit to your lawyer may generate a lot of conversation about small corporations, estate planning, wills, etc. All of these are tied together. The lawyer who points out the desirability of having a will, of integrating your business with your estate plan, of having arrangements to handle the orderly buy-out of a business partner, and of providing certain retirement and insurance benefits through your corporation is doing a good job for you. In fact, if your lawyer does not do these things, I think you are being shortchanged. However, the decision as to whether you want all these things and if so when you want them is entirely up to you.

Except for rather simple services such as drafting a will or forming a corporation, a lawyer will almost always charge by the hour. Some lawyers prefer a retainer arrangement, by which you pay them a certain amount per month to be available for consultation whether you use them or not. *My advice is to avoid retainer arrangements.* My experience has been that in almost all cases, one or the other party feels cheated. Either you call the lawyer too much and ask for many services which do not really require his or her time, thereby requiring more time than the retainer covers, or you do not have any questions or problems and are paying money needlessly.

An hourly arrangement places a premium on trying to reduce the time the lawyer must spend on routine or nonproductive things, such as calling you to obtain answers to questions which you should have been able to answer in the first place, writing a letter when none is called for, or coming to visit you at your home or office.

The best way to obtain good and economical legal advice is to think about the problem yourself as much as you can, do as much background work as you can, provide your lawyer with as much data as possible, and then use your lawyer for what he or she gets paid for: providing you legal advice and counsel and making sure the relevant documents are clear and legally sound.

The example on structuring purchasing and sales forms for your new company (discussed in Chap. 10) is illustrative. If you simply ask your lawyer to prepare some purchase order and sales agreement forms for you, it is likely to be a rather costly job. Your lawyer must find some samples, spend considerable time thinking about which terms and conditions would be best for your company, discuss the matter with you and your sales and purchasing people, and then go through several drafts before the final product is completed. There is certainly nothing wrong with this approach; it is just going to cost you a lot more money than if you use the advice contained in Chap. 10. *Do your own homework.* Give your lawyer a draft of the purchasing and sales terms and conditions which you think are good for your business. Give him or her samples of other companies' forms which you think are good. Ask your lawyer to put the finishing touches on the product by making sure that the terms and conditions do satisfy your particular needs. This approach will also give you a better product because you are going to be focusing on each of the terms and conditions. You know your business and your problems. Your own involvement in the process will not only help the quality of the end product but also make you more knowledgeable as to how it should be used.

Another rule in using a lawyer is that you should not be afraid to discuss fees. On the other hand, you should realize that a lawyer does not know in advance exactly how long it is going to take to do certain jobs. However, there is no reason why you should not be given an approximation. Also, there is no reason why you should not know the hourly rate that your lawyer charges and how the time is recorded. There are many ways lawyers use to record hours. I have seen both extremes— even inside a single firm. One extreme was a partner whose theory was that she spent eight hours a day doing legal work for about half a dozen main corporate clients. Therefore, at the end of the day she simply divided up her eight hours among the clients, depending on approximately what she had done that day. This approach was inexact, but it saved her a lot of time, and over the long haul, it was basically fair. Another lawyer at this same firm had a chart which divided the total day into *tenths* of an hour. Thus, a short phone call was a minimum of 1/10 of an hour. A half-hour phone call was *precisely* 0.5 hour, etc. Most lawyers fall somewhere in between these two extremes. It should be noted that the end result of these two extremes was approximately the same. The lawyer with the tenths-of-an-hour chart recorded fewer total hours during a year, but was forced to charge a higher per-hour rate. Lawyers, like most other professionals, focus on their annual income, not necessarily the per-hour charge.

This is a matter you should feel free to discuss with your lawyer. If you know there is a minimum 15-minute time-recording procedure, there is no point in using five or six phone calls which perhaps might be reduced to two or three with a little advance planning. By the same token, even at an hourly rate of a $150, a reasonably short and to-the-point conversation with your lawyer is only going to cost you about $75—a bargain if you plan the conversation and get some good advice.

Many lawyers will adjust the fees which would be charged by strict use of an hourly rate to reflect what they feel is the reasonable value of their services. This can work both ways. In some cases, a lawyer may increase the fee if the job required only a small amount of time but was very important, or if he or she did it very fast because he or she had considerable experience. For example, if you ask a lawyer to draft a lease for a commercial building, and the lawyer has just drafted one for another client for substantially the same kind of deal, the lawyer may charge you more than an hourly rate particularly if a lot of money is involved. Conversely, if you ask a lawyer for a commercial lease and it is the first one he or she has ever drafted, the lawyer may spend a lot of time educating himself or herself and charge you less than the number of hours worked times his or her usual hourly rate. As a general rule, these adjustments will work in your favor. If your lawyer is expert on a certain job, you will get a better product at a lower price. If your lawyer is not expert, he or she should cut the fee because some of the time spent is for his or her own education.

For your purposes, however, these special situations don't change the basic ideas in this chapter. You and your lawyer should still have a mutual understanding on fees, and the cornerstone of that understanding should be an agreement that, in most situations and certainly for all telephone calls and meetings, the lawyer will charge you only for the time he or she spends on your work, and only at rates which have been explained to you.

I recommend that all business people keep their own files. There is no reason why your lawyer has to keep documents which are important to your company. Keep your own. In the first place, it is much more convenient to get to them. In the second place, you never know when you will want to change lawyers, and it will be much easier to do this if you do not have to go get your files. There is no reason why your lawyer cannot keep copies of everything that relates to your business, but the originals should be in your possession.

What If You Are Not Satisfied with Your Legal Services?

If you are not satisfied with your legal services for any reason, you have a problem that should be addressed. Do not let the matter fester. The first thing to ask yourself is why you are unhappy. Maybe you have decided that you do not like your lawyer. If that is the problem-and it can be a very real one—do not hesitate to change lawyers promptly. After all, this is somewhat of a personal relationship, involving trust and confidence. If you do not have trust and confidence in your lawyer, just try again.

Assuming, however, that you have more objective complaints, I suggest an effort to correct the problem before making a switch. Switching lawyers will be time-consuming and possibly emotional—it is a good thing to avoid if possible.

How do you go about trying to correct a problem? Following are some commonsense methods which I have seen work. (I have also seen them fail.)

- List the problem(s) and openly discuss them with your lawyer.

- Talk with other lawyers. A friend of mine in the executive recruiting business was upset with his lawyer because he charged $125 for a relatively simple employment contract which my friend thought took at most only half an hour's time. When I explained that even simple letter agreements may require at least two drafts, proofreading, telephone calls to the client, etc., and that even though the lawyer may have spent only a half-hour actually dictating the first draft, there was much more time involved than that, he was satisfied.

- In many cases, your objection will be fees. Discuss this with your lawyer and get the facts as to how charges are made, for what, etc. Some lawyers send itemized bills, some very general statements. If you have a concern about fees, ask for a detailed bill. If your lawyer refuses to provide it, I say change. There is no reason why a lawyer—like anyone else—should not be prepared to explain fully what he or she is doing for your money.

- In some cases, your problem may be personal incompatibility with one member of the firm, but a better feeling about other members of the firm. Many attorney-client relationships have been saved by simply switching the person in the firm with whom the client deals.

- If you feel that your problem is second-class treatment because the firm is busy with other clients, you can certainly discuss that. Sometimes a discussion clears the problem up right away. Other times it clears it up—but only temporarily.

- If your problem is that you think your lawyer is not using any initiative to provide constructive legal advice, try asking other business associates about their lawyers. Maybe you are expecting too much.

What About Getting Business Advice from Your Lawyer?

Over the years, I have seen some attorney-client relationships which were built almost entirely on the fact that the attorney had a very high business acumen. One attorney I worked with during the early days of my career actually saved one of his major clients from bankruptcy through his management skills. Needless to say, the attorney had a client for life. I have seen other attorney-client relationships in which more phone calls were placed to the lawyer by the client about purely business questions than about legal questions. If your lawyer has this kind of business acumen, for heaven's sake do not waste it just because he or she also has a law degree.

Caution. Be sure you understand when your lawyer is talking business and when he or she is talking law. Lawyers have a unique power to say no to proposed transactions. Few prudent business people will go ahead with a deal over a lawyer's strong objection if the lawyer's objection is based on legal considerations. However, if your lawyer's business judgment is different from yours, you have much more latitude in overruling or disregarding it.

Getting sound business advice from your lawyer requires not only good business judgment on the lawyer's part, but a good attorney-client relationship in which you discuss proposed business transactions with your lawyer while they are still in the formative stages.

Somewhat related to business advice is negotiation advice. Many times, your lawyer will be a better negotiator than you. Partly, this is because of training, but more often it is simply because of the fact that he or she is a lawyer, with all the connotations that brings to the bargaining table, and also because he or she always has an out if things start going badly. A lawyer can simply say he or she has no authority to make a certain concession and must check back with you, the client. Having your lawyer negotiate for you can be a big plus. Do not overlook the possibility if the situation is right for it. Proper use of your lawyer in negotiations depends on a joint effort by the both of you. Normally, it is economically feasible only in substantial transactions such as the buying or selling of a business.

Should You Get Personal Legal Advice from Your Business Counselor?

Almost all corporate attorneys consider personal legal advice to the principals of their business clients to be an important part of corporate practice. This is because so many personal things are inextricably woven into the corporation. The stock of the corporation may be the individual's principal asset. The asset may be very valuable, but not liquid. Thus, paying estate taxes can be a problem. Many forms of insurance are most economically provided through group policies taken out by the corporation. If the corporation consists of more than one stockholder, it may be appropriate to have restrictions on the transfer of stock, and a requirement that the stock be sold back to the corporation or to the other shareholders upon death or separation from service with the corporation. A very important asset of the principal shareholder or his or her estate may be the pension or profit sharing plan of the corporation. Also, one of the principal reasons for establishing a qualified pension or profit sharing plan might have been to provide substantial benefits for the controlling shareholders.

During my years representing small businesses, a great deal of the work I did for the firm's clients would fall into this category of business-personal planning. After all, while the lawyer may represent the corporate entity, the person who retains the lawyer and who pays the fees is usually the principal shareholder.

All these matters are so interwoven that, in my judgment, it is almost impossible to get efficient and economical legal services unless you have the same law firm responsible for all of them. Of course, it is not impossible. I have seen arrangements where the corporation had a lawyer and where the principal shareholder had a lawyer. Most of these, however, were situations where the principal shareholder was not actually running the corporation. I have never seen a situation where a controlling shareholder who was actively running and managing a business saw fit to use different lawyers for corporate and personal matters of the type mentioned above.

Of course, your corporate lawyer is not going to be much help to you in personal injury, domestic relations, or criminal matters. If you are using a law firm, there may be other attorneys in the same firm who can help you. If not, your corporate counsel will undoubtedly have attorneys to recommend.

2
Starting Your Business

When you decide to go into business, the first thing you will want to do is to decide what legal form to use. This is very important-and a decision which will be made automatically if you do nothing.

What Are Your Choices?

There are basically three ways to set up a business:

1. Operate as a *sole proprietorship*. You own the business assets in your own name, and all the income is yours. You pay tax on all the income the business makes, and you are personally responsible for all the debts of the business. You can use another *business name* if you want — e.g., Bill Hancock DBA Business Laws (DBA means "doing business as").

2. Form a *partnership* with one or more other people. The partnership will be a business entity, but *not* a tax entity. You and your partners will have to pay tax on all the partnership income whether or not you actually take that income out of the partnership. You and your partners will also be responsible for all the partnership debts. Any member of your partnership can bind the partnership and all the rest of the partners to business transactions. Doctors, lawyers, accountants, and other professionals have traditionally practiced in this form because, until recently, state laws did not allow them to incorporate. Now, however, most state laws do allow professionals to incorporate so they can take advantage of the federal income tax benefits allowed corporations.

3. Form a *corporation* — either by yourself or with your business associates. Here there is a big legal difference. You have a separate legal and taxpaying entity, which receives the income from the business operations and pays taxes on that income. The corporate entity is responsible for the debts of the business. You and fellow shareholders are not responsible for those debts unless you affirmatively guarantee them. You, as owner, are entitled to salary and dividends.

If you do nothing, you will have a proprietorship. Forming a corporation requires formal legal action — you have to send documents to the secretary of state. If you go into business with others and do nothing, you will have a partnership. The terms of your partnership would simply be the state partnership law. That law is fairly uniform among the states and is generally fair to all parties. Of course, if you elect the partnership route you certainly should have a lawyer draft a partnership agreement for you.

What Should You Do?

There are many compelling reasons to form a corporation. You can test the water by starting your business as a sole proprietor, but in my judgment, you should limit operations as a sole proprietorship to very small undertakings. I would never recommend going into *any* partnership without a complete partnership agreement. Since it is generally more costly to have a lawyer draft a good partnership agreement than to form a corporation, and for the reasons stated in the remainder of this chapter, it is unlikely that a partnership would be the best form of business for you.

Many business counselors tell me that I am simplifying the picture too much, that incorporation is a decision which is not necessarily best for everyone and that the proper analysis is much more complicated. I agree that *potentially* the analysis can get very complicated. However, in the overwhelming majority of cases, you will find that after you do the analysis the decision is clear — a corporation is best. That raises the obvious question: How much should you pay a lawyer or accountant to do a complicated and detailed analysis and explain all the possible alternatives to you when chances are extremely high that the result will be to simply form a corporation? My answer to that is straightforward: Not very much. I hope that your lawyer does explain the various alternatives to you, but that he or she doesn't try and make too big a deal out of it.

There are two exceptions. The first is where the business is just *so* small that no legal fees or state registration or franchise fees are justified. A hobby-business (e.g., selling some of your photographs or short stories, or an occasional sale of antiques you collect) would be an example of a business which may be just too small to justify any expenses. The second exception is real estate ventures or tax shelters. These kinds of deals almost always depend principally, if not solely, on the tax benefits to be economically feasible. Typically, they generate tax losses, and you must be able to deduct those losses from other income. A partnership or limited partnership is therefore necessary.

Why Should You Form a Corporation?

A corporation offers the business owner a number of benefits.

1. Required decisions will be made early. Forming a corporation is relatively easy, but there are some decisions which must be made. By forming the corporation, you will focus on these problems at the beginning of your business when they are easy to solve. If you let them go, they will only get more complicated. Examples of those decisions are the following.

a. Who owns the corporation? You personally? You and others? You and family members? Forming a corporation requires you to issue shares, and you will have to issue shares to somebody. It forces the issue as to who you are in business with and who owns what percentage of the business.

b. What are you putting into the business? When you form a corporation, you have to spell out in the documents what you are putting into the business.

c. Whom are you going to use as lawyer and accountant? I do not recommend forming your own corporation without a lawyer. That is not because it is hard to form a legal corporation—you can go into any business form store and get the forms, call the secretary of state and find out the fee and where to send the forms, and you have a "corporation." However, there are a number of important long-range decisions which should be made when you incorporate. If you don't do it in the most advantageous way, you will sacrifice many of the benefits incorporation can give. Getting a good lawyer and accountant early is a benefit. A secondary benefit is that you can evaluate your lawyer and accountant early on a relatively easy job. You can see how much they charge and whether they explain enough to you, or waste too much of your time on details and technicalities. In short, you can have sort of a trial marriage before you get into any serious legal or accounting problems, and I think that is a benefit.

2. You will build a good base for the future. Forming a corporation is simply a good, businesslike thing to do if you are going to run a business. You build a solid foundation for making sure that your business operations are kept *separate* from your personal affairs. *This is very important.* Many tax problems small business owners encounter arise out of their failure, in one way or another, to respect their corporation as a separate and independent entity and to keep records which substantiate the fact that it is a separate and independent entity. The corporation facilitates this process, and that is a benefit.

3. Many future transactions are simplified. When you start your business, you will be tempted to get the paperwork over with in the fastest, cheapest, and easiest way. That is fine, up to a point. However, you should spend some time thinking about possible future developments and, if it can be done easily and cheaply, plan for them. For example, a corporation facilitates estate planning. You can give your children or spouse an interest in your business much more easily by giving them stock than by giving them a share of a partnership or proprietorship. In fact, for practical purposes, it is almost impossible to transfer interests in any business other than a corporation. Theoretically, you can transfer a partnership interest, but as a practical matter, this requires so much legal and accounting effort that it can be a real problem. Also, in a corporation, you insulate the ownership from the management of the business. That, of course, is no big deal when you are both owner and manager. But, what if you get sick or want to do something else and have a new person manage your business? It is much easier to make these arrangements with a corporate entity where you have shares of stock — perhaps both common and preferred — to use.

4. It is cheaper to incorporate before you have a going business. Forming a corporation at the beginning is usually about a $500 deal — give or take a few bucks and not counting any planning that your attorney or accountant does. Forming a corporation into which you are intending to put a going business can be a much more substantial task. It usually requires much more legal and accounting effort — and therefore the fees are higher. When you talk about the benefits of incorporation as against the costs, the costs are relatively small. Delaying incorporation will almost undoubtedly increase the costs.

Corporate Taxation

As we all know, tax laws have been changing so rapidly in recent years that anything you read in a book relating to specific tax rates and specific tax rules has to be viewed with suspicion. It may have been changed even between the time it was written and the time the book was published, much less by the time you read it. For purposes of this book, however, all we talk about are a few fundamental rules.

The cardinal rule—to which there are no exceptions—is that you should always do a thorough tax study of the pros and cons of incorporation. The advantages of a corporation listed above are very important, but they are subjective and don't result in hard dollars in your pocket. Even in a relatively small business, we can be talking about quite a bit of money on your total tax bill. A few ideas from your lawyers or accountants can pay big dividends; conversely, a few mistakes can cost you a lot of money. A good tax analysis of your proposed new venture is absolutely essential.

Subchapter S and Subchapter C Corporations

In tax jargon there are essentially two kinds of corporations: Subchapter S and Subchapter C.

The Subchapter S Corporation is so-called because the sections in the Internal Revenue Code describing the taxation of this type of corporation is Subchapter S. The Subchapter S Corporation has all of the legal and other benefits of a corporation on the one hand, with the entire business taxed as a partnership or a sole proprietorship on the other. This, I caution, is a gross oversimplification, and there are many exceptions to the general statement that, "A Subchapter S Corporation is taxed like a partnership or an individual." The exceptions, however, tend to be on the fringes of the transaction and involve some of the details of your planning, such as employee benefits and qualified pension and profit sharing plans.

The Subchapter C Corporation (the provisions governing it are found in Subchapter C of the Code) is what we might call the "normal" corporation. Let me describe some of the fundamental rules involved in this form of business:

1. A Subchapter C corporation is a separate taxpayer. The corporation pays taxes on its income, at its corporate rates, in substantially the same way as an individual.

2. A Subchapter C corporation has its own tax rates which are essentially as follows:

$0 to $50,000	15%
$50,000 to $75,000	25%
$75,000 and over ·	34%

The tax rates for individuals were increased in 1990. Before that, the top rate was essentially around 28 percent for most high bracket taxpayers. It is now about 31 or 32 percent, depending on the individual taxpayer's situation. This means that before 1990 there was often a direct and substantial tax advantage in having a Subchapter S corporation so that all the income would be taxed at a 28 percent rate rather than a 34 percent rate. During the years that this rate differential was in effect, hundreds of corporations did in fact make the Subchapter S election. Now, with the rate differential being a little smaller, the amount of the difference between the top individual and corporate rates has been reduced. In many cases, however, there will still be some differential in favor of the individual rates. In addition, having a Subchapter S corporation means that there will be only one tax on income, whereas in S subchapter C corporation, we will have to pay a tax at the corporate level, and then again when the income is paid to the individual.

3. C corporations can deduct from their income 85 percent of any and all dividends they receive. This includes investment dividends from public corporations received by privately held corporations. For example, if a corporation invests $10,000 in a common stock paying a 10-percent dividend, that will give the corporation $1,000 of income. The corporation will also have a deduction of $850, thus having only $150 on which it must pay income tax. If you personally had that $1,000 dividend income, you would have no such deduction and would have to pay a tax on the entire amount. Thus, one of the big advantages of a C corporation is the ability to invest in dividend-paying stocks and avoid any tax on those dividends. Note that a Subchapter S corporation does not enjoy this advantage. The dividends received by a Subchapter S corporation are passed through to the shareholders and they must pay tax on them as if they had received those dividends directly.

4. Corporations can also deduct salaries, including a salary paid to the sole shareholder, as long as the salaries are reasonable. Thus, the economic effect of a corporation earning $50,000 and paying $50,000 to a sole shareholder is substantially the same as if the shareholder earned $50,000 himself or herself. Going back to our tax rate analysis, then, we can see that one way of achieving the desired result of having a corporation's income taxed at the lower individual rates is to simply pay all of the income out as salary. That is, in fact, one of the major planning tools you should consider in a Subchapter C corporation.

Unfortunately, it has some limitations. The main one is that the salary has to be reasonable. If you are successful in your business, you may make so much money that, in order to pay all of the profit to you as salary, the amount would be too high to be reasonable, and the Internal Revenue Service would disallow some of it. Also, if you want to pay some salary to people who are not really actively involved in the corporation, such as a spouse or a child, the salary may be too high to be reasonable. For example, if you decide you want to pay a child $2,000 or $3,000 a year, and the child really doesn't do any work for the corporation, that $2,000 or $3,000 a year would not be reasonable. The Internal Revenue Service would disallow that as a salary deduction. They would say it was a dividend to you, and a gift by you to the children.

5. Corporations cannot deduct dividends. Thus, if a corporation earns $50,000 and pays the sole shareholder a dividend of $50,000, there will be one tax at the corporate level and second tax at the individual level. This double tax is the biggest drawback of a corporation. You must avoid it wherever possible. As the preceding discussion points out, the labels that you put on a transaction are not controlling. Calling something a salary doesn't necessarily make it so. If it is unreasonably high, the Internal Revenue Service may characterize it as a dividend, thus denying the deduction to the corporation while still requiring payment of tax by the person who received it.

6. As long as you respect certain formalities, and as long as the transactions are bona fide, you can loan a corporation money and receive interest, and you can lease the corporation property which you own and receive rent. The interest and rent will be deductible by the corporation and taxed to you as ordinary income—but not as salary, with all the the payroll taxes that salary payments entail. Since payroll taxes are so substantial these days, another area of important planning is to structure as many payments to you as you can in some way that avoids those payroll taxes. Interest and rents are usually two categories to consider.

7. A very important factor in a Subchapter S corporation is that all of the profits, as well as the losses, that the corporation earns are passed through to the individual shareholders. For example, if you feel that your corporation will have losses during the initial startup period (as is common), you may want to have those losses pass through to you so that you can offset them against your other income. There are limitations on this but, in general, it is possible to structure some new startup operations so that some of the initial losses can be offset against other income. The Subchapter S corporation is the route through which that is done.

8. You must keep in mind one overriding tax principle: Everything you do with your company must be bona fide and must reflect economic reality. For example:

   a. Salary is deductible by a Corporation even if paid to a sole shareholder so long as it is reasonable. But if it is unreasonably high, the IRS will call it a dividend.

> *b.* Rents and interest are deductible by a corporation so long as they are ordinary necessary business expenses. If they are a sham, the IRS will disallow the deductions.
>
> *c.* Interest must, under the tax law, be computed and paid at a reasonable rate. If you make the rate too high or too low, the IRS can impute interest and tax the transactions as though a realistic interest rate had been used.
>
> *d.* If you elect a Subchapter S corporation and pay yourself an unreasonably small salary so that all of the rest of your income is characterized as dividends so as to avoid the payroll taxes, the IRS can recalculate your salary also.

One professor of law uses a skinny pig and a fat pig to illustrate the concept. If you are a skinny pig you can get fatter, but fat pigs go to market. In tax matters, this translates into an ability to structure your deals with your corporation to minimize taxes within a reasonable range. If you do that, you can "get fatter.' If you go outside the reasonable range and get too greedy, you will more than likely "go to market." This is one of the big reasons you should get a good tax adviser as soon as possible. Unless you want to do a lot of studying and reading yourself, you are probably going to need help to tell you when you are staying within reasonable ranges, and when you are getting too greedy.

9. Due to some technical limitations on an S corporation, not everybody can qualify. Two big limitations are that you cannot have any more than 35 shareholders and that other corporations cannot be shareholders themselves. Thus, if you are going to have a lot of shareholders in your group, or if one of the investors that is going to get common stock is itself a corporation, you will not be able to make the S election.

Summary

The bottom line of your tax analysis is very likely going to be twofold:

1. If your anticipated corporate profit is going to be small and you do not have a lot of other outside income, there may be some temporary short-term advantage in containing some of the corporate profits in the corporation for growth purposes. I emphasize "short term" because you do not want to forget about that second tax when you finally take those profits out for yourself.

2. On the other hand, as soon as the money numbers start to get larger, there may be a substantial advantage in electing an S corporation status. You will have only one tax at a 31- to 32-percent level if you elect an S corporation status, and if you do not, you will have an initial tax

at a 34-percent level followed by another tax at a 31- or 32-percent rate when you take that money out of your corporation.

Two Final Tax Notes: Unreasonable Compensation and Unreasonable Accumulation Penalty

Two disadvantages of a Subchapter C corporation are the rules on unreasonable compensation and unreasonable accumulation.

Unreasonable Compensation Unreasonable compensation may take the form of "too high" a salary. A subchapter C corporation can deduct salaries but not dividends. If you pay yourself or any other shareholder an amount that is disproportionate to the value of your contribution to the company, the Internal Revenue Service may very well recharacterize a payment, which you have called salary, as a dividend. This would result in an additional (or double) tax because the corporation would be denied a deduction. For examples if you were to pay yourself a salary of $200,000 per year but the Internal Revenue Service felt that only $100,000 was reasonable, your corporation would be denied a deduction for that second $100,000. If your corporation were in a 34-percent tax bracket, that would be $34,000 more in taxes plus interest and penalties.

Salary payments may also be "too small," the motivation being to save payroll taxes. Since you are going to be taxed on the entire profit of the S corporation anyway, you can minimize taxes by minimizing the amount of your income that is characterized as salary. The rest would be dividends.

The unreasonable compensation problem can also come up in the context of relatives who may work for you. For example, suppose you hire your son as a waiter in your small business restaurant and pay him a dollar an hour above the going rate. There would probably not be any problem with that. However, if you paid him two or three times the going rate, the IRS could say that this was not reasonable compensation and, in reality, you received a dividend and made a gift to your son.

Unreasonable Accumulation Penalty Because of that very important double tax problem in a C corporation, there is often a temptation to simply accumulate profits in the C corporation and never pay them out to the shareholders. If the accumulation of profits is deemed unreasonable, a penalty can be levied.

This unreasonable accumulation penalty is entirely inapplicable to S corporations as, at least from a tax point of view, there is never any accumulation at all. Each year the individual shareholders pay tax on the entire profit for that year. It does not matter whether the S corporation actually pays that profit to the shareholders or keeps it in the corporation for business use. The tax is paid anyway.

For a C corporation, however, you may have to keep one eye out for the unreasonable accumulation penalty. It is usually easy to deal with. First, it applies only at fairly high levels, with a $150,000 exemption. Thus you can accumulate $150,000 of cash in your corporation and invest it in dividend paying stocks without any unreasonable accumulation problem.

Also, the penalty applies only if the accumulation does not have any valid business purpose. It is usually easy to justify rather large accumulations. You may need to purchase a building or other business assets, or you may have other business investments in mind which require a lot of cash. All you need to do is have those business needs well documented. For example, you may want some corporate minutes regarding purchasing the building, or you may have some proposals made regarding capital equipment.

Limited Liability

One of the best-known advantages of incorporation is that it limits the liability of the shareholders to their investment. Shareholders are not personally liable for the debts of the corporation. This seems important indeed. Why, then, do I list it last?

I agree that it is important, but don't forget about the following two factors:

1. Liability for personal injuries of people should be covered by insurance. Further, many times shareholders of corporations are found to be personally liable for personal injuries in spite of the corporation. It is extremely dangerous to rely on the limited liability aspect of a corporation in the context of product liability or personal injury. There are just too many reasons why a jury could find the shareholders liable—sometimes even pure sympathy would be enough.
2. When you borrow money from a financial institution, it will almost always want personal guarantees from the shareholders.

That leaves trade creditors as the principal debt that is purely corporate and will rarely be imposed on shareholders. If you're in the kind of business where trade creditors constitute a large part of your debt, limited liability is important. However, if you are not, it may be an over-stated benefit.

Another problem with the limited liability aspect of corporations is the legal doctrine of "piercing the corporate veil." Under this doctrine, the courts sometimes look through the corporation and hold the indi-viduals actually running the business liable for debts, taxes, or personal injuries. Courts will pierce the corporate veil whenever it appears that the people running the corporation have not respected the corporate entity themselves. For example, if you form a corporation but don't have separate corporate bank accounts, don't keep separate corporate books, comingle the corporation's money with your own, and don't re-spect the corporate entity by dealing at arm's length with it, courts may well not respect the corporate entity either. It is very important to keep in mind that the corporation is a separate and distinct entity. If you bor-row from or loan to it, if you enter into a lease with it, or if you buy from or sell to it, there must be proper documentation and the trans-action must be reasonably fair. If you don't respect your own corpora-tion, the courts may not respect it either.

Forming the Corporation

Sold — I'll take one corporation — how do I get it?

Corporations are creatures of state law. The way you form a corpo-ration depends on your own state laws — but the following is typical. It is a very easy procedure. The hard part is not forming the corporation, but figuring out exactly what to contribute to capital, what kind of shares to issue, how much debt the corporation should have, and the other matters mentioned in this book.

The first step is generally to file articles of incorporation with the sec-retary of state. The articles of incorporation make you a legal corpora-tion. They also keep anyone else in your state from using the name you picked. Conversely, if you happen to have picked a name already reg-istered, the secretary of state will refuse to register your articles until you change the name. The fee is relatively modest, often $100–$200. The articles of incorporation establish the capital structure. They say what classes of shares the corporation can issue and what the voting rights of those shares are. Here is where you authorize preferred and different classes of common stock if you want.

The next step is to prepare documents which show what you are go-ing to put into the corporation. This can be done in a simple letter, but if you are actually transferring automobiles, contracts, or real property, you will have to eventually assign or transfer these items just as you would in any other sale. The incorporators then accept this offer and issue the shares to the persons making the offer. Now you have a corporation and shareholders.

The shareholders then meet to adopt a document which Ohio calls a Code of Regulations and most other states call bylaws. It spells out the relationship between the shareholders, how and when they meet, etc. Essentially, it is a boilerplate document for a small business. The shareholders also elect the directors. Now you have a corporation, shareholders, and directors.

The directors then meet to elect the officers of the corporation. That's just about it. You can do all this in writing—you don't have to actually meet. Almost all states have special statutes which recognize the fact that closely held corporations don't follow the same formalities as large publicly held corporations. Most states allow any action which could be taken at a meeting to be taken by simple written consent.

This practice is so standardized that every lawyer has a set of preprepared forms. Legal clinics even advertise the formation of corporations at low fees—typically less than $500. Most corporate lawyers charge a little more, but not much. We are talking here about a simple corporation. If it is complicated—perhaps because you are incorporating an existing partnership—the fees will be higher.

This chapter contains some sample incorporation documents. *The intention is to show you how the process works, not to recommend you incorporate yourself without professional help.* Only the key documents are included.

What Kind of Stock Should I Use?

There are two basic kinds of stock available for use by small corporations—but a tremendous number of hybrids which can be used to satisfy special needs. In fact, one of the big advantages of a corporation is the availability of all these different kinds of ownership.

The two basic types of stock are *common and preferred.* Typically, the common stock owns the equity of the company and has the right to control it through the election of the board of directors. The preferred, on the other hand, has no right to elect directors and has only a right to the dividend assigned to it. Upon liquidation of the company, the preferred receives "preference" as to assets. The preferred shareholders will get paid before any of the common shareholders. The law requires only that corporations have common stock. Everything else is a matter of individual preference. Within wide latitude, you can create any kind of stock you want. Following are some hybrids which have been used frequently in the past.

Two classes of common stock with different voting rights can sometimes satisfy the requirements of investors with different interests. For example, perhaps one investor wants to have at least 50 percent of the voting power of the company but has only a small fraction of the capital. There could be a class A voting common, and she could be given 50 percent of that. There could then be a class B nonvoting common which would be given to the other investors who invested more capital.

Classes of stock which become voting on specified events, or which are voting for specific purposes, are also used. For example, preferred stock is normally not voting, but it can be given voting rights if the corporation doesn't pay the preferred dividends for two years in a row. Preferred stock can be cumulative or non-cumulative. Cumulative means that if the corporation does not pay a dividend on the preferred, it would be required to pay all past dividends on the preferred stock before any dividends were paid on the common. A noncumulative preferred would not have this requirement.

Convertible preferred stock can be used to advantage in some cases. This kind of stock starts out to be normal nonvoting preferred stock, but can be converted into voting common at some prescribed rate at the election of the shareholder.

While these hybrids are useful in some instances, the standard preferred stock is still the most often used additional stock for small corporations. One of the nicest things about preferred stock is that its value is fixed. For example, a $100 preferred stock is worth $100. There is no need for any subjectivity in valuation if you want to give it away for estate planning purposes or if you want to redeem it. That value will also stay the same throughout the life of the corporation. Dividends on preferred are paid at the discretion of the board of directors. It is like the common stock in that respect. Thus, you can pass the dividends on the preferred during the early years of the corporation if that is appropriate.

Caution. One of the rules for using the Subchapter S Corporation is that you can have only one class of stock. Thus you cannot have both common and preferred shares if you want to use a Subchapter S corporation. You would need to stick with the normal, or Subchapter C, corporation. Also, the one-class-of-stock requirement is somewhat of a trap in that notes or other instruments that people might at first consider to be a "class of stock" might be so considered by the IRS in an audit. If you do use a Subchapter S corporation, it is doubly important for you to always check with your professional advisors before issuing stock, notes, or any other instrument that could possibly be characterized as a "different class of stock."

The Issuance of Shares Is Highly Regulated

The issuance of shares of stock in a company (or for that matter any "security") is highly regulated at both the federal and the state levels.

At the federal law level, the general rule is that you cannot issue any securities without registering them with the Securities and Exchange Commission, a cumbersome and costly process. Luckily, there are many exemptions for small businesses, including exemptions for stock issued in a so-called *private placement* and for stock issued in only one state (the so-called *intrastate offering exemption*). When you are joining together in a small business with several other people all in one state, these exemptions allow you to issue your stock without registering it. Further, at the federal level, these exemptions apply automatically, so that in many cases involving closely held companies you do not have to file any documents at all with the federal government or Securities Exchange Commission. It is, however, important for your lawyer to know exactly what shares you are issuing and to whom. Your lawyer must be able to verify that there are no federal securities law registration requirements.

At the state level the situation varies widely. In many states the documents you need to file with the state securities law people are relatively simple. On the other hand, there is often an express filing requirement so that you can claim whatever exemptions from registration might be applicable for small closely held companies.

In some states failure to file these documents is only a technical violation of the securities laws, but it can be very serious. Technical violations of either the state or the federal securities laws are serious because such violations will usually give the person to whom the shares of stock were sold a right of recession. As a practical matter, you have guaranteed that the person will not lose any money. If the corporation falls on hard times, the people you have issued stock to might have a right of recession so that they can require the corporation to buy back their shares of stock at their original price.

Example

You form a corporation with $25,000 of capital, putting in $15,000 yourself and selling the other $10,000 worth of stock to two other individuals for $5,000 each. The state in which this occurs has a requirement that you file a document claiming the applicable exemption from the state security laws for this transaction, but no such document is filed. Thus there is a technical violation. One year later the corporation has fallen on hard times and the two other shareholders want out. You calculate that the fair value of their shares at that time is only $1,000. However, they may be entitled to a right of recession, which means that instead of giving them the fair market value for their shares, you have to give them back the original price they paid, $5,000 each. In other words your failure to satisfy the state securities law requirements—even though it was only a technical oversight—has amounted to a guarantee to the other shareholders that they will always get their original investment back. This is why it is so important for you always to discuss any issuance of shares with your legal counsel before you actually do so.

Note. Most state securities laws and certainly the federal securities laws have a very broad definition of the term *security.* Certainly it includes shares of stock but may also include notes, interests in partnerships, or any other documents that evidence ownership of or even interest in your business. For example, suppose our hypothetical business with $10,000 of its capital being sold to others were formed as a partnership, with the partnership interests being divided the same as the corporate shares of stock. Many state laws would require a registration. In some states, the failure to dot all the securities law i's and cross the registration t's may allow those partners a right of recession.

What Should I Put in the Corporation?

By asking this question, you are halfway to the answer. Too many times persons starting out in business just put the business assets in the corporation because they are "business assets." That is a very logical thing to do, and has *economic* merit. Unfortunately, it usually has a rather high tax price tag, and that is why most practitioners do not recommend it.

Instead, the corporation should be "thinned" by putting in only part of the assets as a contribution to capital and loaning the rest. Of course, this may not be possible. When I started my business, the entire capital contribution was $500 in cash and some office furniture that I had around the house. Obviously, no room for thinning there. You may be in roughly the same position. However, if the circumstances warrant, thinning the capital structure of your corporation initially will usually reduce taxes and get more money in your pocket.

Let's assume that you have $100,000 to put into a business. This can be either $100,000 cash to start a new business or $100,000 to buy an existing business. For this purpose, you would use exactly the same analysis either way.

The first possibility would simply be to form a corporation with $100,000 of capital stock. You put in $100,000 in cash, you get back all the common stock of the corporation, and the corporation then buys the business or uses the money to start the new business. You would have a capital structure of $100,000 capital and no debt. Solvent indeed, but probably not the best thing to do.

Let's thin the capital structure of the corporation by putting in only $50,000 capital and loaning the corporation the other $50,000. The terms of the loan would be 8 to 12 years with an interest rate of 12 percent. Notice that we have not changed the economic deal. The business still has $100,000. However, if you thin the capital structure of the corporation in this way, you will get the following benefits:

1. The debt can be repaid tax-free. Remember that putting money into the capital structure of a corporation is very easy and involves no tax problem. Getting it out again is an entirely different matter. In many situations there is simply no way to get your money back out again without some tax. However, if you loan the money to your corporation, it is just like a loan to anyone else — when you get repaid, there is no tax.

2. You can get interest on the money. That is a plus because there are many additional costs involved in salary payments. Even assuming you are well under the levels where you have to be concerned with unreasonable-compensation problems, salary payments will necessitate social security contributions for both you and the corporation and a fairly substantial and increasing array of other state and federal payroll taxes. Interest, on the other hand, is deductible to the corporation and taxable to you — but there are no other incidental taxes.

Using the cash example presents the clearest case of thinning the corporate capital structure. However, you can also accomplish the same thing by retaining certain real or personal property and leasing it to the corporation.

Real property is perhaps the most obvious way to get money out of the corporation via rent. As a general rule, you will want to analyze the situation carefully before you contribute real property to a corporation or have a corporation buy real property with its own funds. It is usually a substantial investment, and the opportunity to have the tax benefits involved in real estate ownership available to the individuals directly is often appealing.

Key Rule.   Remember that it is easy to put money or property into a corporation tax-free, but very difficult to get it out again without paying taxes. Before you make sizable contributions of money or property to the capital of a corporation, analyze the effects of that contribution because once done, it will be hard to undo.

Tax Reality

Not to belabor the point about tax reality, but I think this is another area where some fairly obvious questions will arise and where this discussion is important to you. Remember that the reason for this discussion is to highlight the need for professional tax advice — not to make you your own tax planner.

You may ask, If it is good to put $50,000 in as debt, why don't I just put all, or almost all, of the money in as debt? If a little is good, a lot is better — right? Further, why do I have to lock myself up for 8 to 12 years? What is wrong with using a demand note or one which has a one-year maturity which I can extend if I want? After all, I'm the sole shareholder. Further, why do I have to have 12-percent interest? I don't want interest right now from the corporation, and the corporation needs the money more than I. How about an interest-free loan at least for a while?

The IRS is not stupid, and the tax law — mostly — reflects economic reality. When you contribute money to a new corporation in exchange for common stock, the tax treatment is simple.

- There is no tax when you incorporate.
- Your basis in the stock equals the amount you paid for it.
- When you sell the stock in the future, gain will be measured against that basis.
- The corporation cannot "repay" the amount you contributed, because it is not a loan but a contribution to the capital of a corporation.
- Dividends paid on the stock are taxable to you and not deductible to the corporation.

What if you simply called the capital contribution a loan, though it did not have traditional loan features such as a maturity date and a fair interest rate? If you did have a maturity date, assume you made it 100 years. Alternatively, assume you made it "on demand."

Now, you say, the $100,000 you paid in is debt so that:

1. You can get it out tax-free as a repayment of a loan.
2. The payments to you based on the $100,000 are interest and, therefore, deductible by the corporation.

Do you really think that the IRS is going to believe that the $100,000 is debt and not stock just because you called it debt? Of course not. The IRS is going to say, quite properly, that the money you paid in was a capital contribution, and they are going to disallow the deduction to the corporation of the "interest." If you take your $100,000 back, the IRS is going to say that it is a dividend, taxable to you and not deductible to the corporation. Why? Because that is the economic reality of the transaction. You have tried to be *too* greedy.

Take the other assumption—you set a short maturity date for the "loan." If you repay the loan at the maturity date, that is all right. However, this is a new corporation and its earning power is uncertain. Suppose you set the maturity date at 1 year, and after the year you do not have enough money in the corporation to pay the debt. Are you going to go to a bank and borrow the money at high interest rates just to pay yourself? Of course not. You are going to extend the loan. Okay, so you extend the loan—what is wrong with that? Put yourself in the position of the IRS. If they come in and find that you extended a loan which was supposed to be paid, are they going to believe that you really intended to pay the loan on maturity in the first place? Probably not. They are going to say that this was just a paper sham—you really made a capital contribution and never intended to pay it back in one year, even though you had a paper that said you did. Suppose you extend the payments again a second time. That looks even more suspect.

Suppose you make the contribution payable "on demand." The IRS is going to say no dice—in a closely held corporation where you are both the lender and the lendee, that just isn't kosher. *Again, you got too greedy.* You tried to have your cake and eat it too, and that will almost always cause tax problems. I give advice to stay out of trouble. If you are audited and have to spend your time and money for professional fees— you lose even if you "win." Further, your odds of winning cases like those I have described above is poor—at best.

If you want to "get creative" with the suggestions I give you, see a lawyer or tax accountant first. Even if you do not want to get creative, it is worth the money to have a good professional handle your incorporation—it may cost you a few dollars, but I think it is worth it.

In summary, then, whenever possible, seriously consider thinning your capital structure and follow the following guidelines:

- Do not contribute more than 50 percent of the money in the form of debt. Try to keep a one-to-one ratio between the equity and the debt. This is very conservative advice, but it is guaranteed to please the IRS and not cause you any problem.

- When you contribute "debt," make it *real*. Generally, this means a maturity of between 8 and 12 years. A shorter period runs the risk of not having the money available and having to extend the maturity. A longer period runs the risk of having the contribution look like capital rather than debt. Either way, the IRS will more than likely challenge the transaction. The 8-to-12 rule is a conservative and safe approach.
- Make the interest rate somewhere between what the IRS charges and the prime rate.

Conclusion

Let's summarize what you've learned from this chapter.

1. When you start your business, you should think carefully about the legal form that you are going to use. I think you will usually find that a corporation is best. Under today's tax rules, an S corporation is often very attractive.
2. However, forming a corporation is only a part of the initial structuring of your business. You have to decide:
   a. What kind of stock the corporation should authorize and issue
   b. What should be contributed to capital and what to debt
3. During the course of the discussion you saw—I hope—that incorporation, redemption of stock, issuance of preferred stock, and many other things which go into proper tax planning are rather technical. Forming the corporation was easy, but for the other parts of the deal—those which save the tax money—professional advice is a good investment.

That is basically it. Many lawyers use a preprinted package of material which contains a nice-looking binder and some fancy share certificates. The package sometimes also contains a preprinted copy of a sample code of regulations and a seal. In Ohio and most states, a seal is not required.

One of the most important things a lawyer can do for a small business client is to help plan for changes of control, either because of death or disability, or because one of the business owners simply wants out of the business. This is tremendously important, at least as measured by the number of lawsuits by business people who do not follow this advice. Remember that it is much easier to make such arrangements early, when the business is being formed. Therefore, while they are technically not essential, experience teaches us that you will be well advised to try and address the issue during the formative stages of the company. Admittedly it is difficult. It is a little like trying to plan for a possible divorce during the honeymoon. However, we believe it is a very important consideration.

Sample Incorporation Documents

The following sample incorporation documents are based on Ohio law and procedure. Documents in other states are similar but may differ in some respects.

Caution. The forms on the following pages are for illustration only. They have not been included with the intention that they would be used in any specific case. They are slightly abbreviated and not necessarily in correct form for actual use. *I do not recommend forming your own corporation without a lawyer.*

Articles of Incorporation

In Ohio, the secretary of state will provide you with a form for articles of incorporation. All you have to do is fill in the blanks. It is that easy if you want a very simple corporation with one class of common shares and no special provisions enlarging or restricting the rights and powers of the shareholders, directors, or the corporation itself. Most articles of incorporation fall into this category. Remember that articles of incorporation can always be amended to add these things later if appropriate.

ARTICLES OF INCORPORATION
of

_____
(Name of Corporation)

The undersigned, a majority of whom are citizens of the United States, desiring to form a corporation, for profit, under Sections 1701.01 et seq. of the Revised Code of Ohio, do hereby certify:

FIRST. The name of said corporation shall be _____

SECOND. The place in Ohio where its principal office is to located is
_____County.
   (City, Village or Township)

THIRD. The purpose for which it is formed are:

To engage in any or all other lawful acts or activities for which corporations may be formed under Sections 1701.01 to 1701.98, inclusive, of the Ohio Revised Code.

FOURTH. The number of shares which is authorized to have outstanding is 750 common shares.

FIFTH. The amount of stated capital with which the corporation shall begin business is five hundred dollars ($500.00).

IN WITNESS WHEREOF, We have hereunto subscribed our names, this _____ day of _____, 19_____.

_____
(Name of Corporation)

_____
_____
_____

Note. Ohio law also requires a form for appointing a person to accept service of legal process.

SIMPLE LETTER OFFERING MONEY AND A FEW ASSETS TO THE CORPORATION

Incorporator's name (your own name if you are the incorporator)

Address

Gentlemen:

I hereby offer to give the _____ Corporation the sum of $5,000 in cash and the following described personal property (or the property listed on an attached page) in exchange for your issuance to me of 100 common shares of The _____ Corporation, which shall be all the issued and outstanding shares of the corporation. The transfer shall take place on the date you accept this offer.

(Signed and dated)

Gentlemen:

(The Corporation), an Ohio corporation, does hereby accept the foregoing offer.

(Incorporator [s])

That is really all there is to it. It can, of course, get much more complicated than that. You may have a going business to offer to the company and you may want to thin the corporation by offering the property in exchange for both stock and notes. There may also be leases of real or personal property involved. However, many small companies are formed with documents just this simple.

After you have filed your articles of incorporation and had them approved by the secretary of state, you then have a first meeting of the shareholders. In this case, you are the only shareholder, the offeror of the money/property, and the incorporator. You have executed the Offer and Acceptance as noted above. Since there is no use in having a "meeting," you simply use the state procedures allowing actions to be taken by written consent and execute a document which looks something like this.

ACTION BY SHAREHOLDER BY WRITTEN CONSENT

Pursuant to Section 1701.54 of the Ohio Revised Code, the undersigned, being the sole shareholder of (name of corporation) does hereby take the following action in writing.

1. The action of the incorporators in accepting the offer from _____is hereby ratified.

2. The following people are hereby elected directors of the corporation to serve for a period of one year or until their successors are duly designated or elected. [I recommend at least three directors and possibly four—they can all be family members even if they are not active in the business.]

3. A Code of Regulations for the company is hereby adopted in the form attached hereto. [I have not included a copy—they can be quite long, and they are not very important for a small company.]

Signed_____

Now you have yourself a corporation with directors. You still need officers and you probably need a banking resolution. Your bank will supply you with a copy of the resolution it uses.

ACTION OF DIRECTORS BY WRITTEN CONSENT

Pursuant to Section 1701.54 of the Ohio Revised Code, the undersigned, being all the directors of_____ , do hereby take the following action in writing.

1. The following people are hereby elected officers of the company, to serve for one year or until their successors are duly designated or elected. [There are very few requirements here. The following is a usual list—sometimes one person holds more than one office, but you should have separate people as president and secretary (or vice president and assistant secretary) because many documents require the signature of both these officers. You may want your lawyer to service as an assistant secretary.]

President_____

Vice President_____

Secretary_____

Treasurer

2. The company hereby adopts the following banking resolution. [Use the bank's form — they will want a copy attested to by the corporate secretary.]

                                                    Directors

Date:_____   _____

                                     _____

                                     _____

                                     _____

                                     _____

3

Involving Other People in Your Business

From many years of practicing law, I can say without any qualification whatsoever that the single biggest problem — by several orders of magnitude — in operating any business is maintaining the good relationships with the other key people in that business. This includes your fellow stockholders (or partners) and the key employees in the company who feel that they have some important stake in the success of the enterprise. We all know sorry tales of people who started out with the best intentions but came to unhappy and costly partings of the way because of differing views as to what should be done with the business or how it should be done.

Further, if I had to pick the one area which is the subject of most dispute, it would be the proper dividing of the corporate pie. Everyone involved will have a higher view of his or her contribution to the success of the corporation in relation to the contribution of others. Those who supply the money will think that they should get the lion's share of the profits; those who do the work will think the opposite.

On the other hand, except in the very smallest of enterprises, the involvement of other people is going to be key to the success and profitability of that business. We all know that you simply cannot do everything yourself and that it is extremely difficult to hire good people in a small business unless they have some piece of the action.

First, let me state my personal preferences so that you will understand my biases in reading the rest of this chapter. Despite the fact that you cannot do everything yourself and despite the fact that it is difficult to hire good people on a straight salary, I always strongly recommend that this approach be carefully considered and analyzed before you let someone else into the action of your company. Further, when you do have to let somebody in on a piece of the action, I recommend that you try to do it via the employment contract approach, where the person's salary or compensation is based on increased profits or some other rather easily measurable criterion. If you need additional capital, explore debt, leasing, or preferred stock before giving up equity for money. I recommend sharing the ownership or the responsibility for managing your corporation with other people only as a last resort. These personal biases are partly the result of my psychological makeup, but they are also the result of 25 years of reading case after case involving all forms of wrangling among business partners.

I would like to devote the rest of this chapter to discussing the legal problems involving the use of other people in your business. I think it is useful to divide this discussion into three categories, because virtually all of the cases I have read and the problems I have personally encountered can be grouped into one of these classes.

1. The partnership and the problems of partnership law
2. The problems of having more than one common stockholder in a corporation
3. The problems and opportunities inherent in the employer-employee relationship—specifically employment contracts.

Partnerships

A partnership is a form of doing business where two or more people join together to share the profits of an undertaking and do not form a corporation. As was discussed in the preceding chapter, a partnership is a business entity but not a tax entity. The partnership will not save you any taxes, but on the other hand, if there is a loss, it will allow you to deduct your share of the loss from your other income. Partnerships are generally of two types: general partnership, which is the kind I have been talking about, and limited partnership.

Limited partnerships are used in real estate syndications and other tax shelter investments where the investor wants the tax advantages of a partnership but not the unlimited liability that typically goes with being a general partner in a general partnership. In a limited partnership there is one or more general partners and then a group of "limited partners" who are only investors. Essentially, these people are much like the shareholders in a corporation. Their liability for business losses extends only to the money they have contributed to the partnership. Thus, if someone sells you a limited partnership interest for $10,000 in a million-dollar real estate venture and the whole thing goes bankrupt, you are subject to losing only your original $10,000 contribution. You will not have to make good on the hundreds of thousands or even millions of dollars of liabilities which can be generated when one of these big deals goes down the drain. Limited partnerships are useful for tax shelters but are not generally used for business deals.

In a business deal, the typical pattern is that two or three people will get together to informally conduct a business and will not bother to incorporate. They will simply shake hands, or perhaps draw up a very sketchy agreement which says that they will all work together for the common good of the company and share the profits on some basis — usually the same basis on which they contributed capital.

Though informal, that kind of arrangement does have legal implications. *The law will infer a partnership.* The fact that you may not have any partnership agreement does not matter. The terms of your partnership will be those contained in the Uniform Partnership Act, which provides for the following key rules:

1. Any partner can bind the other partner or partners to business debts.

2. Partners are *individually and personally* liable for partnership debts if those debts exceed the assets of the partnership. (In our real estate deal, if that was a general partnership rather than a limited partnership and you contributed $10,000 to a deal which went bankrupt because it had liabilities of $1,000,000 more than its assets, you would be individually and personally liable for the entire $1,000,000.)

3. Any partner can terminate the partnership at any time for any reason. If the partner has contracted not to terminate the partnership, there may be a cause of action against the partner for damages, but that does not change the basic fact that a partnership can be terminated at the virtual whim of any partner.

4. The death of any partner automatically terminates the partnership. You can usually work around this problem in a well-drafted partnership agreement, but it is a rather complex and cumbersome problem.

5. The liability of a partner for partnership debts is *joint and several.* This means that *each* partner is liable for *all* the partnership debts. If you are 50-50 partners with someone, you can be stuck with 100 percent of the debts if the other partner turns out to be insolvent or skips town.

6. You cannot change any of this by contract. You can, of course, enter into any kind of partnership agreement you want which establishes the rights *as between partners*. But, when the creditors are involved, there is simply nothing you can do to change these basic rules about liability. Creditors cannot be cut off from these rights by any private deals you make with your partner.

7. A partnership interest is subject to the normal rules of family law. If your partner gets divorced, you may find yourself in partnership with the spouse or, more likely, the spouse's lawyer. If the court awards the spouse all or a portion of the partnership interest in your partnership, there is simply nothing you can do to prevent it other than terminating the partnership.

8. Essentially, the same thing is true for tort liability. If your partner runs over someone and gets sued for more than the insurance coverage, the injured person can attach the partnership interest and you could end up in a very difficult situation.

These are the kinds of problems that make lawyers very nervous when clients want to enter into a business partnership.

Two Cautions.   First, if at all possible, try to avoid going into business as a partnership. Second, if there is some reason why this must be done, be sure to have a comprehensive partnership agreement drafted by a good lawyer, and be sure to read and understand that agreement.

Corporations and Shareholders

I would like next to discuss the legal principles involved in corporations and shareholders in terms of how a corporation is run and who has the power to make major decisions.

A corporation is a creature of state law, but in all states the principles for how a corporation is operated are substantially the same. The corporation is owned by the common shareholders. The common shareholders have one principal right, and that is to elect the directors. *A shareholder has absolutely no right whatsoever to participate in the management of the corporation.* The shareholders' only right is to elect directors. All states provide that a corporation shall be run and managed by its board of directors; and further, that the board of directors will operate by majority rule. Thus, on a five-person board of directors, any three directors can effectively dictate the course of action of the company.

Further, the officers of the company who are in charge of the day-today management of the company, subject to the direction of the board of directors, are all elected by the directors. Again, the majority rule applies. A majority of the directors can elect the officers of the company.

These basic principles seem to effectively preclude participation in the corporate entity by the minority shareholders—and indeed, they do. But in order to protect minority shareholders, the law has given them certain rights and imposed certain obligations on the majority. For example, a corporation must deal fairly with the minority shareholders. If the corporation's assets are to be sold, the minority must be given their fair share of the proceeds. Many states have a so-called right of appraisal and buy-out, whereby in certain key transactions, such as the sale of all the corporate assets or the liquidation of the company, the shareholders who disagree with the majority are entitled to have the corporation buy their shares at a fair value. Of course, exactly what is fair in these kinds of situations is always subject to much dispute.

Minority shareholders have other rights, too. The chief one is to bring lawsuits against the company. A minority shareholder is entitled to attend the annual shareholders' meeting; to vote for directors (even though the minority holding may not represent enough votes to elect any directors); and usually, to examine the books and records of the company. In short, minority shareholders do not have any important *substantive* rights to dictate how the company is run, but they have a lot of *procedural* rights which they can use to harass the company and make a general nuisance of themselves. For this purpose, a minority shareholder is anyone who holds even a single share.

If you stop and think about the above general legal principles for a minute, you can see some of the obvious problems.

1. If you give your good associates a few shares of your company, you have not given them anything except the right to cause you a lot of trouble if they get mad at you.

2. If you are going into business with somebody in the form of a corporation, and you end up with 49 percent of the stock and they end up with 51 percent, they control the *entire* company and you have *almost nothing* to say about it. Essentially, your rights are the same as they would be if you had only one share. You can cause a lot of trouble, but you cannot really do anything important.

The right of the majority to run the business, as a practical matter, includes the right to substantially dilute the interest of the minority. Suppose, for example, that you have a company with a net worth of $100,000 and majority shareholders of 51 percent, with you holding the other 49 percent. There is virtually nothing in the law—except for vague concepts of fairness and fraud—which would prevent those 51-percent shareholders from paying themselves salaries sufficient to reduce the assets of the corporation substantially. They could then liquidate it, and while you would be entitled to 49 percent of whatever was left when it was liquidated, that might not be very much.

Suppose you have a 50-50 ownership of your corporation. This will effectively prevent the other party from taking advantage of you because you will have an effective veto power over everything. By the same token, the other party has an effective veto power over anything important that you want to do, and so you have the classic standoff.

Because of these problems, I do not recommend any of these kinds of transactions. I will explain this in more detail later on, but let us look again at some things which don't strike me as being a very good idea.

1. Giving a few shares of stock to employees or friends can cause you nothing but trouble. You haven't really given them anything important (except perhaps psychologically), but you have given them the opportunity to cause you a lot of legal headaches if there is a falling out later on. I recommend you don't do it.

2. A 51–49-percent deal is very good if you have the 51 percent and very bad if you have the 49 percent.

3. A 50-50 deal has a lot of problems, the key one being that there is simply no good way to break a deadlock. While you and the other 50-percent shareholder are wrangling about some problem, the whole business can go down the drain, and there is nothing either of you can do about it unless the other agrees.

The above discussion assumes we are talking only about common stock. Common stock, you will remember, is the voting stock of the corporation, and the common shareholders are those who own the equity interest in the corporation on and are entitled to elect the directors. The directors, in turn, manage the company. There are, however, other kinds of stock, and indeed, there are many different kinds of common stock. Because of these other alternatives, you do not have to get involved in the above three kinds of situations which present so many problems. Let us take them in order and see how they can be dealt with.

Instead of giving friends or relatives common shares of your company, you could give them preferred stock or nonvoting common. Depending on what you want to accomplish, it seems to me that some other arrangement besides giving away voting common shares of the company could accomplish the same result. For example, suppose you had two classes of common, class A being entitled to vote for directors and class B being nonvoting. If you wanted to allow other people to participate in the equity growth of the company, there is no reason why you could not create a class B stock and either give some of it to them or let them purchase it. By the same token, if you wanted to give someone income, you could create preferred stock and give him or her that so you could pay dividends on the preferred and provide the income that way. If you wanted to provide someone with a share of the current profits, you would not have to use stock at all; you could simply use a contractual arrangement to pay them a bonus equal to whatever share of the profits you thought appropriate, calculated in any way you think appropriate.

Going to our 51–49-percent deal, it seems to me that the problem here is the fact that the 49-percent shareholder has almost enough stock to control the company, but not quite. It is one thing to get frozen out if you have only one or two shares and quite another to get frozen out if you have 49 percent of the stock — although legally these amount to approximately the same thing. Assuming you want to have an arrangement where one party has the sole and complete right to run the company but the other has a very important share in the profits and income of the company, there are a number of ways you can do this and safeguard the 49-percent shareholder. Again, nonvoting common and preferred stock can be used for this purpose. For example, you can have one person own all of the voting common and another person own all of the nonvoting common. That way you have it spelled out right up front that the person who does not own voting common stock cannot vote for the directors and is subject to the rights of the people with the voting stock to control the company. That strikes me as a lot fairer than a 51-percent–49-percent deal.

The 50-50 deal is much more difficult. It is a classic problem for which lawyers really don't have many good solutions. If you want to have a 50-50 deal, you are simply going to have to live with the deadlock problem. You can minimize it to some extent by trying to reach an agreement as to how you will break a deadlock while you are still friends, rather than waiting until after a problem occurs, when you may not be on the best of terms. You can appoint an arbitrator, who may be your lawyer, an accountant, or a neutral business associate; or, if you think it is necessary, you can go into an elaborate arbitration arrangement pursuant to the rules of the American Arbitration Association. Essentially, these rules provide that each of you picks an arbitrator, those two arbitrators pick a third, and the three arbitrators together resolve any dispute.

In my judgment, the common denominator is that you should get professional help in drafting the documents and issuing the appropriate kinds of stock. I have touched on only a few of the problems and opportunities involved in joint ownership of a corporation. Indeed, there are many books written on the subject, and your flexibility is limited only by your own imagination and that of your lawyer.

One of the key things which would have avoided a lot of the disputes I have seen is simply a meeting of all the parties in question, where corporate counsel explains clearly to each person exactly what his or her rights and obligations are and, correspondingly, what rights he or she does not have. I know that when you are starting a business the last thing you want to do is to get all of your people together for an afternoon in a lawyer's office to discuss this kind of thing. The last thing on any of your minds is that there will ever be any kind of dispute among all you good people who are going to help one another make this business a success. I certainly hope that is true for you, but my experience has shown that it may not be. Getting everything out on the table and all of these problems thrashed out while you are still friends can be done in an afternoon in a lawyer's office. If you wait till a problem comes up, it is going to take many afternoons with many lawyers.

Caution. The issuance of securities of any kind, including shares of stock in a closely held company or for that matter even partnership interests in a closely held partnership, is often highly regulated at both the federal and the state levels. You should never issue shares of any corporation—remembering that shares can also include debt instruments, such as notes—without having discussed this with your legal counsel. Some state or federal registration requirements may be necessary; if you fail to follow these rules, the persons buying those shares might be entitled to a right of recession. (See Chap. 2.)

Buying Out Other Shareholders

As a corollary to all of this, after you have decided exactly what kind of working arrangement you are going to have, it is necessary and appropriate for you to decide how the various parties are going to be either bought out or redeemed out should they die, become disabled, or desire to withdraw from the business. Again, the rationale is very simple. These kinds of arrangements are standard and very easy to work out so long as everyone is friends and no one knows who will die or become disabled first. They can be difficult and costly to work out later on, when the interests of the parties become adverse. There are an infinite number of ways to deal with these problems. Many of them involve life insurance. If you are going to buy someone out when he or she dies, life insurance can be used to provide the money to do it with. Even this can become complex, however. Consider the following questions:

1. Should one shareholder take out life insurance policies on the lives of all the rest so when anyone dies, the others have money to buy the deceased shareholders' interest?

This works for up to about five people (25 life insurance policies in that case), but this relatively simple approach can get terribly complicated if many people are involved.

2. Should the *company* take out the life insurance so that the company redeems the shares of the deceased shareholder? If the company takes out the policy, is the money paid on the death of the shareholder to be considered an asset of the company?

Example

> Suppose you and another person form a company with $50,000 capital each, and agree that if one dies, the company will redeem the deceased person's shares. To provide the money, the company takes out a $50,000 policy on each of you. The other shareholder dies the next day, and $50,000 is paid to the corporation. The assets of the corporation are, at that point, $150,000 — $50,000 that you each contributed and $50,000 from the insurance company. When the company redeems the shares of the deceased shareholder, should it pay half of $100,000 or half of $150,000? The answer you choose makes a big difference.

There is no right or wrong approach, but failure to agree on this point when you enter into the redemption agreement is definitely bad and will certainly cause a dispute later.

If you think it is difficult and complex to work out a simple arrangement to redeem or purchase the shares of a shareholder when life insurance can be obtained, try figuring out a way to do it if one or more of the shareholders are uninsurable, or if neither the individuals nor the company can afford enough insurance.

Death is the easiest of all situations to deal with. There is no problem in determining when someone is dead, and in most cases, life insurance can provide all or at least most of the cash necessary to take care of the problem. However, what about disability or a failing out? Those are more difficult problems because there is no easily identifiable event and perhaps no money. They can and should be dealt with, however, while neither party knows who will become disabled first, and while both are friends and neither has reason to blame the other for a falling out. Corporate lawyers have an arsenal of tools for dealing with these problems. Legal form books are full of sample agreements. Your job is to make sure the problem is dealt with in a planning mode — not in a dispute-settlement situation. If you wait until after a dispute arises, the only winner is likely to be the lawyer.

What to Tell Your Lawyer When You Discuss Buy-Out or Redemption Agreements

The above problems have become so standard that all lawyers have buzz words which they use to discuss them—namely, redemption agreements, which refers to cases where the *corporation* redeems the shares of a deceased or disabled shareholder; and cross-purchase agreements, which refers to situations where the individual shareholders purchase the shares of the deceased or disabled shareholder. These documents are not terribly long or complicated, but they require some very important decisions. As always, taxes play a very important role. Therefore, the key thing you have to do is lay all the financial cards on the table and ask your lawyer or accountant to make a recommendation as to which approach is best for you. I recommend against asking an insurance advisor for this advice because of the extremely large number of contracts (and therefore commissions) which can be generated by the cross-purchase arrangement. I have seen insurance agents literally set up for life on one of these deals. While it may be best for you, I think you should have that determination made by a lawyer or accountant who has no particular ax to grind. Redemption and cross-purchase agreements will cost you just about the same in legal and accounting or tax planning fees.

Here is a very brief list of things to think about before you call your lawyer. It will save both of you a lot of time (and should save you money):

1. What contingencies do you want to cover? Death is certainly going to be the first, but what about
   a. disability? (How are you going to define disability?)
   b. withdrawal from business or retirement?
   c. business disputes or breakup of the company?

2. How are you going to determine the value of the corporation? This is the most difficult point. Everyone who writes about the subject seems to say that book value is not a good measure. I agree that it *may* not be a proper measure, but I think it is usually a very good measure. It certainly is simple. Perhaps the best way to determine value is to execute a schedule with the agreement saying what the value is, and then reexecute it every year with a revised value. The problem I have seen with this approach is that people forget to do it, and when someone dies there is no recently agreed-upon value and therefore nothing whatsoever on which to base value. That almost always causes a dispute and possibly a lawsuit. Remember that your lawyer is not going to be too

much help here. He or she can suggest alternatives, but *you* have to make the judgments. Your accountant is in a slightly better position to help you, but it is still your business, and its value is always going to be very subjective.

3. Tell the lawyer about the age and physical health of each party. Remember that insurance is a good way to get money only if it is available and not prohibitively expensive. If one or more of the shareholders is in ill health or old, insurance may not be a viable alternative.

4. Be prepared to share your personal balance sheet (or at least the important parts of it) with your lawyer. He or she cannot do a good job on this problem without knowing what the individuals involved can reasonably afford to do. If all the parties are independently wealthy, your lawyer is going to have an easy job. If all the parties are young and their principal asset is going to be stock in the business, your lawyer's job is much more difficult.

5. Be prepared to share your views on what to do if someone becomes disabled, and be prepared to talk about what you consider a disability. What if someone has a heart attack and simply has to cut back? What if someone is completely and totally disabled for one year (or two) but can work thereafter? Again, your lawyer cannot make these decisions for you. He or she can ask you questions and provide alternatives, but you have to make the decisions.

6. Be sure to give some thought to the precise mechanics of how the deal is going to work out. What if everyone agrees on a cross purchase agreement and everyone promises to take out the necessary policies? Upon the death of the first shareholder, you find that someone forgot to do it. Should there be a trustee to physically handle all the insurance policies and make sure the premiums paid when due? It may not be a bad investment. Then again, it may be wasted money. You have to decide.

Summary of Sharing Ownership

To summarize up to this point: Do not form a partnership unless there is virtually no other way to do business, and do not let things drag out before forming a corporation because, if you do, the courts will impose a legal partnership in the interim. Instead, use the corporation and all the flexibility that it provides to solve the problems inherent in doing business with others. Learn from experience—which has shown ownership-sharing arrangements to be the single most frequent cause of disputes and litigation between business people. Use your corporate counsel and get your full measure of value from him or her by asking for his or her legal judgments and expertise on how to spell out almost everything beforehand while those involved are all still friends. Remember the oil filter commercial, and pay your lawyer a small amount for an "oil filter" now rather than a large amount for an "engine overhaul" later.

Employment Contracts

In order to avoid the difficulties of equity arrangements wherever possible, I recommend the use of employment arrangements as an alternative. If you want to recruit a hotshot sales representative, manager, or engineer and motivate that person to join your company and do a good job, the way to do it is usually money. You do not have to give stock and cause all the problems discussed previously. An employment arrangement which provides that the person gets a salary plus a certain share of the profits ought to be sufficient. This, however, creates its own set of problems—albeit less serious ones than those mentioned above—so I would like to discuss employment contracts in the remainder of this chapter. The reason I have separated the two is that I think that it is impractical to expect a businessperson to deal with the tax and corporate problems inherent in shared ownership arrangements as discussed above. On the other hand, any businessperson can prepare a good draft of an employment contract with the help of this chapter. If you do your homework, your lawyer and accountant should be able to review your work and provide useful comments for minimal fees. In contrast, I should warn you that the legal fees for establishing corporations with different classes of stock, drafting redemption or cross-purchase agreements, or effecting arbitration agreements to break a deadlock will be rather substantial if the lawyer does a good job for you. These are complicated and time-consuming jobs.

I do not generally favor employment contracts. I think businesses, both large and small, are generally better served by having employment relationships simply be employment at will. However, there may be some circumstances which call for a contract.

An employment contract may be necessary when you want to recruit people who have a good bargaining position and who want to have their rights spelled out in a contract. Also, if you are going to recruit someone based upon a sharing of the profits or some other formalized kind of incentive compensation, you will probably need a contract to spell out exactly how much money the person is entitled to.

An employment contract is not necessary when all you want is to assure that the employee respects the confidentiality of private information or that you will get the benefit of any inventions the employee makes on company time. In these cases, a simple employee confidentiality agreement or an agreement requiring the assignment of inventions will accomplish the desired objective. A sample of such an agreement is contained in the chapter on intellectual property (Chap. 13). However, if the main purpose of the agreement is to keep the employee from going into competition or working for a competitor after he or she leaves, the better approach is the execution of an employment contract.

What Kind of Employment Agreement Do You Need?

Assuming that a contract is necessary, the next question is what kind? Basically, there are three types.

1. The first type is the so-called *letter agreement*, which is a very short form frequently used by many companies, both large and small. It seems to serve quite satisfactorily despite the fact that it does not cover very many contingencies. Generally, a letter form can be used when it is thought difficult or inappropriate to negotiate with the prospective employee on all of the incidental terms which would be included in a more formal contract, but either the employee wants the assurance of continued employment at a stated salary or the company has one or two very specific requirements which it feels could be set forth in a letter agreement.

2. The second form is what might be termed the *general form*. While there is no actual form by this name, there is a basic contract which is frequently used in an attempt to compromise between the very short, informal letter agreement and the extremely elaborate full form employment agreement which is used when one or the other parties feels that virtually every contingency must be provided for. This basic contract, which is simply called the general form for lack of any better designation, is the one which is discussed herein and is set forth as an example.

3. The third type is the *full-form employment agreement*, where the parties attempt to cover every conceivable contingency. While this kind of contract may be necessary on some limited occasions, it is very difficult to negotiate because the parties must focus on and bargain for virtually every single term.

Considerations in Employment Contracts

Following are some of the important considerations which must be decided in drafting an employment contract.

The Essentials of the Deal.   This, of course, is the most important part of the contract and should include the following:

1. A clear identification of the parties.

2. A statement of the length of employment and what happens at the end of the term, if anything (e.g., is the contract renewable at someone's option).

3. A description of the basic duties of the employee and to whom the employee reports. You should consider the question of moonlighting and whether or not the employee is going to be required to devote his or her full time to the company. A popular approach is to require the employees to devote "substantially" all of their time to the company, except for reasonable vacation periods. The word "substantially" clearly allows the employee to continue to participate in a limited number of outside deals related to passive investments such as managing a stock portfolio or participating as an investor in real estate or other syndications, but would not include a second job or a part-time business.

4. The pay. This is, of course, one of the most important terms of the agreement. While there naturally can be no form for this, it usually breaks down into the following four parts:
    a. The basic salary.
    b. A bonus, an incentive compensation, or deferred compensation of some type.
    c. The fringe benefits, which, rather than being explained in detail, are usually stated to be simply the same fringe benefits that everybody else in the company gets.
    d. A catchall provision including such other items of compensation as may be agreed upon. These could include the use of a company car and possibly a different vacation period than would normally be allowed an employee with comparable years of service.

If the new employee is to be granted stock options or other rights to invest in the company, it is essential that this provision be drafted by a lawyer. The employment contract is not intended to be used for that purpose.

A troublesome problem in contracts which base the compensation of the employee on the profits of the company is the definition of the term *profits*. Following are some considerations:

1. It should be clear whether the profits are to be computed before or after taxes. Also, the effect of the employee compensation should be made clear, as this naturally has an effect on the profits of the company.

Example

> If the employee is to be paid $10,000 if the profits of the company are $100,000, it should be made clear whether the profits of the company have to be $100,000 before or after the payments to the employee. Obviously, if the company made $100,000 and was then called upon to pay $10,000 to the employee, its profits would, at that point, be only $90,000.

2. Tax considerations are also important. If the company desires to take into account the payment to the employee in the year in question, there will be a very complex set of calculations because the payment will reduce taxable income, which reduces taxes, etc. This can be worked out, but it is difficult. The best approach is usually to base the payment to the employee on profit *before* taxes.

As you can see, then, a seemingly simple employment contract can generate complex legal and accounting problems. I always recommend that any employment contract which includes a formula for paying the employee be reviewed by the company's accountant to make sure that the accountant can actually make the computations which are necessary, and that all parties are in agreement as to how those computations should be made. Lawyers live in fear of deals in which each party is depending on the good faith of the other rather than a clear legal document. Remember that if either party goes to see his or her lawyer about the proper interpretation of an employment contract, all is not well. At that point, amicable agreements are exceedingly difficult to achieve.

The Restrictive Covenant. Perhaps second in importance to the essentials of the deal is the restrictive covenant. Restrictive covenants are important because in the absence of such a provision, there is no legal rule prohibiting an employee from competing with his or her former employer unless trade secrets or some kind of fraudulent or unfair methods are involved. The provision contained in the sample form has been constructed to attempt to work around a number of legal problems which will be obvious from a reading of the provision. In any restrictive covenant, it is important to include limitations as to time and area.

The restrictions must be reasonable, or the courts will not enforce them. What is reasonable will vary from case to case. Your lawyer can help you make this determination; it is a combination legal-business judgment. However, even with your lawyer's help, there may be no clear answer. My view is that it is better to have a shorter period in a smaller geographical area which is clearly enforceable than to have something the company clearly feels protects itself but which is of doubtful enforceability. Another aspect of the reasonableness question is the extent of the trade secret or confidential information which may be involved. For example, in a case involving Orkin Exterminating Company and one of their employees, the Arkansas Supreme Court held that an otherwise reasonable noncompetition agreement was not enforceable because there were no trade secrets or confidential information involved. The court said that the basic flaw in the noncompetition covenant of the agreement was that it was directed not against unfair competition but against competition of any kind on the part of the former employees. A reading of the majority and dissenting opinions in this case points out the essential problem.

The majority said that it would have sustained the restriction if trade secrets, special training, or confidential information or access to lists of customers were involved. However, it said that the pesticides used by Orkin were commercially available; that the training was available in numerous colleges; and that although Orkin did train its employees, it did so only as a matter of self-interest, to make them proficient in their jobs. The court said further that:[*]

> If Orkin's position is sound, then any employer in any business devoted to selling—whether the sales be of insurance, real estate, clothing, groceries, hardware, or anything else—can validly prohibit its former salesmen from engaging in that business within the vicinity for as long as two years after the termination of employment. Needless to say, the law does not provide any such protection from ordinary competition.

The following quotation from the dissent, however, suggests that there were, in fact, a considerable number of facts which supported the argument that a valid trade secret existed and that some of the information in question was confidential.

> Admittedly, Orkin's confidential technical manuals told its sales and service personnel how to service its customers. An Orkin employee taught Weaver procedures. Confidential technical bulletins prepared by Orkin's research and development section disseminated

*Orkin Exterminating Co. v. Weaver, 521 S.W. 2d 69, 1975.

among its employees, disclosed the latest ideas and recommendations of the employer in treating procedures and on chemicals that can or cannot be used in particular areas. The chemicals are not specifically found on the market, but since Federal law requires that the ingredients be shown on the label, an employee can learn which chemicals to buy on the open market in order to provide service to a customer. Orkin has patent rights, not on the chemicals, but on the mixtures. One can buy the chemicals that go into Orkin's mixtures but not the mixtures.

To operate successfully in the pest control business, one must have a working knowledge of the problems that could be encountered in a particular business being served, of the various insects that might be anticipated, how they multiply, where and how they hibernate, the areas to be searched, the particular chemical to be used to treat the specific infestations found, the strength to be achieved by mixing chemicals, and the types of areas in which applications should or should not be made. All these techniques, chemicals and application procedures are kept confidential. Weaver did have access to all Orkin's mixtures of chemicals, methods of applications and techniques, all of which were confidential.

The last portion of the restrictive covenant form that I have included has been carefully drafted to assure maximum enforceability, even though some court in some jurisdiction may determine that some part of it is unenforceable. However, this provision should not be used to justify a basic restriction in terms of time or area which otherwise may be unjustified. In other words, the first line of defense should be that the provisions are reasonable.

So long as a company continues to pay an employee's salary, it can restrict that employee from any kind of competition anyplace in the world. The problem comes when the company stops paying the salary and then attempts to prohibit the employee from earning a living. Courts react against this and closely examine restrictive covenants and, in many cases, hold them unenforceable. The lesson to be learned from this is that if the employee could really severely damage the company by going into competition, then the basic term of employment should be for what the company feels is a long enough period to protect itself. This way, the maximum risk it runs is simply having to pay the salary of the employee at a time when he or she is not performing any service for the company.

This is also a technique I used in order to determine from clients and management just how important the noncompetition agreement was. When the client would first mention the subject, I would be told that it was very important, and that if this employee were not restricted from doing anything even vaguely related to the present job anywhere in the world, disastrous consequences would result. Therefore, I was asked to draft the most restrictive clause I could possibly create. When I agreed to do this but said that the company would have to agree to continue to pay the employee's salary after termination to make it enforceable, the matter was viewed in a different perspective. I suggest you take the same approach. Ask yourself what restrictions you *really* need, and be able to articulate precisely why you need them to your lawyer.

Confidential Information and Inventions   Perhaps the third most important subject to be dealt with in the employment relationship is confidential information and inventions. As mentioned before, however, I recommend that this be handled in a separate document. This document can simply be incorporated with the form employment contract I have suggested (see Chap. 13 for a sample).

Other Considerations   Following are some other considerations which can arise in drafting an employment contract and which could be extremely important in certain circumstances.

1. *What do you do about the sale or discontinuance of the business?* Unless there is something in the contract covering this point, the sale of your business does not, in and of itself, give you the right to terminate a contract of employment if that contract is for a fixed term which extends past the sale date.
2. *What do you do if the employee fails to perform as anticipated?* Despite the best of intentions, it may be that person is not productive for you. The general law on this is rather unfavorable to the employer. Unless you have something fairly clear on which to base your action, you cannot discharge an employee who has a contract. Of course, if there is a deliberate and willful failure to perform, or if the employee embezzles money, becomes an alcoholic, or simply does not show up for work for an extended period of time, you would have the right to cancel the contract. If, however, the problem is simply a dispute as to the value of the employee's services—a question of whether or not the employee is earning his or her keep—it is extremely unlikely that you will be able to discharge someone who has an employment contract. At the first sign of trouble, the best thing for you to do is to start building a record and to try to establish some objective criteria for measuring the employee's performance. Even this, however, is extremely difficult. Talk to your lawyer early if you have a problem like this.

3. *What about changes of duties?* A few cases have illustrated the need for the contract to stipulate that the employee's duties may be changed by the employer. Absent such a provision, it has sometimes been successfully asserted by an employee that a change of his or her duties by the employer amounted to a breach of contract.

4. *State laws.* As alluded to above, an employment contract is going to be governed under state laws, and these are not uniform. Some states will simply not enforce restrictive covenants at all.

5. *What if the employee already has an employment contract with somebody else?* If you intentionally induce an employee to leave the employment of someone else, you may be guilty of interference with a contractual agreement and subject to damages by the other employer. The general rule is that unless you have actual knowledge of the prospective employee's other contractual relationship, you cannot be guilty of inducing a breach of it. However, when you have *actual knowledge* and when you do not is subject to what the judge or jury believes when they hear all the evidence. You might want to ask the employee if he or she is subject to any other contract. This rule can operate in your favor if someone with whom you have a contract is negotiating with someone else. If you have an idea that this might be happening, you can enhance your legal position by informing the other company of the employment contract the employee has with you.

6. *Employment contracts for sales representatives.* If a sales representative is given an employment contract and if his or her compensation is based on commissions, some additional considerations become appropriate.

   a. The method of calculating the commissions should be made extremely clear. This issue causes many disputes. Some things which should be considered are the following:

      (1) Are the commissions paid on all orders forwarded by the sales representative or only on those accepted by the company?

      (2) Does the company have the right to reject orders? (The company should have the right to reject any order either because of the lack of credit of the customer or for any reason deemed appropriate by the company.)

      (3) Is the commission on the total sale, or are such things as returns, freight allowances and discounts, and bad debts or other similar items subtracted from the base?

      (4) When are the commissions payable—when the sales representative sends in the order, when the merchandise is shipped,

when it is received by the customer, or when it is actually paid for by the customer?

(5) Will the sales representative receive a drawing account or some other type of advance on future commissions?

b. What about expenses? Must the sales representative defray all of his or her traveling and other expenses, or will the company pay for a portion or all of them?

c. What kind of paperwork in terms of reports to the sales representative, etc., should be undertaken by the company? Generally, the company should furnish some kind of report to the sales representative, perhaps on a monthly basis, showing all information necessary to calculate the commissions payable.

SAMPLE EMPLOYMENT AGREEMENT

This Agreement is made and entered into this _____ day of _____, 19 _____, but effective as of _____ ("Effective Date") by and between _____ a corporation with offices located at _____ (The Company) and _____ of _____

(Employee)

WHEREAS, The Employee has certain valuable experience in the business conducted by The Company, and

WHEREAS, both the Employee and the Company feel it would be beneficial to enter into an employment arrangement and both desire to have the terms of such arrangement set forth in an Agreement, and

NOW THEREFORE, in consideration of the mutual agreements herein set forth, the parties agree as follows:

1. *Duties*

Upon the effective date, the Company shall employ and the Employee agrees to be employed by The Company to perform the following duties:

[Herein specify the *general* duties to be performed by the employee— but do not be too specific. Also, be sure to include the clauses set forth below to specify that the duties may be changed, and state to whom the employee is to report.]

The Employee shall also perform such additional or different or other duties related to the business as may from time to time be delegated to him or her by The Company. The Employee shall devote substantially all of his or her time to such duties except for reasonable vacation periods, and shall observe and abide by the reasonable company policies and decisions of the Company in all business matters and shall be responsible to and report to the Chief Executive Officer of the Company.

2. *Term*

The Employee's employment shall continue for a period of _____ years, beginning on the effective date of this Agreement and ending on _____.

3. *Compensation*
The Company shall pay and the Employee shall accept as full consideration for the services to be rendered hereunder compensation consisting of the following:

a. [Salary.]

b. [Any other bonus, etc., which might be paid.]

c. The Employee shall also receive such other benefits as may be made available from time to time to other management employees of The Company with similar age and years of service as Employee.

d. Such other items of compensation as may be agreed upon by Employee and The Company from time to time, including but not limited to, reasonable vacation periods, expense accounts, and the use of company automobiles.

4. *Illness, Incapacity or Death*
If at any time during the term of this Agreement the Employee becomes disabled or is unable for any reason, substantially, to perform his or her duties hereunder and he or she has not breached any of the provisions of this Agreement, compensation shall continue to be paid to him or her as provided in paragraph 3 but only as to the first six-month period, during which he or she shall be so disabled. The Company may, at its sole option, continue payment of Employee's salary until he or she is able to return to work or for such period greater than six months as The Company elects, or may terminate this Agreement. If Employee should die during the term of this Agreement, Employee's employment and The Company's obligations hereunder shall terminate as of the end of the month in which his or her death occurs.

5. *Restrictive Covenant* [must be reasonable as to time and territory.]
The Employee and The Company agree that The Company's business depends, to a considerable extent, on the individual efforts both in sales and design of Employee. Accordingly, Employee covenants and agrees that he or she will not, for the period of his or her employment hereunder and for one year from the date of expiration of this Agreement (but in no event for less than four years from the date hereof in the event of earlier termination of his or her employment hereunder for whatever cause) engage directly or indirectly (either as principal, agent or consultant or through any corporation, firm or organization in which he or she may bean officer, director, employee, substantial shareholder, partner, member or be otherwise affiliated) in any activity anywhere in the United States competitive with the business being conducted by The Company at the time of termination of his or her employment hereunder, including without limitation [specify general nature of business].

6. *Confidential Information and Inventions*

Employee shall execute and abide by an "employee invention and confidential information agreement," in the form attached hereto as Exhibit A and incorporated herein by reference.

The covenants of Employee contained in paragraphs 5 and 6 hereof shall each be construed as an Agreement independent of any other provision in this Agreement, and the existence of any claim or cause of action of Employee against The Company, whether predicated on this Agreement or otherwise, shall not constitute a defense to the enforcement by The Company of either covenant. Both parties hereby expressly agree and contract that it is not the intention of either party to violate any public policy, statutory or common law, and that if any sentence, paragraph, clause or combination of the same of paragraphs 5 or 6 (including the provisions incorporated by reference) is in violation of the law of any state where applicable, such sentence, paragraph, clause or combination of the same shall be void in the jurisdictions where it is unlawful, and the remainder of such paragraph and this Agreement shall remain binding on the parties hereto. It is the intention of both parties to make the covenants of paragraphs 5 and 6 binding only to the extent that it may be lawfully done under existing applicable laws. In the event that any part of any covenant of paragraph 5 or 6 is determined by a court of law to be overly broad thereby making the covenant unenforceable, the parties hereto agree and it is their desire that such court shall substitute a reasonable judicially enforceable limitation in place of the offensive part of the covenant, and that as so modified the covenant shall be as fully enforceable as set forth herein by the parties themselves in the modified form.

7. *Miscellaneous*

a. Governing Law.

The validity, construction, interpretation and enforceability of this Agreement and the capacity of the parties shall be determined and governed by the laws of the State of _____.

b. Assignment.

This agreement is personal to each of the parties hereto, and neither party may asssign or delegate any of the rights or obligations hereunder without first obtaining a written consent of the other party.

c. Rights and Remedies.

Both parties recognize that the services to be rendered under this Agreement by Employee are special, unique and of extraordinary character. Either party may, at its option, terminate this Agreement or elect to institute and prosecute proceedings in any court of competent jurisdiction, either in law or equity, to obtain damages to enforce specific performance of the Agreement to enjoin the other party as appropriate and to recover reasonable attorneys' fees and costs of prosecuting such action in the event of the occurrence of any of the following:

   i. If there is a substantial breach by either party of any of their terms and conditions of this Agreement (other than those set forth in paragraphs 5 and 6 herein), and such breach remains uncured after the expiration of sixty days from the date of receipt of written notice by other party, or

ii. If there is a breach by Employee of any of the covenants of paragraphs 5 and 6 of Agreement.

Termination for any cause shall not constitute a waiver of The Company's rights under paragraphs 5 and 6, nor a release of Employee from his or her obligations hereunder.

The rights and remedies provided each of the parties herein shall be cumulative and in addition to any other rights and remedies provided by law or otherwise. Any failure in the exercise by either party of its rights to terminate this Agreement or to enforce any provision of this Agreement for default or violation by the other party shall not prejudice such party's right of termination or enforcement for any further or other default or violation.

d. Collateral Agreements.

This Agreement constitutes the entire Agreement between the parties respecting the employment of Employee, and there are no representations, warranties or commitments, except as set forth herein. This Agreement may be amended only by an instrument in writing executed by the parties hereto.

e. Notices.

Any notice, request, demand or other communication hereunder shall be in writing and shall be deemed to be duly given when personally delivered to an officer of The Company or to Employee, as the case may be, or when delivered by mail at the following addresses:

(_____)

(_____)

(Signatures)

A Final Note on Securities Law Issues

A troublesome development since the first edition of this book is the holding by several courts that when a company buys back shares of stock held by employees, even pursuant to a written agreement specifying the price of the stock, the company has a duty to tell the shareholder about material developments. We normally think about such a duty only in the context of public companies where such disclosure is obviously relevant to the stock market. However, cases have extended it to the private context.

Example

A company has three shareholders. Two have 40 percent each and one has 20 percent. The two shareholders with 40 percent each buy out the 20-percent shareholder (or the company redeems the 20-percent shareholders' shares) at what everyone appears to agree on as a fair price. However, six months later the company is bought out by a larger public company at a high premium. There were, in fact, some very preliminary discussions between the company/40-percent shareholders before the 20-percent shareholder sold out. Can the 20-percent shareholder sue the company/40-percent shareholders under the securities laws for failure to disclosure those discussions? One court held yes.

Example

A company has a program whereby employees are allowed to purchase shares at book value, but when the employee leaves, the shares have to be sold back to the company at book value. The basic idea is that if the employee works hard and the company is successful, book value should increase and the employee should benefit. The employee decides to leave the company for his or her own reasons. (In the case involved, the reason was simply that the employee's wife did not get along with the employee's mother and wanted to move to another city—nothing whatever to do with the company.) The employee leaves, sells the shares back at book value, and then a public company buys the private company at a substantial premium. Can the employee who left sue the company for failure to disclose the negotiations that had already taken place? Again, the court held yes.

What do we conclude from cases like these? My advice is to *be very careful about giving employees shares or letting them buy shares.* Of course, discussions about a possible buy-out and employees selling their shares to the company or management, it is important to keep your legal counsel informed of all the details. There may be some duties of disclosure, and there may be some situations in which you simply cannot purchase the shares of minority holders.

4

Buying a Going Business

In my judgment, it would be a mistake to attempt to buy any going business without a good corporate lawyer being thoroughly involved in the transaction, including the drafting of a complete purchase agreement. I will, therefore, devote only a little space to this subject.

What Are Your Options?

There are two basic ways to buy a going business. First I will discuss the major alternatives, and then I will give you my personal preferences. To have a concrete illustration to work with, let us assume you want to buy a home improvement center. It is now conducted in corporate form by a person you know. That person desires to retire, and no family members or employees are in a position to take over the business, so it is for sale.

One way to buy the business is to *buy the stock* of the corporation. If you choose this route, you could accomplish the transaction by simply giving the seller a check for the purchase price in exchange for his or her shares of stock. Of course, you would want your lawyer to have analyzed the company first to make certain that there were no other shareholders, that the stock was not subject to any restrictions, and that, in general, there were no legal problems in the transaction. Your lawyer's job, however, would be relatively easy.

The other option is to *buy all the assets* of the company. Here, you would have to literally count all the pieces of lumber, hardware, etc., and make a complete inventory. Then you would have to assign a value to each item and total it up. Further, in the case of trucks or real estate, you would have to get the appropriate titles reissued in the name of your new corporation.

All other options for buying a going business are variations on these two basic methods. You can pay the seller in installments whether you buy the assets or buy the stock. You can buy the entire business, or the seller can retain some of it. For example, in some transactions the seller may retain the real estate used by the company and lease it to the new buyer. If the seller is to be involved in the new business, part of the deal can be an employment contract or a consulting contract for the seller. The variations are almost endless, but when all is said and done you almost always end up with a transfer of either stock or assets.

Is it better to buy stock or assets? The benefits of either option depend on which side of the fence you're on. In my judgment, a buyer is almost always better off buying assets than stock. On the other hand, in many cases, the seller will be much better off from a tax perspective selling you stock rather than assets. The decision is therefore often a function of both economics and the negotiation skills and postures of the parties.

Here are some basic rules most of which have several exceptions and variations (buying a business is a fairly complex practice):

1. In the first edition of this book the distinction between ordinary income tax and capital gains rates was often useful to keep in mind. At that time the capital gains rate was approximately half of the ordinary income rate. It was therefore advantageous to structure a transaction so that any taxes were paid at the capital gains rate and, correspondingly, to minimize ordinary income.

Now, however, there is no difference between the rates for capital gains and ordinary income. On the other hand, there is much talk in Congress about changing our tax laws so that there will be a lower rate for capital gains than for ordinary income. This makes planning rather difficult. You may, for example, structure a transaction with a five-year employment or consulting agreement for the seller. At this time it wouldn't make any difference to the seller whether income was received in the form of a consulting or employment agreement, or as payment for stock or assets. The tax rate is going to be the same. However, the seller will be paying taxes not only in the year of the transaction but for the next four years. Suppose that during that time the capital gains rate is reduced and the ordinary income rate increased—a likely possibility. Now the transaction may not be as attractive because the seller will be paying taxes at higher ordinary income rates.

In other words, the present tax law, which has no distinction between capital gains and ordinary income, is at once a simplifying and a complicating factor. If the transaction is an all cash deal and doesn't extend into future years, the single rate makes things rather simple. There really isn't any advantage in shifting portions of the purchase price either away from or into employment agreements, consulting agreements, and the like. If, on the other hand, the transaction calls for payments over a number of years, the existing political climate forces us to gamble on future tax rates.

2. Another very important feature of our current tax law—which is different from the time of the first edition—is that the seller almost always pays a very substantial tax penalty when selling assets. Specifically, if the seller sells the assets of a corporation there will be two taxes. The first will be a tax on the gain that the corporation realizes in the sale of the assets, and the second tax will be on the money paid to the individual. This change in the tax law has been very important in structuring transactions. In years past it was possible to structure a transaction so that, whether the buyer bought assets or the stock of a company, the seller's tax was essentially the same. Therefore, the seller didn't have any reason to seriously object to the buyer's preference for purchasing assets rather than stock. Now, however, the seller may have a very important reason for wanting to avoid an asset transaction.

The following example points out the magnitude of the problem.

Example

> A seller has a company worth $1,000,000 in which the cost basis is substantially zero, so that if the seller sold the whole company for $1,000,000 the profit would be all taxable. If the seller sold the stock for $1,000,000, he or she would have a tax at an ordinary income rate of 28 percent for a total tax of $280,000 and a total aftertax profit of $720,000.
>
> Suppose instead that the buyer purchased all the assets of the company for the same $1,000,000. Assuming a corporate tax rate of 34 percent, this would be a tax of $340,000 with a net left over to the corporation of $660,000. Then, when the corporation distributed that $660,000 to the shareholder there would be an additional tax of 28 percent, or $184,800 of tax. We now have total taxes of approximately $524,800 and a total net to the shareholder of only about $475,200. As you can see, the seller's tax situation makes a sale of assets almost prohibitive.
>
> These calculations represent a gross oversimplification of the situation. When you actually work out the numbers it might not turn out quite that badly. You will always, however, have to deal with that second tax at the shareholder level which will almost always make the seller push hard for a stock deal rather than an asset deal.

Note. The 1990 tax rate changes would alter the calculations a little, but the basic point is still the same.

3. From a corporate law perspective, it is usually desirable for a buyer to purchase assets rather than stock simply because, by purchasing as-

sets, the buyer can pick and choose the exact assets that the buyer wants. Perhaps more importantly, the buyer can avoid acquiring the unknown or contingent liabilities of the corporation. Suppose, for example, you buy all the stock of the corporation and then the tax returns are audited and additional taxes are due. Suppose there are lawsuits filed after you bought the company but arising out of transactions that occurred before. All of those contingent or unknown liabilities would now rest on the buyer's shoulders rather than the seller's. There are ways to minimize problems like these, such as putting some of the purchase price in escrow and getting representations and warranties from the seller, but all of those techniques are less than perfect. They usually depend, for example, on the seller remaining solvent and available to make good on the warranties.

4. Taxes aside, in some situations it may be better to buy the stock of the company than the assets. This will usually occur when the company may have favorable contracts that cannot be assigned. We all know that in most contracts which prohibit assignment, the definition of assignment includes not only an actual assignment of the contract but also a change in ownership or control of the company. For example, if you are buying a distributorship it may be that the contract with the manufacturer not only prohibits assignment, but allows the manufacturer to terminate the distributorship if all of the stock or controlling interest in the stock is sold by the owners. In that case simply buying all the company's stock would not get around the necessity for getting the consent of the manufacturer. There may, however, be some cases where preserving the original corporate identity is important.

The Importance of the
Legal Audit

The foregoing problems are only some of the examples of why it is so important for you to invest in a "legal audit" whenever you buy a business. Lawyers have checklists of things that they will look into so that all the potential risks and liabilities are on the table. After those things have been ferreted out, you, your lawyers, and the parties on the other side of the negotiation table are in a better position to structure a deal that works out best for both parties.

A legal audit does not have to be done entirely by a lawyer. In fact, there are some obvious advantages in you doing some of the work yourself (in close consultation with the lawyer). For example, someone has to get copies of the major contracts that the business to be acquired has already entered into. Since those contracts are now going to be your contracts, it is to your advantage to read them so that you fully understand what they say. In addition, however, you should have your lawyer read over at least the major ones because there are some important legal concepts that you might not catch. The point is that, as mentioned earlier in this chapter, contracts are either assignable or unassignable; if a contract is unassignable, what is the effect of a change in control of the company? This is only one example of the many things to be covered in a legal audit.

What About Buying a Business Where the Seller Stays on to Help You?

One of the best ways to learn a business is to have the person who built it up show you. If it can be arranged, I like this kind of deal — with some cautions. Of course, the facts may not allow it. The reason the seller wants to sell may be because of ill health or another business venture which will take all his or her time. However, one possibility which is definitely worth your consideration is to ask the seller to stay for at least a limited time to help you. This has at least the following advantages:

1. Obviously, the seller knows more than you about all aspects of the business.

2. If the seller is going to be staying on, he or she is more likely to be candid and forthright in the negotiations than if he or she is going to take the certified check to the Caribbean the evening of the closing.

3. If problems come up, the seller's advice and counsel can be worth its weight in gold to you.

My only caution here is to make sure you spell out exactly what you expect of the seller and what the seller is committing to do. You need a contract of some type. It can be an employment contract, as discussed in Chap. 3, or a consulting agreement. Experience has shown that while this is a common and desirable arrangement, it can also produce a lot of conflict. That is why I recommend the carefully negotiated and discussed agreement. I think you should negotiate it yourself, if at all possible. Your lawyer may also be able to negotiate the deal. Perhaps your lawyer could even negotiate a better deal than you could. However, keep in mind that your lawyer is not going to have to work with and rely on this person during the crucial initial stages of the business. After you negotiate everything you can think of and are as clear as possible in your own mind about exactly what your relationship with the former owner is going to be, then have your lawyer draft the appropriate documents. Remember that this business may be almost like a blood relative to the former owner. The transition is likely to be traumatic. Someone else is now going to be coming into his or her business and calling all the shots. That is the biggest reason why you need a carefully drafted agreement to avoid trouble.

Making the salary or fees you pay to the former owner depend on the performance of the business gets mixed reviews from most counselors. On balance, I think a *fixed fee or salary* is best. The contrary argument is that a formula based on sales or profits gives the former owner an incentive to do a good job and give you good advice. If you do have some kind of formula agreement, however, what I said above about lawyers and the need for a full and comprehensive agreement is doubled — and you should get the accountants in on the act too.

What About the Employees of the Business—Should They Get Employment Contracts?

This is a difficult question to answer in the abstract. My general preference is *not* to have employment contracts unless there is a rather clear reason for them. In the case of a former owner, there is a clear reason. In the case of other key employees, there may also be compelling reasons. In fact, it may turn out that one of the principal assets of the business is its people. In that event, you will want to carefully consider employment contracts with the key employees—as well as noncompetition agreements.

In summary, then, before you buy a going business be absolutely sure that you have done all your homework. You are going to be spending a lot of money all at once. There are many advantages to buying a going business, but there are also a few disadvantages, and the large initial capital outlay is one of them. All those little problems that come up one at a time when you start a business from scratch may be presented to you all at once if you buy a business that is already established. If you get a good corporate lawyer who approaches the purchase of the business in a systematic way and who drafts a comprehensive purchase agreement, not only will you be assured of a relatively hassle-free transaction on the purchase itself but, more importantly, you will have a sound base to continue that business in the future. Remember, also, that all the considerations we talked about at the beginning of the book apply here. You still have to form the corporation and decide on the capital structure, what kinds of stock you will have, and whether you elect Subchapter S.

Legal Fees for Buying a Business

Start out with the assumption that you are going to need the same legal help to form the corporation and evaluate your alternatives as if you were starting a business from scratch. That is a minimum of $300 for the smallest and simplest deal and a maximum of $2,000 or so for one which is larger and a little more complicated. (Of course, I am talking here in very general terms and concentrating on *small* business.) Therefore, you have to remember that these fees are a baseline that you must work from. *Everything the lawyer does to help you in the actual purchase agreement is going to cost extra.* These transactions are too individual for me to provide a general cost estimate in this book. However, in a specific case, your lawyer should be able to give you an estimate.

I recommend against any percentage fees. Some lawyers like to charge a certain percentage of the sales price when they represent a buyer or seller of a business. I do not like those arrangements. Make your lawyer tell you exactly what he or she is going to do, how long it is going to take, and approximately what it is likely to cost. Drafting a purchase agreement can be either a big or a little job, depending on how you use your lawyer. If you are a poor negotiator and your lawyer is a good one, you want to use your lawyer for more than just legal help. I find this to be the case in many situations. On the other hand, if you feel that you are the best person to negotiate the deal, do not waste time and money by dragging the lawyer around to all the meetings. Do, however, make sure you get legal advice on important points before you start negotiating.

Do not try to save legal fees by not having a *complete* purchase agreement. Remember that your interests and those of the seller are different. The seller is going to get a certified check at the closing and has little use for any agreement. He or she takes his or her money and can disappear if he or she wants to. You have to live with the business and all its problems. *You are the one who needs the agreement.* The seller is likely to want to push for the simplest, quickest deal possible. *Slow down.* Do not let the seller talk you into buying the stock on a handshake. Buying a business is likely to be one of the most important investments you ever make, and it is foolish to try to save a few dollars of attorneys' fees here. The same is true for the legal audit. Let your lawyer do a good job for you.

5
Franchising

If you want to start your own business, you have essentially three ways to do it: Start your own from scratch, buy one that is already established, or enter into a franchise agreement. There are a wide variety of franchise arrangements, and it is probably safe to say that just about any kind of usual business which you could either start yourself or buy is available in a franchise format from somebody. Of course, we all know about the typical examples—McDonald's, Howard Johnson's, Holiday Inn, Midas Muffler, all the gas stations, bookstores, and last but not least, print shops.

In 1980 there was a very important development in the law regarding franchising. The Federal Trade Commission announced a rule which said, in effect, that franchisors had to provide each franchisee with a booklet which explained all the important aspects of the franchise in plain English and gave the net worth and background of the franchisor. This ruling came about in response to widespread dissatisfaction among franchisees, who often felt they did not get what they bargained for from the franchisor. It was the old story of salespeoples' puffing. Franchises can be extremely lucrative things for the franchisor and are sold by sales representatives who are usually on commission. In the past, that situation made for some high pressure and a bit of abuse. Of course, the major companies such as McDonald's did a good job. On the other hand, there were a number of less reputable companies that did not do a very good job of telling the franchisees what they were going to get for their money. Many times, when the franchisees found out, they were extremely disappointed.

Now, however, by federal law, the franchisor must give you a document explaining all of the important things about the franchise. Federal law does not, however, require that you read it, You will also be given a copy of the franchise agreement. Likewise, federal law requires the franchisor to deliver a copy of it to you but does not require you to read it. Should you so desire, you are well within all your legal rights in simply believing everything the sales representative tells you, looking at the nice, pretty pictures he or she will give you and writing out your check without ever reading any of these documents or consulting your attorney. Obviously, I do not think this is a particularly desirable course of action, but history shows that it happens all the time.

What Is a Franchise?

As discussed in this chapter, a *franchise* is simply a license to use the trademark of the franchisor. In most cases, we are talking about a package deal, where the franchisor allows you to use its trademark, tells you how to set up and run the business, and gives you certain prescribed assistance, such as site selection and a model bookkeeping procedure you can follow. The franchisor sometimes also undertakes certain continuing obligations, such as advertising, training, quality control, and free business advice. Normally, the price for all this is a fixed fee *plus* a certain percentage of sales. I should add at this point, however, that there are many, many different types of franchise arrangements. We are only talking about the most typical format.

The franchisor usually retains some rights as to quality control and advertising (e.g., McDonald's food has to meet certain standards, and the Golden Arches trademark must be used at the location). However, you run the business. Typically, the franchisor is the helper and counselor, but you are the businessperson. The franchisor helps you reduce the risk of starting out in business yourself by providing you a tested and proven package. However, a franchise does not guarantee success.

Why Do You Need a Lawyer in a Franchise Deal?

You need a lawyer in a franchise deal for two reasons.

The first reason is that you probably ought to form a corporation for your franchise just as you would if you were developing the business yourself or buying a going concern. Everything we said about forming a corporation is equally applicable to going into business via the franchise route. The franchise arrangement typically will not say anything about the form in which you do business. That is up to you. You can use a sole proprietorship or partnership if you want to. The franchisor may advise you to form a corporation or to at least discuss the possibility with your lawyer, but the decision to do so and, of course, the actual mechanics and cost of accomplishing that are up to you. Further, such matters as thinning the corporation, electing Subchapter S, and providing buy-out arrangements if you have more than one shareholder are all your responsibility. The franchise arrangement deals with the business aspects of the deal (how to run that print shop, hotel, restaurant, etc.), not with general business-legal rules such as those involved in forming and operating any corporation.

The second reason for having a lawyer in a franchise deal is that your first major transaction is going to be the execution of the elaborate and very important franchise agreement. The explanatory document the Federal Trade Commission requires is supposed to be written in plain English. It usually will be. You should not have any trouble understanding it if you take the trouble to read it. The actual franchise agreement, however, is another story. It is likely to be many pages of fine print together with a lot of legalese. Your lawyer can make sure that you understand exactly what the agreement says and does not say. You can match your lawyer's interpretation of the franchise agreement with the things the sales representative told you and make sure they square with one another. You can also negotiate the franchise agreement. Obviously, your flexibility in negotiating depends on the franchisor. In most situations you do have at least some bargaining position. If a clause in the franchise agreement is particularly burdensome to you or gives you some special problem, it is usually subject to negotiation. Your lawyer can both point out the problems and help you in the negotiation.

Keep in mind that the explanatory booklet required by the Federal Trade Commission is only a disclosure document. It only requires the franchisor to disclose the facts to you—it does not require that they be "solid" facts. If the franchisor is bankrupt or close to it, all it has to do is state its net worth in the disclosure statement. It is up to you to read that statement and understand what it means. Your lawyer can help you. Also, remember that our definition of a franchise included many undertakings on the part of the franchisor. It is up to you and your lawyer to make sure that you completely understand what the franchisor will and will not do, that your understanding is accurately set forth in the franchise agreement, and that you have some reasonable basis to believe that the franchisor will be around in the future to carry out its part of the bargain. The government will not help you on any of this—except to require the disclosure statement, which makes your job a bit easier.

Franchise Example

Let me give you a brief example of starting into the instant printing business by the franchise route.

Instant printing is usually started at one location – a typical storefront operation consisting of around 1,000 square feet of space and around $35,000 worth of equipment. Most of the equipment consists of a printing press and a camera for making the offset plates which are used on the printing press. The typical franchise fee for this kind of instant print shop is about $50,000 and a percentage of your sales. For this, the franchisor will find a location for you, select all the equipment and install it, and train you in how to use it. The franchisor will also give you some training on how to keep an elementary set of books, how to advertise, who your customers might be, etc. In addition, you will get a trademark license to display the franchisor's name at your store. In short, the franchisor will assume that you know absolutely nothing about the instant printing business, nothing about how to operate the equipment, and nothing about how to keep books.

If you wanted to start a print shop without using a franchise, you would have to select the location, buy all of the equipment, and learn how to use it. Without counting the value of your time, we have already said that this would cost you about $35,000. Essentially, you can buy the equipment for just about the same price as the franchisor, and you can also finance it at just about the same rates as the franchisor. Indeed, the companies that sell the equipment will usually be happy to lease it to you and to give you some training on how to run it. When you are done, you have spent a lot of time, but you have saved about $15,000, and you do not owe any franchise royalties. However, you also do not have the right to display a franchisor's name, and you do not have anybody to call for help or advice for free.

The decision as to whether to go into business via a franchise or by yourself depends on how much you value what you get from the franchisor and how much the trademark is worth. Pursuing our print shop example, I am afraid that the trademark is not usually worth too much. Do you seek out a particular franchisee when you want instant printing? That leaves you with the other items. Taken as a whole, I think it is fair to say that they are worth the $15,000 and the percentage of sales. However, what if you already know how to operate printing equipment and where to buy it, and you know or can easily figure out how to keep books? Perhaps you have even worked in a print shop and know how and where to advertise. Then you start taking away from the benefits *to you* of the franchise, but you still keep that $15,000-plus-royalties price tag.

The decision of whether to start a business through the franchise route or go it alone is largely a personal one. The function of your lawyer should be to make sure you completely understand exactly what you will be getting so that you can make that personal decision based on your own needs and desires. His or her other function is to make sure that the documents you sign obligate the franchisor to do what is required.

In summary, then, make sure you take advantage of the federal laws which require you to receive a booklet describing the franchise in plain English. Study that book carefully, comparing it with the actual franchise agreement and discussing both of these documents with your lawyer to make sure you understand exactly what you are going to get for your money. Involving a lawyer in your franchise should not cost you a lot of money. Once you do all the homework by assembling these documents and explaining to your lawyer exactly what you want to do, he or she can review them rather quickly. It should not take your lawyer more than a few hours to read these documents and make sure that you understand them completely. That is money well spent in a deal this size.

Franchise Danger Points

Remember that no lawyer can make a bad deal into a good one. Nor can a lawyer make a franchisor live up to the promises contained in a franchise agreement. Your lawyer can, of course, help you sue the franchisor if that becomes necessary, but that is not what you went into business for. In my experience, the biggest danger points in franchise deals are the following—most of which are only marginally "legal."

1. Franchisor either cannot or will not live up to the promise made during the sales pitch. There are two things you should do to minimize this problem:

   a. Read carefully the portion of the franchise disclosure statement which describes the net worth and experience of the franchisor. It may be that the people selling you the franchise have a net worth which is less than the market value of your home, and their experience in the business in question is extremely limited.

   b. Consult with other franchisees. Get their personal experiences as to how this franchisor has performed.

2. You don't make as much money as the franchisor said you would. Franchisors will almost always give you projections as to how much

money you will make. They will state clearly that these are not guarantees and you may not make this much money. They will also state that you could make more. However, you will often fail to hear or understand these qualifications, and when you do not strike it rich, you may tend to blame the franchisor. Of course, there are two sides to every story. I tend to think most of this problem is caused by false expectations which basically already exist in most people's minds and which the sales representative for the franchisor certainly does nothing to diminish. In short, make sure your expectations are reasonable. When someone comes to me with a proposed franchise deal and shows me projections, I carefully cross-examine that person as to their reasonableness. After we scrub these projections down, *I cut them in half.* The net effect of doing this is that it takes the franchisee twice as long as he or she projected to reach an acceptable level of profitability. That, in turn, raises the need for working capital and perhaps even living capital. While this is certainly not a legal matter, I feel that making the client focus on this possibility and being certain that the client can make a go of the operation even on these reduced assumptions is a positive thing. If the client does not have enough working or living capital to succeed on the basis of my arbitrary halving of the assumptions, I counsel extreme caution.

3. You underestimate the amount of money you will have to spend to start the business. Typically, a franchise agreement will contain a listing of "all" the things you need to start your business. Hopefully, this list will clearly state exactly what the franchisor supplies as part of the franchise fee, and what you have to buy yourself—perhaps with the franchisor's assistance. This listing will, in most cases, be relatively complete and may make you feel that it is absolutely complete. When something additional comes along, you may feel that the franchisor has misled you. Again, this is a two-sided question. Any person who makes a list of "everything" needed to start a business thinking that the list will be 100-percent complete is just not being realistic. There are too many incidental or indirect items. You simply must realize this and make sure you have sufficient capital to take care of this common problem. However, you should also do everything possible to make the franchisor spell out everything you will need in the agreement. Just because you cannot be 100-percent accurate does not mean you should not come as close as you can. If you use my arbitrary halving technique mentioned above, this problem will not be too significant, because you will have allotted sufficient working or living capital to handle these unforeseen, and perhaps unforeseeable, items.

4. The fourth item, really a variation on the above, is that the franchisor does not do what the agreement provides in the time pro-

vided. This is another reason for my halving approach. However, it is absolutely necessary to make sure that your franchise agreement spells out not only exactly what the franchisor will do, but also when these things will be done and what your remedy will be if they are not done on time. This is a sensitive point. The franchisor will say, in essence, "Trust me." I would not do it. I have just seen too many problems resulting from such faith. Make the franchisor write up a timetable, and provide remedies for you if the franchisor does not make the deadlines. If you fail to do this, even my halving approach will not be sufficient. Things could drag out so long that a greater cushion would be necessary.

As you can see from this discussion, almost all of the franchise danger points involve a breach or possible breach of contract by the franchisor. If you have the agreement drafted and at least partially negotiated by your lawyer so that the franchisor knows you are represented by counsel, I think you can minimize these potential problems. If the franchisor is stretched for time and money—as many franchisors are—the franchisor will delay progress for you unless you are represented by a lawyer who knows your contractual rights and is prepared to insist on them.

State Franchise Law

In addition to the general rules in federal law, some states have much more restrictive franchise laws to protect the investor. In these states the franchise laws not only require disclosure, but also provide the franchisee with certain substantive rights. The state franchise laws are beyond the scope of this book, but you should know that they exist. Before buying any franchise you should check the laws of the state in which the franchise is located. You should also check your own state laws as they may be applicable. One of the things your lawyer should do for you in any franchise transaction is to tell you what state laws would be applicable and what protections they provide.

6
Pension, Profit Sharing, and Deferred Compensation Plans

One of the truly great opportunities for tax saving through your corporation is the ability to establish a qualified pension and profit sharing plan. Here are the key benefits:

1. Your company can deduct the money it pays into the plan in the year in which the contribution is made.

2. The employees do not have to pay any tax on this money until they actually receive it—usually during retirement.

3. All the earnings from money while it is being held in the pension or profit sharing trust are tax-free.

Let us look at a simplified example to see how this works.

Suppose your company establishes a qualified profit sharing plan into which it contributes 10 percent of its aftertax profits every year. The percentage share which is attributable to each employee depends upon the employee's compensation. To make our case simple, let us assume you have four employees including yourself. You earn $60,000 and the others each earn $20,000. Suppose further that the contribution to the plan turns out to be $10,000 a year. When the company contributed the $10,000, it would have a tax deduction. Thus, its income tax would be reduced for that year. Assuming the company was in the 34 percent tax bracket, that is a saving of $3,400 for that year. Each employee's share depends upon his or her compensation, and since your compensation is half the total, 50 percent of that contribution belongs to you. The other 50 percent would be divided three ways among the other three employees. However, none of you have to pay any income tax on this amount, even assuming it is fully vested, which means that employees are entitled to it even if they quit the company. Further, that $10,000 contribution is going to be invested in some income-producing securities, and since the trust is tax-free, you can invest in high-income securities without worrying about paying tax. Thus, for example, you can invest in corporate bonds, which are currently paying around 10 percent interest. That money can be compounded tax-free during the life of the trust without any income tax. When an employee receives a distribution from the profit sharing plan (because the employee either quits or retires), a tax will be payable.

The ability to establish the so-called qualified plans is perhaps the single most important benefit of a corporation. You can form these kinds of plans even if you are the only employee.

There is, however, a very important problem. This highly beneficial income tax treatment is not given to you for nothing. There is a trade-off. It is a social as well as an economic one. Congress has decided that these kinds of benefits must be available to the employees as a whole, not just to yourself and the highly paid executives. Thus, in order to achieve these tax benefits, you must have a plan which satisfies numerous technical requirements designed to assure that substantially all the employees participate in the tax bonanza. Taking our preceding example, you could not have a plan that covered you as the $60,000 employee but eliminated the three $20,000 workers. That is the biggest problem in establishing one of these qualified plans. You have to decide whom you must cover and whom you want to cover, and then you have to see what kind of benefits are going to be available to you after you provide the necessary benefits to everybody else.

Obviously, the clear cases are easy to analyze. If you have a one-person corporation, there is nobody with whom you have to share the wealth, and you are absolutely foolish not to have one of these qualified plans. On the other hand, suppose that you run a business where you are really the only "majordomo" and you have 50 other employees. If you establish a qualified plan under these facts, you are going to have to provide benefits to a lot of people, and the percentage of the benefits directly attributable to you may be relatively small. Of course, there are two sides to the question: One is the actual economics and the other is the employee benefits side. You may need a profit sharing plan or a pension plan simply to recruit and keep good employees. The tax benefits may be secondary. However, my personal experience in the case of small businesses is that this is not the case. The owners of the business (and perhaps a rather close group of highly paid officers and family members) desire to have the major benefits. They are willing to share the benefits with the other employees only if it does not dilute their own benefits too much.

This is an exceedingly complicated subject, and I cannot deal with it adequately in this book other than to explain the very basic rules to you and to strongly suggest that you discuss this matter with your lawyer. I can say without much doubt that there will be some kind of plan which will provide you significant tax savings—even if it is only the individual retirement account which you establish personally.

Why Is This Subject So Complicated?

Here is a very brief and abbreviated review of the factors that make this such a complex area.

1. The social security system has grown to such an extent that your corporate and individual retirement plans—and even your disability and death benefits—*must* be coordinated with social security benefits. Those benefits, however, are difficult to determine unless you are close to retirement age. Further, social security is a politically sensitive issue. It would be foolish to assume that the entire system is going to go broke, but it would be equally foolish to assume that the system will be the same 20 years from now as it is today. Certainly, there will be changes of some sort, and they are out of your control.

Many pension and profit sharing plans today must, as a matter of sound economics, be integrated with social security. This means that in some way, the wages covered by social security give less benefits in the plan than wages over that. Thus, employees who make under the social security amount obtain limited benefits under the plan, and the more highly paid workers get larger benefits. Integration of the plan with social security means that you can usually design a qualified pension or profit sharing plan which provides a substantial portion of its benefits to you and your highly paid executives even though the plan may technically cover all your employees.

2. The number of "experts" in this field is astonishing. I went to a seminar on the subject sponsored by our local chamber of commerce and heard presentations from lawyers, accountants, actuaries, people

from savings and loans, banks, insurance companies, brokerage houses, and consultants ranging from those who specialized in the entire area of retirement planning to those who limited themselves to one aspect, such as investment of the plan assets. Each of them had some kind of ax to grind. They also, of course, had their personal preferences and biases. It is going to be very difficult for you to obtain a complete, unbiased, and accurate explanation of all your alternatives.

3. Whatever you do, it is likely to cost you quite a bit of money. Even a standard off-the-shelf or prototype defined benefit pension plan offered by a financial institution is likely to cost you $2,500 in fees by the time you get it instituted and about $1,000 a year in fees and costs to keep it going after that.

4. There is a bewildering array of different types of arrangements. I will list the basic ones for you, but you must keep in mind that there are very many variations.

The Profit Sharing Plan

A profit sharing plan is a system whereby a company puts in a certain amount of its profits into a trust. The employees as a whole share in the trust—usually in direct proportion to their salary. The example I gave above is typical, but there are a number of ways to divide the pot in a profit sharing plan. The key things which distinguish a profit sharing plan from most other arrangements are the following:

1. Money must be contributed out of profits. If you do not make any profit, you cannot make any contribution.
2. You do not have to make contributions every year. You have much more flexibility in a profit sharing plan than in most other arrangements. If you make it big in one year, you can make a relatively large contribution, and correspondingly, if you have a bad year, there is no problem in skipping a contribution. Most plans provide for almost complete discretion in the amount of the contribution so long as it comes out of company profit.

Pension Plans

There are many different types of pension plans. In fact, the range of possible pension plans extends from only a slight variation on a profit sharing plan to something which is akin to a private social security benefit. Following are some of the major types of plans which I have seen used by small business.

1. *A money purchase plan.* In a money purchase plan, the company makes a defined contribution which, for example, can be a certain percentage of pay. The money then goes into a trust which is invested, just as in the profit sharing plan we talked about. While there may not be separate individual accounts, there is a separate individual accounting system whereby each individual is entitled to a certain amount. That amount, however, depends on the balance in the employee's account, which, in turn, is a function of the company contributions and the earnings of the money while it was in the trust. When an employee retires, he or she gets a benefit of whatever that amount will buy—hence, the name "money purchase." This kind of system is usually used in conjunction with an insurance company. The company pays its contribution to the insurance company, and when employees retire, they get an annuity based upon whatever their account will buy.

2. *A defined benefit pension plan.* The most typical pension plan in large companies—and the one many smaller companies also use—is a so-called defined benefit plan. There are many ways to define the benefit, but the usual one is to define it as a certain percentage of the employee's salary. For example, an employee may have a benefit equal to 60 percent of his or her average salary for the highest five years. In order to provide enough money to pay the employee this benefit, you have to get an actuary to make numerous computations. The company then makes contributions into the pension plan which, according to the actuary's estimate, will assure that the plan has sufficient money when the employee retires to pay the benefits.

While there are many more types of plans available, my experience has been that a small business which operates in corporate form and which warrants a specifically tailored plan uses either the profit sharing plan, the money purchase pension plan, or the defined benefit pension plan. Special cases, however, dictate special plans, and that is why I strongly suggest you find and use a good consultant.

Prototype Plans

Many financial institutions, including banks, savings and loans, and brokerage houses, have already drafted a standard or prototype plan. All you do is fill in the blanks. Obviously, this saves a lot of money. To some extent, it decreases your flexibility, because the prototype plan only offers certain options. Nevertheless, for many small businesses, the prototype plan is the way to go. There is simply not enough money involved to justify having a team of lawyers and actuaries and accountants specifically design a plan for you. As a very gross generalization, I would say that if you have 50 employees or less, a prototype plan is best for you. On the other hand, if you have 50 employees or more, I would say that it would be worth your while to at least carefully consider a specifically designed plan which takes into account your particular circumstances-including most importantly the number of employees that you have, the salaries that they all make, and the kinds of benefits that you want.

Employee Retirement Income Security Act (ERISA)

In the mid-1970s, Congress became concerned about a number of abuses in private pension plans. Perhaps the most important concern was *vesting*, that is, the point in time at which the employee's interest in the plan belongs to the employee, even if he or she quits the company. If, for example, a company or union had a 30-year vesting plan and you worked 29 years and 9 months and then got fired, you got nothing. This appeared to Congress to be extremely unfair. Some pension plans had very long and arbitrary vesting requirements.

Accordingly, one of the important things Congress did in the pension reform legislation was to require that qualified plans have certain minimal vesting requirements so that this kind of thing did not happen. These vesting requirements are important, because they present both problems and opportunities. While you must allow employees to have a vested interest in your plan at some relatively early date, there is still quite a bit of flexibility.

The actual vesting rules are not only quite complex but they change frequently. Even our own very simple profit sharing plan, originally established to have very liberal vesting requirements, has been amended several times in the past few years because of statutory or regulatory changes. For example, at the outset the plan offered 100-percent vesting after three years of employment and attaining age 25. At the time that was very liberal. Even at that, however, the rules were changed so that we had to lower the age to 21 years and lower the three years to two years. The point is that one of the more important decisions you will have to make in designing the specifics of your pension or profit sharing plan is the method of vesting. My advice is to be more conservative than the law requires so as to avoid having to amend the plan every time there is a change in the law or regulations. Even if you adopt a conservative approach, as we did, you still may find that periodic amendments are necessary. To some extent the rules on pension and profit sharing plans are highly political.

Another factor that makes qualified pension and profit sharing plans a little technical is the coverage requirement. The general rule is that these plans cannot discriminate in favor of officers, shareholders, or highly paid people. As a practical matter in the small business context this often means that you cannot have a plan covering only the owners and top management, and leaving everyone else out. It also means that you cannot have a plan that ostensibly covers everyone but, as a practical matter, provides the lion's share of the benefits to those top people. Again the details are complex but you are going to have to make some decisions. You can be aggressive and adopt the most restrictive coverage provisions possible under existing laws and regulations, or you can be a little bit more conservative. I suggest that you consider being a little more conservative for the same reason as being conservative about vesting. These rules are always changing and you don't want to be in a position where you have to amend your plan every time there is a minor change in the rules.

Summary and Conclusions

If your company is at all profitable it is highly likely that you can benefit substantially from some type of qualified pension or profit sharing plan. There are two tax benefits that are so favorable that it is almost impossible not to take advantage of them to some extent. They are:

1. The ability to make a contribution to the plan for the benefit of the employees and have that contribution deductible by the corporation with no corresponding income to the employee

2. The ability to have that contribution earn interest and dividends tax free

On the other hand, these very favorable tax benefits are circumscribed by an area of law and tax regulations that is so complex that even the simplest of plans requires technical and expert help.

Our final conclusion is that history and experience teach us that these rules change so rapidly that, in our judgment, you are ill advised to allow experts to talk you into a plan that tries to exploit these advantages 'o their ultimate maximum. Our concern is twofold.

1. If you should happen to step over the boundary line of legality, the tax problems are severe. The corporate deduction may be disallowed, income may be imputed to the individuals, and the income earned by the money in the trust may be taxable.

2. Even if you successfully stay just inside the boundary lines, you can assume that the laws and regulations will change so that you will have to

be constantly alert to necessary amendments. As a practical matter, this means that you will have to be paying your expert consultants more than might otherwise be necessary to keep close watch on the details of your plan.

Don't pass up the tremendous advantages of a qualified pension or profit sharing plan, but don't get too greedy either.

7
Your Payroll

One of the first things you will have to do when you start your business is to set up a payroll. Any corporation must do this even if it has only one employee. This can appear to be a formidable task at first, but it is really rather easy because most of it is mechanical. However, your payroll does have some important legal implications, which will be discussed in this chapter.

If you have an accountant, many of the processes described in this chapter will be taken care of in the accountant's normal procedures. Accountants are just as good and efficient at setting up a payroll as lawyers are about forming corporations. It is an easy and routine job. The accountants will usually be of less help, however, on ensuring compliance with the wage and hour laws. It is not difficult and there is a lot of good help available from the various government agencies. Very briefly, here are the things you have to do to set up a payroll.

1. Get the federal income tax package of materials which explains about withholding and payment of social security and federal unemployment taxes.
2. Get applicable state or local income tax forms which explain about withholding for those taxes.
3. Make sure each employee is covered by workers' compensation insurance.
4. Make sure you have filed appropriate forms for state unemployment compensation.
5. Make sure you understand and abide by the wage and hour laws.

Federal Income Tax

You have an obligation to withhold federal income tax from employees' wages according to prescribed charts. These provide exact amounts that you have to withhold according to the number of dependents the person claims and the amount of money he or she makes. All the charts and tables will be included in the package that the IRS gives you, and they are not hard to understand. You also have to withhold from each employee's wages a proper amount for social security (FICA), and you have to match that amount yourself. In addition, you have to withhold from the employee's wages a certain amount for federal unemployment tax. That amount, however, can be affected by state unemployment taxes. If there is a state unemployment compensation tax, it will be deducted from the federal unemployment tax. Payroll taxes present two potential legal difficulties which I would like to discuss.

The first problem is the withholding—and the fact that you are holding the government's money. The tax procedure requires you to deposit taxes you withhold from your employees fairly promptly. The exact times depend on how much money is involved—usually you must fork over the money within three banking days. This is a sensitive point with the IRS. Payroll taxes are not the place to delay payments. The IRS will assess penalties. Further, if you borrow some of this money for your own use, the IRS will get very mad and is likely to attach your bank accounts.

The second problem is that you and your employees will be tempted to try to find ways around these payroll taxes. There is certainly nothing wrong with doing this so long as the ways you select are legitimate. If they are not, however, you are asking for trouble. Here are some of the many ways *not* to try to avoid payroll taxes.

1. Paying people in cash instead of by check
2. Paying wages to someone else besides the person working—such as an elderly relative or child—so as to avoid reporting taxable income for that person
3. Trying to treat an employee as an "independent contractor" without any justification, thereby avoiding all withholding

Both you and the employee have a common interest—reducing taxes. However, this does not mean you have a common interest in fraud—and that is what some of these things amount to. Be careful to avoid going too far in minimizing payroll taxes.

Independent Contractor

Small business people sometimes try to minimize payroll taxes by using independent contractors. Use of independent contractors also has many other advantages including possibly a savings on your employee benefit cost (health insurance in particular). You should be alert to the areas where you might be able to substitute an independent contractor for an employee. You should not, however, try to treat people who, in reality, are employees as independent contractors.

The line between an employee and an independent contractor is often very difficult to draw. The same facts can sometimes be characterized either way. Take normal maintenance workers.

Example

> Suppose your building requires 40 hours of maintenance work a week. You have essentially two choices. You could hire a person, put him or her on your salary, and have that person do the 40-hour a week job. You could also hire a contractor to provide your maintenance. You would simply enter into an (written) agreement that spelled out how the individual would do the maintenance work, the duties, and the compensation. The compensation would likely be a fixed fee although you can have an independent contractor arrangement where the compensation is stated as an hourly or daily rate.
>
> There is quite a bit of litigation involving which category someone falls into. Pursuing our maintenance person example:

1. What if the person is injured and tries to collect workers' compensation?

2. What if you canceled the contract with this person and he or she tried to collect unemployment compensation?

3. What if, during a routine tax audit, the auditor feels that the payments should have been wages and assesses a deficiency because you failed to pay the appropriate payroll taxes and do the appropriate withholding?

4. In addition to payroll tax issues, there are also issues of liability. What if this person negligently injures someone while doing the maintenance work for you?

In each of these cases there could be a judicial inquiry as to whether the person was, in reality, an employee or an independent contractor. All of the facts would be examined.

How does the small business owner tell the difference between an independent contractor and an employee? I think we can all see the clear cases:

A Clear Independent Contractor Situation: The truly independent contractor would do maintenance work not only for you but for other companies, buy all of its own equipment and supplies, has a clear contract specifying exactly what maintenance operations are supposed to be performed, works independently of close supervision—perhaps at night—and has been an independent contractor for years. In addition, you have had your maintenance work done by independent contractors for many years.

A Clear Employee Situation: The employee has no other source of income, works during the day subject to detailed instructions issued by your people on what to do, when to do it, and how to do it. The individual does not have any of his or her own equipment or supplies—the company supplies all of them—and the company has historically had a full-time maintenance worker as an employee.

Most cases fall somewhere between those two clear situations, and it is often a close call as to whether in any given case an individual is an independent contractor or an employee. There is, however, one absolute rule: It doesn't make any difference how the parties themselves characterize the arrangement. In other words, even if the company and the independent contractor fully agree that it is an independent contractor relationship and not an employer-employee relationship, either the law or the taxing authorities can recharacterize the arrangement in accordance with their view of the reality.

What are the most important factors in deciding whether your independent contractor characterization will hold up? In my experience there are basically two.

1. *Day-to-day control:* The more day-to-day control over the details of the work, the more it looks like an employer-employee relationship.

2. *History:* How you have historically treated the person is the second most important factor because this whole area is politically sensitive. There is tension between the Internal Revenue Service and Congress over the possible revenue loss involved in characterizing an arrangement as an independent contractor when it really is an employer-employee relationship. Often the IRS wants to crack down but Congress, sensitive to the political realities, often tries to preserve the status quo. As of late 1990, the standoff continued and the Internal Revenue Service is operating under the basic idea that past practices

will be respected—as long as they are at least fairly reasonable. In other words, if you have historically treated your maintenance worker as an independent contractor, and you have at least a respectable argument as to why that is appropriate, you can be fairly sure that IRS won't attack that (at least today). Similarly, however, if you have historically treated your maintenance person as an employee and then changed that treatment in order to take advantage of the possible payroll tax savings, you would have to be concerned about a possible IRS recharacterization.

Note.   This problem is much less severe, or becomes altogether nonexistent, if you go through another corporate entity which does pay the appropriate payroll taxes. In other words, the concern arises only when the independent contractor maintenance worker has a direct contractual relationship with you. If you instead have a contract with a maintenance firm or a temporary agency, which in turn hires the maintenance person, and pays appropriate withholding taxes, and so on, there would be hardly any risk of someone recharacterizing that person as your employee. This would be true even if there was a considerable amount of day-to-day control over the work.

Workers' Compensation

I have included workers' compensation under the payroll chapter simply because, as a mechanical matter, the way you pay workers' compensation premiums is usually to calculate your payroll, apply the percentages given by the state workers' compensation authority for the occupations in question, and send that money to the appropriate place.

Workers' compensation laws are *state* laws, and they differ rather widely among the states. In some states there is only one official state workers' compensation bureau, and you have to deal with it for all matters including payment of premiums. In many other states there is more flexibility. The program is still a "legal" one with a lot of legal implications, but private insurance carriers are allowed to actually handle the insurance portion. In some cases, you can even self-insure, but that is usually an option only for large companies.

There are, however, some common denominators to workers' compensation matters, and they involve legal risks which will be described here in some detail. I will be discussing Ohio laws, but the problems and advice would be essentially the same in most other states. For specific advice, you should touch base with your lawyer.

Workers' compensation was probably the first "no-fault" insurance program. It removes fault as a criterion for an award. Injured workers are entitled to medical care and replacement of a portion of their lost wages for any work-related injury without regard to any negligence either of the employee, the employer, or any fellow worker. *Conversely — if you are not protected by workers' compensation insurance, you enjoy no such immunity.* That, then, is the biggest problem. Make *absolutely sure* that all the workers in your facility are covered so that if they are injured on the job, they cannot sue you and recover those large personal injury awards. Here is a brief rundown of the most troublesome areas.

- "Normal" employees should not present any problem so long as you file the appropriate forms and keep the appropriate records as called for by your state system.

- Employees of other people working on your facility can present a problem — e.g., a painter who is painting the outside of your building. You obviously do not cover them because they are not on your payroll. What if their own employer does not cover them either? You could have serious exposure. Ohio law imposes responsibility for workers' compensation not only on the employer but on anyone contracting with an employer who does not comply. Thus, if the painter did not have workers' compensation insurance, and he or she fell off a ladder and was injured on your job, *you* could be sued. *Moral:* Make sure *everyone* working on your premises is covered, not just your own employees. The usual way to do this is to make sure you include in your contract with painters, repair people, etc., a provision which requires that they have coverage. If they are small operations with doubtful financial resources, you probably should go further and require them to actually furnish evidence of coverage to you.

- People who may come in to your plant informally to help out with a project are also a source of difficulty. If you actually get the person's name on the payroll — even if he or she only works one day — that is all right. However, putting someone on the payroll for a single day is cumbersome, so you may want to have some other arrangement. For example, suppose one of your employees is assigned to do a large project over a weekend and wants to have a friend come in to help. The friend would not be put on the payroll; the employee would simply turn in twice as many hours as really worked and turn over half the pay to the friend. You may find this attractive for a number of reasons, the simplicity and lack of paperwork being the most important. However, I recommend against it because of the workers' compensation problem. You have someone working in your facility who is not going to be covered. If he or she is injured, you may become involved in a very large lawsuit. Instead, use a temporary help service. They will take care of all the paperwork and make sure everyone is covered by the necessary insurance. They will even let you pick the person. You will be charged a percentage (about 25 percent) of the person's salary. It may cost you a few dollars more, but I think it is well worth it.

- What about other insurance? Won't your normal liability insurance cover this kind of thing just as if the person were a visitor? *Maybe not.* In Ohio, for example, if someone should be covered by insurance and is *not*, no other insurance can be called upon to pay the claim. That is because Ohio has a state system, and no private insurance coverage can be used to pay claims which should be dealt with by the system. Your state may have similar rules; consult your insurance advisor to make sure. It depends on two factors—the state law and your particular insurance coverage.

Workers' compensation is big business. There are many lawyers who specialize in representing injured workers before the relevant authorities to get the maximum amount possible out of the system. As in any other insurance program—especially one involving something as subjective as disability—there are gray cases. There is also fraud. When I worked for a large multinational corporation, our payroll people told me that they were able to save *millions* of dollars by hiring expert firms and consultants to monitor workers' compensation claims in various states to make sure that only proper and legitimate claims were paid—and then only in proper and legitimate amounts. As a small company you will not have this big a problem, but the theory must be kept in mind: *Workers' compensation is no free lunch.*

Most states use a system where all companies are *experience-rated.* The state fund computes your premium by multiplying your total payroll for a given job classification by a factor which represents the general or industry wide rate of hazard and a special factor for your own company which represents *your own claim experience.* The possible premium range is large. If you assume, for example, that a given job represents a certain *general* hazard and would generate $1 of premiums without experience rating, experience rating can affect your premium by a factor of 85 percent either way. That means the premium could be reduced to 15 cents or increased to $1.85. It is easy to see how a good safety program to reduce accidents and a good program to monitor your workers' compensation could pay handsome dividends.

Unemployment Compensation

Unemployment insurance is also a creature of state law. Generally, it is mandatory and provides that if someone gets laid off for lack of work or fired without just cause, he or she can get unemployment benefits in the amount provided by state law. In Ohio, that is roughly half of what the worker earned, up to certain maximums. The benefits can last as long as 26 weeks. This too is somewhat experience-rated. Employers who fire people more often, or have layoffs more often, pay a higher percentage of payroll as the premium. The same cautions are appropriate here as for workers' compensation. You have to keep in mind that it is not a free lunch, and if you try to be too nice, it is probably going to cost you money.

Unemployment compensation problems usually deal with whether a person is entitled to a benefit. If someone is fired for proper cause, or quits without proper cause, he or she is not entitled to unemployment benefits. Exactly what is proper cause is subjective, and that is where the problem is. As you might expect, the law is heavily weighted in favor of the worker. Ohio, for example, even pays unemployment to people out on strike! Nevertheless, when someone applies for unemployment, the employer will be notified and given the opportunity to contest payments. This is a rather minor problem. Unlike workers' compensation, there is no possibility for huge awards against you. It is only a matter of a few dollars more or less on your premium, and for a small company it usually is not worth hiring a lawyer to contest a claim. You might simply write to the relevant state authority yourself and tell your side of the story. If that does not work, you may just have to forget about it.

Overview of Wage and Hour Laws

This section will discuss the basic requirements of the federal wage and hour laws. This is a very simplified discussion because the laws themselves are lengthy, technical, and complicated. However, in most cases, the actual requirements you have to comply with are relatively straightforward.

One of the difficulties in summarizing the wage and hour laws is that there are two parallel—but somewhat different—sets of rules: one for businesses which are engaged in selling products or services to the government and one for all other businesses. Essentially, the differences are in overtime pay and minimum wage requirements. In private industry The Fair Labor Standards Act requires overtime pay only for hours worked in excess of 40 hours in one week. For government contractors, the Walsh-Healey Act requires overtime pay for hours worked in excess of 8 hours per day. The Fair Labor Standards Act establishes fixed minimum wages for all workers, and the Walsh-Healey Act establishes minimum wages which are fixed periodically by regulation and which depend on comparable pay in private industry in similar jobs and similar locations.

The following are the important requirements of the wage and hour laws which small businesses should keep in mind.

1. The law requires certain *minimum wages* to be paid to all covered workers.

2. The law requires overtime to be paid for hours worked in excess of 40 hours per week—or 8 hours per day in the case of government contracts.

3. The law provides rules on when employees must be paid for commuting or other travel time, as well as when compensable work time starts and stops.

4. The law imposes restrictions on the employment of minors and people doing work for the company in their own homes.

5. The law imposes restrictions on the amounts of wages which may be garnished.

The first thing you should do as a business owner is to determine if the wage and hour rules apply to you. Therefore, the first thing I will discuss is the exemptions. After that, I will very briefly discuss each of these requirements.

Exemptions from Minimum Wage Requirements

Perhaps the most important exemption from the wage and hour rules is for businesses whose total annual salaries are less than $500,000. There is an additional requirement that the business be engaged in interstate commerce, but almost any kind of activity has been held to satisfy this requirement. There are other limits for certain specific types of businesses.

Whenever you want to rely on an exemption from this or any other law, I think you should take some extra steps besides just reading a summary of the law yourself and deciding that you are exempt. Those extra steps include, at a minimum, getting a complete copy of the law and regulations, carefully reading them, contacting the local office of the government agency in charge of enforcing the law, and discussing your exemption with the people there and being sure they agree. Remember that these federal statutes have serious penalty provisions. If you make a legitimate mistake, and if you can show you were reasonable in your actions (such as by a discussion with someone in the government agency or your lawyer) your penalties will likely be very small. Conversely, if the government thinks you deliberately did not comply with the wage and hour law—or any other law—the penalties will be much more severe. Also, remember that if you choose the route of going to the government agency yourself, you have to be completely honest and disclose all the relevant facts. You must also make a careful record of what you said, what the person you talked with said, whom you talked with, and what information you provided him or her.

In addition to the general exemptions from the wage and hour laws, there are several specific exemptions *from the minimum wage rules only* which apply to certain special cases. However, these exemptions require specific permits or approvals from the government. You cannot just assume that they apply even if you meet all the criteria listed below, and even if you have discussed the exemption with the government or your counsel. These exemptions are:

1. *Learners* can be paid less than the minimum wage if the Department of Labor approves the program. Many industries have learners' programs. The requirements and the amounts that have to be paid differ. Office and clerical jobs do not qualify.

2. *Apprentices* can be paid less than the minimum wage. There are special regulations. Apprentices differ from learners in that apprentices are in a training program for a skilled job.

3. *Handicapped* people can be paid less than the minimum wage under certain rather formal and approved arrangements.

4. *Full-time students* may be employed at less than the minimum wage in retail or service establishments, and in colleges if the Department of Labor finds that employment at the lower wage is necessary in order to prevent curtailment of opportunities for employment.

The key thing to remember if you think one of these exemptions might apply to you is that you need specific advice and approval from the Department of Labor—Wage and Hour Division. First, get their publications describing the general rules, and then go and talk with them to see what specific rules might apply to your situation. Your lawyer can do this for you, but there is generally no reason why you cannot do it yourself.

Minimum Wages

The minimum wage requirements are fairly straightforward. They provide that, with the exceptions noted above, you must pay a minimum wage to all your employees — currently $4.25 per hour.

The minimum wage requirements for government contractors are not so straightforward. First of all, you must decide which statute is applicable. This will usually depend on the kind of work being done. The applicable statutes include the following:

1. The most widely applicable statute is the Walsh-Healey Act. The requirements of this statute will be covered in this chapter.
2. The Davis-Bacon Act covers minimum wages paid to workers engaged in public works contracts. This act is usually applicable in the construction industry.
3. The Service Contract Act covers workers employed by government contractors and subcontractors who provide services to the United States.

Unfortunately, the technical requirements of each of these laws differ, and space does not permit a complete listing of all the requirements of each act. However, the general thrust of the minimum wage laws for government contractors is that there are no set minimum figures in the statute. Instead, the minimum wages are fixed periodically by the administrative agency and published in the Federal Register. Further, the minimum wages are different in many cases, depending on the industry and the geographic location. The following section of the Walsh-Healey Act states the general principle:

> All persons employed by the contractor ... will be paid ... not less than the minimum wages as determined by the Secretary of Labor to be the prevailing minimum wages for persons employed on similar work or in the particular or similar industries ... currently operating in the locality.

Overtime

The general rule regarding overtime is that a company must pay workers one and one-half times their regular rate for hours worked in excess of 40 hours per week. The trouble comes in defining regular rate.

Regular rate is *not* necessarily the normal hourly rate at which people are paid, nor even their hourly rate computed by dividing their weekly salaries by the number of hours actually worked. In most cases, either of the above would be approximately right but not necessarily absolutely correct. While the Fair Labor Standards Act speaks in terms of hourly rate, it is not necessary to pay workers on an hourly basis; they can be paid weekly, daily, twice a month, monthly, or at whatever other period suits the employer. However, for purposes of computing their regular rate, the whole thing must be factored down to an hourly figure.

Another problem in the overtime area is deciding exactly who is covered. The Fair Labor Standards Act and the Walsh-Healey Act contain the concepts of exempt and nonexempt employees, and it is only the nonexempt group which must be paid overtime. Exempt people include the administrative, executive, and professional employees; nonexempt people include the hourly employees and the salaried people who do not meet the requirements of being exempt. It is easy to get into considerable legal difficulty by failing to pay overtime to people whom the company thinks are exempt but who are later termed nonexempt after analysis of their duties. Typically, the problem will arise when someone who has been classified as exempt either becomes disenchanted or gets fired and sues for back pay. The court or the Department of Labor will then conduct an elaborate analysis of the person's duties to ascertain whether he or she was in fact exempt. If the conclusion is no, the company will have to make up for any lack of overtime pay. In larger cases involving many employees, the Department of Labor may itself institute suit. The concepts of regular rate and exempt versus nonexempt employees deserve further elaboration because these are the cornerstones of the wage and hour laws.

Regular Rate   The employee's regular rate is the basis for computation of overtime pay and is, therefore, very important. The trouble usually comes in nonstandard payments. Beginning with simple examples, an employee who is paid a certain amount per hour for a normal work week and receives no other form of compensation would have a regular rate equal to this hourly rate. Similarly, a salaried secretary who works 40 hours a week would have as a regular rate the weekly pay divided by 40 hours.

The trouble will come when some nonstandard payment is made either in the form of cash or otherwise. The regular rate includes all of the employee's compensation, not just the base compensation. Thus, if the employees are paid a bonus in addition to the weekly or hourly rates, this bonus would have to be factored into the employee's regular rate. For example, suppose that a company decided to institute an incentive program and pay all the workers a bonus of $25 per week if the company made certain sales or profit levels for that week. In that case, the $25 bonus would have to be cranked into the regular rate, and if an employee worked overtime, his or her overtime pay would have to be based upon the regular rate which was augmented by that bonus. Thus, the employer would be in a position of having paid what it thought was a legitimate bonus, only to find out that it must recompute every nonexempt employee's wage and make an additional payment to those who might have worked overtime during the relevant period.

Fortunately, a number of statutory exclusions minimize this problem. Bonuses seem to present a frequent problem. In order for a bonus to be excluded, it must be either truly discretionary or part of a standard profit sharing plan. The typical incentive bonuses, which are based on profits, production, etc., do not qualify under either exclusion. However, it should be observed that even if the bonus is not exempt, if it is computed as a percentage of pay rather than a per capita amount or a fixed amount based on some other factors, the overtime problem will automatically take care of itself because, in essence, the pay on which it is based will already have had the overtime pay included so the bonus will be increased by the proper amount. Thus, in the case of a bonus, if it is based on a percentage of pay, there will generally be no problem, but if it is not, either it must fall into one of the exemptions or overtime pay must be recomputed.

A *purely discretionary* bonus is not included in the employee's "regular rate," but the Department of Labor takes a rather restrictive view of what is purely discretionary. Christmas gifts or Christmas bonuses which are not based on hours worked are also not included in the employee's regular rate.

In summary, then, the red flag here ought to be a bonus of any type. If it is a purely discretionary bonus or simply a modest Christmas gift, there is no problem. On the other hand, if you try to gear the bonus to the employee's production or the company's output, you must make sure either that the bonus is calculated as a percentage of pay or that you have taken this overtime problem into account. If you do not, your exposure could be quite high, because a worker or the Department of Labor could cause you to recompute all your calculations for the last two years and make up any differences. In cases where your operation has been running on a substantial overtime basis, this can generate a lot of money.

Informal Arrangements for Time Off   Another danger point in The Fair Labor Standards Act is informal arrangements for time off. A small business, for example, may have a policy that an employee who wants a day off can simply take it and make up the day some other time. One well-publicized case reported in *The Wall Street Journal* involved a small store in New England where the proprietor allowed employees to take time off during the summer and during hunting seasons on the informal understanding that they would make up the days some other time. The employees were simply paid a weekly salary and there was no deduction for the time they took off, nor any addition to their pay for the weeks in which they worked an extra day. The Department of Labor, quite correctly under the law, said that this was improper. The employer was under no duty to dock the workers when they missed a day, but when they made up that day the employer was under a duty to pay time and a half. Therefore, during the weeks the employees worked an extra day, they should have been paid time and a half for that extra day.

The aspect of this case which made it so bizarre, and the point which you should keep in mind, is that the Department of Labor took this position in spite of the fact that virtually all the employees of this company told the Department of Labor they did not want to do it that way. They wanted to have the informal arrangement where they could negotiate with the boss to take a day off and make up the time later. They did not want to be docked during the week they took the day off, and they did not want time and a half when they made the time up.

All this, however, was to no avail. *The Department of Labor says that employees cannot waive their rights under the Fair Labor Standards Act.* If this were not the rule, employers might pressure the employees to sign waivers of their rights, and this would frustrate the objectives of the law. This case, like so many others, was triggered when one of the employees got mad for some reason and filed a complaint with the Department of Labor.

The moral of this story, of course, is that you want to be careful about being too nice when it comes to granting employees time off which will be made up later. This will almost always result in their working less than 40 hours during one week and more than 40 hours during another. If the pay is kept constant, you will have a technical wage and hour violation. Frankly, I believe that most employers simply ignore this technical problem. I think this is probably a very practical solution, so long as it is not a pattern or practice which can give rise to substantial liability over a long term. If you do it once in a while, there ought not to be any problem. But, if virtually all your employees took advantage of this opportunity on a significant scale, the potential liability over a two-year period could be large.

Example

Suppose that you are operating a retail store which does not do very much business in the summer. You have 10 employees, and you make an informal agreement with them that they will work 4 days during the summer and 6 days in the winter. The employees are happy because it gives them an extra day in the summer when they can use it for personal reasons without costing them any money. You may find the arrangement desirable because it gives you more work force when you need it. Technically, however, the fact that the employees gave up the day during the summer does not entitle you to get it back in the winter without paying time and a half. Pursuing the example, suppose 10 weeks are involved. That means 10 days extra in the winter, times 10 employees, times 8 hours per day. Thus, the number of hours worked for which time and a half should have been paid but was not is 800. The statute of limitations is 2 years for a maximum exposure of 1,600 hours. If the average hourly rate of these workers is $6 per hour, half of that is $3 per hour. Three dollars per hour times 1,600 hours is $4,800 maximum exposure.

Contrary to popular belief, there is nothing in the Fair Labor Standards Act about double time for weekends, triple time for holidays, etc. All of those things have been developed over the years through collective bargaining agreements, and they may be common practice in some industries. The law, however, has a very simple requirement: time and a half for hours worked in any one week over 40 hours. It does not matter whether the hours are on Saturday or Sunday or nighttime, or whether there is any holiday involved. Further, there is no requirement that these 40 hours be worked in 8-hour days. Under the Fair Labor Standards Act, there is absolutely no reason why you cannot go to a 4-day, 40-hour week without any overtime problem if you should so desire. However, this would create some problems under government contract rules, which are explained below.

Government Contracts.   Prior to 1986, the Fair Labor Standards Act and the Walsh-Healey Act differed in regard to overtime pay. The Fair Labor Standards Act has always required overtime pay only for hours worked in excess of 40 hours per week. The Walsh-Healey Act also required overtime pay for hours worked in excess of 40 hours per week, or in excess of 8 hours per day. In 1986, however, an amendment to the law stated that employees of all federal contractors could work any combination of hours in a 40-hour week without requiring overtime pay. Overtime compensation would be required only for hours worked in excess of 40 hours per week. The significance of this change is that it allowed government contractors to implement work weeks consisting of four 10-hour days without triggering the Walsh-Healey overtime provisions. This four-day 40-hour work week has proven popular with some employees.

Exempt Employees

Another important concept in the Fair Labor Standards Act is that of the exempt employee. The general rule is that executive, administrative, and professional employees are exempt from the minimum wage and overtime provisions of the Fair Labor Standards Act. The appropriate definitions are as follows.

- An executive is one whose primary duty (generally agreed to be 50 percent or more of his or her time) is in managing an enterprise or department or subdivision thereof. He or she must customarily and regularly direct work of two or more other employees and must be able to hire and fire or suggest changes in status of other employees. An executive must customarily and regularly exercise discretionary powers.

- An administrative employee is one whose primary duty (generally agreed to be 50 percent or more of his or her time) is in performing office or nonmanual work relating to the management policies or general business operations of the company. An administrative employee is one who regularly and directly assists a proprietor or executive or another administrative employee or who works only under general supervision along specialized or technical lines requiring special training, experience, or knowledge and who executes only under general supervision special assignments and tasks. An administrative employee must customarily and regularly exercise discretion and independent judgment.

- A professional employee is one whose primary duty (generally 50 percent or more of his or her time) is in performing work requiring scientific or specialized study as distinguished from apprentice training and training for routine work, or in performing regular and creative work in a recognized artistic endeavor depending primarily on the invention, imagination, or talent of the employee.

The act contains certain presumptions about compensation. If an executive, administrative, or professional employee's compensation is above a certain base level, the employee is presumed to satisfy the requirement. Currently that base level is $250 per week. This will take care of most of the clear situations. It should be noted that there are also minimum rates below which it will be presumed that the person is not an executive, administrative, or professional employee. At the present time, the figures are as follows:

- Executives must make $155 per week and are presumed executive if they make $250 per week or more.

- Administrative employees must make $155 per week and are presumed administrative if they make $250 per week or more.

- Professional employees must make $170 per week and are presumed to be professional if they make $250 per week or more.

It should be noted, of course, that these are only presumptions, and the mere fact that someone makes over the maximum amount stated above does not automatically qualify him or her as an executive, administrative, or professional employee—he or she must still satisfy the substantive requirements.

Obviously, the determination of who is exempt and who is not exempt is very important, because you do not have to pay exempt people time and a half for overtime.

Again, the problem is going to come up when you are trying to be too nice. You may have a loyal secretary whom you want to give a promotion to, but you really do not have a job which qualifies as executive, administrative, or professional. You, therefore make one up, give the secretary a new title and a raise (perhaps a substantial one), and call the employee exempt. The employee works hard for a number of years (including spending evenings and weekends on the job), and then there is a falling out. At that point the employee says that he or she should have been paid time and a half for all those evenings and weekends, and there you have the problem.

The practical solution seems to be this: If there just is no way to classify the employee properly as administrative, executive, or professional, either make sure he or she does not work substantial amounts of overtime and keep records to show this or else simply pay overtime where it is due. On the other hand, if you are in the gray area and if you feel that there is substantial value to your business in giving this employee an exempt status even if it may be a close case, there really is not too much of a risk so long as you are not talking about a lot of people.

If you make a practice of doing this, and you have a considerable number of people on your staff who are not being paid overtime because you consider them to be executives or administrative people but you probably cannot justify that, it would seem that you have a potential exposure. You ought to try to bring the situation more in line with the law.

This area of the wage and hour laws is one where business people and lawyers sometimes get into rather heated arguments. Usually the businessperson says to the lawyer words to this effect: "I hear what you are saying, but good old Millie just would never do that to me." The lawyer tells the businessperson that he or she does not know Millie but does have a lot of books which are full of cases where people just like good old Millie did do it to somebody. My own view is that to a certain degree, the businessperson's judgment is more appropriate in this area.

Exposures are rather low, there are no criminal penalties, class actions are unlikely so long as the number of employees are small, and the government regulatory efforts are extremely light. This is not at all like Title VII of the Civil Rights Act of 1964 or the antitrust laws, where even good-faith mistakes can cost you an awful lot of money. If you enjoy the personal satisfaction of telling your lawyer that you know he or she is right and you appreciate his or her advice, but you are not going to pay any attention, this is a relatively low-risk place to do so.

This assumes, however, that you really are talking about good-faith judgments and that you do maintain the proper records. As in all areas of the law which are governed by a federal statute, the enforcement authorities do have great power to give you a lot of trouble if they feel you are in bad faith. If you deliberately destroy records or do not keep any in the first place so that the Department of Labor cannot possibly audit whether you are paying time and a half or not, they may very well get mad enough to use some of that power.

Child Labor Laws

The child labor laws are part of the Fair Labor Standards Act. Penalties for violation of the child labor laws are, in general, extremely weak or nonexistent. Of course, as always, this presumes good faith violations rather than a deliberate flouting of the act.

On the other hand, there is hardly anything that will cause you to have to sit by yourself in church on Sunday morning quicker than a newspaper story that your company has violated the child labor laws. I do recommend some caution here. Not because you are going to go bankrupt or go to jail if you do not; but because it is just the right thing to do.

Essentially, the child labor laws say that employment of minors (those under 18 years of age) is subject to certain restrictions. The restrictions depend on the age of the minor. Subject to extensive explanation contained in the Department of Labor Regulations, employment of minors between ages 16 and 18 is restricted (but not totally prohibited) in certain high-risk areas, such as manufacture or storage of explosives, motor vehicle driving, coal mine operations, logging occupations, woodworking occupations, roofing, excavating, and operating power-driven machinery. Thus, in the case of minors between 16 and 18 you can employ them unless there is some specific rule that says you cannot.

In the case of minors between 14 and 16, the thrust of the regulation changes—you can employ a minor only in certain areas set forth as being permissible. These include such jobs as office and clerical work, cashiering, selling, modeling, artwork, price marking, assembling orders, packing and shelving, bagging and carrying out customers' orders, errand and delivery work, clean-up work, etc.

The law also contains the concept of an age certificate. If you get the proper age certificate from a minor, you will be protected against an inadvertent violation of the law, even assuming the minor lied about his or her age. If you do not get such a certificate and the minor lied, you will still be liable for a violation.

Child labor laws present both a problem and an opportunity. Employment of minors is obviously highly desirable in many situations, both for the company and for the minor. However, if you want to do this on a substantial scale, I recommend that you talk with the Department of Labor, get their appropriate publications, and read them first. (They are listed in this chapter.)

The Portal to Portal Act

The Portal to Portal Act is a portion of the wage and hour laws which has to do with the calculation of the number of hours employees work. Essentially, the law says that workers need not be paid for transportation from their home to their place of work. Thus, in a normal case, one computes hours worked from the time the worker actually starts work until the time he or she actually stops, and the time spent going to and from home or walking from the plant door to the work station is not counted. Of course, this general rule can be altered by custom or contract.

If you send a nonexempt employee out of town, I simply recommend the commonsense approach. For example, if you send a nonexempt employee to a training class or seminar, the only additional payments I would make are those which are rather clear. If you ask the employee to work an 8-hour day and then travel to the other city at night, that travel time ought to be compensated. On the other hand, if the employee spends 3 days in another city going to a seminar, I do not view it as necessary to compensate the employee for 72 hours. I would simply pay for a normal 8-hour day unless, of course, the actual training periods are longer. The law on this sort of thing is not as clear as it might be, but I think that common sense should prevail.

Garnishments

Garnishments are a point of annoyance. The Fair Labor Standards Act restricts the *amount of wages* which can be garnished. Accordingly, the payroll people must be informed of these rules and must be instructed to comply with legitimate garnishment orders only up to the maximum extent required by law.

The federal garnishment law limits the amount of wages subject to garnishment to 25 percent of a worker's "disposable earnings," which are generally defined as the earnings remaining after withholding for taxes and other amounts required by law, or the amount by which the weekly disposable earnings exceed by 30 times the Fair Labor Standards Act minimum wage, whichever is less.

In my experience, the garnishment forms used by most courts explain this fairly well, and there is not much of a problem. If you do have a question, I would suggest calling the court or the local Department of Labor Office—if you call your lawyer, that is what he or she would probably do.

Also, the federal garnishment law prohibits the discharge of an employee because that employee's earnings have been garnished for "any one indebtedness." The meaning of "any one indebtedness" is not entirely clear, but it should be noted that it is definitely different than any single garnishment. Accordingly, the mere fact that an employee has had his or her wages garnished more than once does not mean that he or she can be discharged. In addition, a policy of discharging employees with excessive garnishments can be considered to violate equal employment opportunity laws if the policy operates discriminatorily—and, statistically speaking, one is very likely to find this to be the result. Before you discharge someone because of frequent garnishments, you want to be sure of at least two things:

1. The garnishments involve more than single indebtedness and

2. You are not using the garnishment policy discriminatorily so that blacks, women, Hispanics, or persons of Asian origin are discharged more frequently than white males.

Record Keeping

Employers subject to the Fair Labor Standards Act are required to keep fairly detailed records concerning their employees. Records must be kept for both exempt and nonexempt employees, although the records for nonexempt employees are more detailed. The reason for the records on the exempt employees is to allow the government to make a reasonable audit to see that they were, in fact, exempt. The reason for the records on the nonexempt employees is to allow for checks on whether or not the provisions of the act have been complied with. The company does not have to keep these records in any specific format, so long as they can be audited.

Getting Help from the Government

The place to go for help on wage and hour problems is the local office of the U.S. Department of Labor, Employment Standards Administration, Wage and Hour Division. They publish a lot of material and usually have capable and conscientious people available to answer your questions. Like government publications in general, many of them are difficult to use. They either simply reprint the entire language of the statute or regulation, in which case they are lengthy, technical, and difficult to understand, or they abbreviate the rules so much that they do not tell you what you need to know. Nevertheless, there are some good publications which you should have. If you get them from the Department of Labor, there will not be any cost.

Overtime Compensation WH Publication 1262 An interpretative bulletin stating the official position of the Department of Labor regarding computation of overtime compensation.

Overtime Compensation WH Publication 1325 A publication for general information; not to be considered official position. Provides basic information in relatively simple and useful language.

Restriction on Garnishment WH Publication 1333 Provides regulations on a section-by-section basis for the relevant laws.

Important Notice—Federal Wage Garnishment Law WH Publication 1436 Provides a shorter, more easily understood statement on the maximum wage limits for garnishment purposes.

Records to Be Kept by Employers WH Publication 1261 Provides the regulations on a section-by-section basis on the record-keeping requirements of the Fair Labor Standards Act.

Child Labor Requirements in Nonagricultural Occupations WH Publication 1330 A very well prepared booklet, summarizing the relevant rules and reprinting the relevant regulations.

Handy Reference Guide to the Fair Labor Standards Act WH Publication 1282 An excellent general overview of the law. Written in plain English.

Executive, Administrative, Professional and Outside Sales Exemptions Under the Fair Labor Standards Act WH Publication 1363   A useful, 10-page explanation of these exemptions from the overtime requirements.

Regulations, Part 541: Defining the Terms Executive, Administrative, Professional, and Outside Salesman WH Publication 1281 Complete copy of all the relevant regulations. Rather lengthy and technical, but complete and accurate.

Summary

In conclusion, we have seen that setting up a payroll can involve considerable paper shuffling, but that adequate help is available from the relevant state or federal authorities. If you take advantage of that free help, there is no reason why you cannot do everything yourself. There are several legal cautions:

- Do not get too greedy in trying to arrange things to avoid payroll taxes or withholding.

- Do not let anyone work on your premises without workers' compensation coverage — even if he or she is working for an independent contractor. Make sure the contractor has coverage and obtain evidence of it if necessary.

- Workers' compensation and unemployment compensation are items of expense which are affected by your experience. Keep this in mind as you conduct your business operations.

- Keep the wage and hour rules in mind as you set wages and schedule work. Do not avoid paying time and a half on the basis of an informal agreement unless you clearly understand the risk involved and are willing to assume it.

8

Employment Practices

In my legal guide for executives of larger companies, the chapter on discrimination in employment is 64 pages long, by far the longest chapter in that book. Even so, it only scratches the surface of the relevant laws. Equal employment opportunity has been one of the biggest growth industries in the legal profession. In fact, it has become so much a part of the daily life of business people that the relevant laws and legal considerations have been digested and reduced to standard practices and procedures, so that personnel people now understand the legal requirements as well as many lawyers. Many seminars teach personnel people about the basic EEO ground rules and help them understand how to steer their companies through the complicated maze of regulations. Having nonlawyers handle many EEO matters is a good idea. Whenever you have a problem this big, you just cannot have lawyers handling it on a continuing basis; it is too expensive.

However, many of the EEO considerations are peculiar to a large company. For a small company, the problems can be quite a bit simpler, and the risks are quite a bit smaller.

EEO laws can usefully be divided into two categories.

1. In the first category are the so-called *antidiscrimination laws*. These are the social laws of the mid-1960s, principally Title VII of the Civil Rights Act of 1964. The basic concept of these laws is that it is illegal for a company to discriminate in any employment matter on the basis of race, sex, age, handicap, national origin, or religion. It is very important to note that these laws are prohibitions. Unless you have already discriminated against these protected groups and need to adopt a

plan to fix that problem, there is no need to have an affirmative action plan to hire and promote minorities.

The federal equal employment opportunity law covers all employers with 15 or more employees. However, almost all states except the southern states have equivalent state laws that cover smaller companies. In Ohio, for example, the antidiscrimination law covers any company with three or more employees. Thus, even the smallest of companies is going to be covered by EEO laws.

2. In the other category of EEO laws are those imposed on *government contractors*, the so-called affirmative action plans. They require that if you are a government contractor, you must have a written affirmative action plan that follows numerous detailed requirements to spell out exactly what positive steps you are going to take to bring more minorities into your company and to promote the minorities you already have into positions of increased pay and responsibility.

By far, the bulk of the administrative work is in the second category. You can easily see why. It applies to any company with government contracts, no matter how good its employment practices have been in the past and no matter how many females or minorities work in the company. Because we are talking about small businesses, I am going to eliminate this second category to simplify the discussion. If you do have government contracts, you must have an affirmative action plan, and you are probably going to need some expert help to draft it so that it passes muster with the government compliance people.

With that brief introduction and overview, I would like to go through some of the trouble spots in the EEO laws so that you can avoid them.

Selection Process

The selection process is one of the most important areas where you can run afoul of the EEO laws. You simply have to evaluate people fairly. We all know that is subjective, but the law and theory are very clear. If you reject employees because they are black, because they are female, or because you do not like their national origin or religion, you are very likely to wind up in big trouble. The EEO laws specifically allow attorneys' fees, thus creating a built-in incentive for people to bring lawsuits. If you discriminate against a black or a female who then gets a lawyer to sue you, you are going to be liable not only for the damages suffered by that person, but also for the attorneys' fees generated in the lawsuit. In the case of the single plaintiff, it is possible that the attorneys' fees could be larger than the damages.

It is very important to understand that this applies to each and every job. Suppose, for example, you say that you are not prejudiced against minorities and you certainly do not mind having women in the company, but for certain jobs you want certain kinds of persons. You want a white male to be your traveling sales representative, a female to be your secretary, a male (either white or black) to run some of the machinery in your plant because it is a very dirty job and you do not think women would like it, a woman to be the receptionist because you think that looks nicer, and so on. All of these selection preferences are clearly illegal. You must apply the equal employment opportunity antidiscrimination laws each time you hire somebody. As a practical matter, there are no exceptions to this rule.

The fact that your customers happen to like a particular kind of employee does not make any difference. Some of the airlines tried to raise this argument in the case of male flight attendants. They conducted surveys and found that the majority of their customers wanted female flight attendants. That did not even get them to first base. Customer preference is totally irrelevant.

Measuring People's Ability

When you hire someone, you obviously want to get the best person you can for the job. The law, simply stated, is that you must measure the person for the job and not the person in the abstract. Thus, almost any arbitrary requirement (such as a college degree) is extremely suspect. You may be able to justify it, but remember that the burden is going to be on you and it is a difficult one to meet. You must clearly define the job and its requirements and do your utmost to select the best person for the job. This you are entitled to do. EEO laws do not require you to hire unqualified people. What you cannot do is simply pull an arbitrary requirement out of the air and say that you will not consider anybody who does not satisfy your preconceived and perhaps arbitrary criterion.

There are certain obvious applications of this principle. If you need a secretary, you are entitled to require that the secretary type a certain number of words per minute, take shorthand at a certain rate, and so on. If you need an accountant, you are entitled to require the person to have an accounting degree from a college. However, if you need a sales representative and you want to say that you are going to hire only someone who has a college degree, you are going to have a problem. You are going to have to show that a college degree is a job-related requirement. Frankly, I do not know whether it is or not, but I do know that it is going to be extremely difficult for you to prove your case in court, and that the law imposes the burden on you to prove it.

There are elaborate rules regarding all forms of tests. These rules say, in substance, that if you give a test and it screens out an abnormally higher number of minorities than white males, the test is discriminatory. Again, the burden is on you to prove that it is job-related. Except in obvious cases such as typing tests for secretaries, this is extremely difficult, if not impossible. The criterion for abnormally higher rejection rates is 80 percent. Thus, a test will be discriminatory if it rejects more minorities than nonminorities by a factor greater than 80 percent. This is very important; let us see how it works.

Example

You have 10 white male applicants and 10 black male applicants. You give them all a test, and all 10 white males pass but only 7 of the blacks. The passing rate for white males is 100 percent, but 70 percent for black males. You put the 70 percent over the 100 percent and you get 70 percent. Since the requirement is 80 percent, the test is discriminatory. It screens out a disproportionately high number of blacks. If eight blacks had passed the test, it would be all right. If the test does not pass muster under this rule, you must validate it.

That is almost impossible except for obvious job-related things. If the job involved inspecting and required the use of a micrometer, and the test measured whether the applicant could read and use a micrometer, I think it would be all right, because this is a clear situation. Just be sure the test actually measured the ability to use and read a micrometer. On the other hand, suppose the job involved general factory work and the test you gave was a reading test. That would not be an obvious job requirement. You would have to validate the test. You would have to show, by the Equal Employment Opportunity Commission's highly burdensome regulations, that the ability to read was a legitimate job requirement.

The use of any paper-and-pencil test is a danger point. I recommend that if you use any such tests, you obtain legal counsel as to their permissibility under the EEO rules. If you are on the wrong side of this rule, a plaintiff has a ready-made case against you, and you are practically defenseless.

Equal Pay

Equal pay for equal work is another high-risk area. If you pay males more than females for equal work, that is a clear violation of the law. The females can bring, and often have, brought, costly suits against the employer for back pay. You simply must pay equal pay for equal work. You must look to the substance of the work.

Example

You call a female employee a secretary and pay her $800 a month when in reality she is an administrative assistant or even an executive assistant. Then you hire a brand-new, bright-eyed white male out of college, give him a fancy title, and pay him $1,600 a month. But if it turns out that he does the same thing your "secretary" has done for many years, you may have to explain that in court.

Many equal pay cases involve essentially these facts.

Another highly sensitive area consists of "female" jobs which, because of history and inertia, females comprise the majority, if not all, of the people doing that work. Testing and inspection in a factory can be prime examples. If you have a large group of females working in the same kind of job, and it turns out to be a lower-paying job than others in your factory, you should look into this situation to make sure there is no discriminatory reason for it.

Still another problem is assigning different titles for equal work. In the banking industry white males would be given the designation of "trainee" and paid higher wages for essentially teller work. Females would be called tellers and paid less, but would actually be doing the same work as the males. If you have a training program, it must be legitimate and nondiscriminatory. Males and females must have equal access to the program, and the program must really lead to positions of increased responsibility.

Treatment of Pregnant Females

Under the equal employment opportunity laws, discrimination on account of pregnancy is equivalent to discrimination on the basis of sex and is prohibited. Thus, you cannot discharge a female because she becomes pregnant, and you cannot require a female to take an unpaid leave of absence on account of pregnancy before it is medically required. Thus, you must, as a practical matter, allow pregnant females to work right up until the date their own doctor says they should stop or until they stop voluntarily.

Further, you must consider pregnancy to qualify for any short-term disability benefits you have, including salary continuation. Thus, if you would pay your secretary for 6 weeks off work for a broken leg, you would have to do the same for 6 weeks off work for pregnancy.

The rules on the treatment of pregnant females are quite complex, but they have been reduced to a set of guidelines and interpretive questions and answers published by the EEOC. It is listed at the end of this chapter, under "Help from the Government," and it is one of the documents I recommend you obtain.

Handicap Discrimination

The Americans with Disabilities Act of 1990 adds handicaps to the list of attributes that are protected by antidiscrimination laws. The original Civil Rights Act did not include handicaps. (Most of this law is effective as of July 26, 1992.)

The bottom line, therefore, is that it is now just as illegal to discriminate on account of handicap as it is on account of race, sex, or age. Basically, the law says that we have to make "reasonable accommodation" to employees or applicants who may be handicapped. Since the law was enacted only in 1990, there are no cases that flesh out the details of that "reasonable accommodation." We can, however, list certain things that the law itself makes clear.

1. AIDS is a handicap. You cannot discriminate against people either by refusing to hire them or by firing them simply because they test positive for the AIDS virus.

2. The act does not prohibit discrimination against anyone who currently uses drugs. We should, however, note that only current drug users are excluded. Someone who had gone through a drug rehabilitation program might very well be considered handicapped and discrimination against such an individual could violate the law.

3. Essentially the same approach is taken with alcohol. You do not have to put up with someone drinking on the job, but on the other hand you can probably not discriminate against a former or reformed alcoholic.

The Act prohibits employers from requiring a preemployment medical examination or making any inquiries into the prospective employee's medical history. The company can use a post-hiring physical examination and make passing that examination a condition of the job offer. There are, however, some fairly extensive limits on that.

While the contours of "reasonable accommodation" are not entirely clear, the following things may be included:

1. Making the employer's facilities readily accessible and usable to the disabled

2. Restructuring jobs, implementing part time or modified work schedules, or reassigning the disabled individual to a vacant position

3. Purchasing or modifying necessary equipment for use by the disabled

4. Providing appropriate training material or programs, including qualified readers or interpreters, tailored to fit the particular needs of the disabled individual

A company does not need to make reasonable accommodation if it would create an "undue hardship." Again, the contours of "undue hardship" are not yet clear but it is defined as "an action requiring significant difficulty or expense." Among the factors that would be included in the evaluation are

1. The nature and cost of the accommodation.

2. The overall financial resources of the company.

3. The size of the company, including the number, type, and location of its facilities. In other words, a smaller company would not be expected to spend as much money as a larger one.

National Origin

The Immigration Reform and Control Act of 1986 established the so-called "Employer's Sanctions" rules relating to the hiring of illegal aliens. It also provided that you could not discriminate against people not only because of their national origin, but because of their citizenship status.

The most burdensome provision of the law is its recordkeeping requirements. For every person you hire, you have to keep a file that shows that you verified that they were legally eligible to work in this country. That might mean proof of citizenship or, if the employee is not a citizen, proof of legal status. The Immigration and Naturalization Service says that you can use a whole host of things to show that you made a good faith effort to ascertain that the people you hired were not illegal aliens. Thus, even in rural areas or those areas of the country that do not have any significant population of illegal aliens, you still have to maintain this paperwork. The government has done a fairly good job of explaining it and providing the appropriate forms. It should, however, be on everyone's checklist of personnel practices. For each hire you must be sure that you have some documents that verify the person's eligibility to work in this country.

Because of the antidiscrimination provisions, you also should add to your training programs a caution that the company cannot refuse to hire people who speak with an accent or who look as if they are "foreign" out of fear that they might be an illegal alien.

At this point, most of the litigation under this law has been for violations of the paperwork and record-keeping requirements. Enforcement is not extensive and is concentrated in larger cities or areas where there are populations of illegal aliens. Nevertheless, since the law is very clear and since there are substantial penalties for failure to maintain these records, we should all be sure to have compliance procedures. The key document is the so-called Form I-9 (Employment Eligibility Verification Form), and the supporting explanations as to how to use it contained in the "Handbook for Employers," published by the Immigration and Naturalization Service just after the law was passed. This is an example of a "do-it-yourself compliance area." There really isn't any need to spend money on lawyers to tell you how to do this. The government forms and explanatory booklets are adequate.

Your Employment Application Form

Many of the employment application forms I have seen are tickets for plaintiffs' lawsuits. My advice is to design an employment application form that asks only for the information you need to evaluate an applicant legally. Some employers put anything on an application form that they think they might want to know for any kind of vague and general reason. I have seen application forms that include the following items that in the view of the EEOC, which enforces the antidiscrimination laws, are discriminatory:

Do you own your own home?

Are you married?

What is your maiden name?

Do you own your own car?

How many dependents do you have?

All of these questions are viewed as discriminatory by the EEOC because they have an adverse statistical effect on minorities. Minorities, partly because of past employment discrimination, do not own their own homes or their own cars in the same percentage as nonminorities. Consequently, if you ask such questions because you feel that persons who own their own home are stable and are going to stay in the community, and persons who own their own car are going to have an easier time in getting to work and are therefore going to have better attendance, you had better be able to prove it. So far, I have not seen anybody do it. In the overwhelming majority of cases, these kinds of questions on an employment application form are nails that hold the lid on the coffin in any lawsuit that might be brought against you. For example, if there is a single job for which a black male and a white male applied, and you chose the white male, the black male may have a very marginal case as to why you did not select him. On the other hand, if you have a bunch of these bad questions on your employment application form, that bad case turns into a good one, and you are very likely to become involved in a lawsuit and have to pay back pay and attorneys' fees. I strongly recommend you examine your employment application forms and make sure the questions are entirely job-related.

Two Cautions. (1) Do not trust published forms, even from fairly reputable sources such as trade associations or chambers of commerce. They may be all right, but I have seen many recently drafted forms that purport to be free of legal difficulty and are not. (2) You may need supplementary forms for special cases. Many questions are proper for one kind of job but not for another. For example, if you are hiring a person who is going to handle money, you can ask if the applicant knows of any reason why he or she might be denied bonding insurance coverage. That question would not be proper for persons who were not going to be bonded. Similarly, if you are going to hire a person to drive a motor vehicle for you, you can ask about past traffic violations, but you cannot ask this question if there is no legitimate reason for your knowing the answer.

Promotions

Substantially everything said about employment applies to promotions also. You must treat people equally on promotions just as you do in the case of the initial hires. Civil rights laws have progressed much past the stage where you could satisfy your obligations by hiring women and minorities but keep them in lower-paid jobs. Today, all that will do is increase the magnitude of the judgment against you, because these minorities having the lower-paid jobs will constitute a class which has been discriminated against. If they institute suit, there will likely be a recovery on behalf of all the members of the class rather than simply for one person who was denied a promotion.

Unjust Dismissal

Federal law and state statutory law remain essentially the same today as they were when the book was first written (with the important qualification that handicapped people are now covered by Title VII). Those laws enumerate only certain specific categories of people and say that a company is prohibited from discriminating against those people or treating them differently from any others. The list of protected people is long and the concept of discrimination rather broad, but in theory, at least, there are a fairly straightforward set of rules that are applied reasonably uniformly throughout the country.

The decade of the 1980s, however, saw the development of a completely new cause of action, the *unjust dismissal*, which goes by different names in different states. Someone who was fired could claim that the discharge, while not discriminatory, was simply unjust. This marked a fundamental change from the so-called *employment at will doctrine*, which was in effect before. In fact, the employment at will doctrine is still stated to be the general rule with all unjust dismissal theories being exceptions. The trouble is, in actual practice in many states, the exceptions have eaten up the general rule. It is now uniformly agreed that the only counseling advice lawyers should give their clients is that all discharges must be able to pass muster on some type of fairness or reasonableness test. Even if you are discharging a white male under age 40 who is not handicapped in any way (and thus not covered by the antidiscrimination laws), that person can still institute a lawsuit if the discharge was unjust. Indeed, that is the context of many of these unjust dismissal suits. They were instituted by employees fairly high up on the managerial ladder, often with many years of experience.

The boundaries of the unjust dismissal theory are still being developed, but the following claims have been successfully asserted.

1. The discharge was illegal on public policy grounds. These cases usually involve "whistle blowers" who supply information to enforcement officials about the company or a fellow employee concerning a possible crime.

2. The discharge was for exercising a basic statutory right. These cases involve discharge of people who had filed claims under workers' compensation laws or who had filed complaints with the Occupational Safety and Health Commission or otherwise exercised their rights under a federal or state law. One of the problems employers have faced is the marginal worker who does file some type of claim. It is clear that simply filing the claim does not give the worker tenure in the job, but it certainly does make the employer's burden of proof a little more difficult.

3. The discharge violates an implied contract. Remember the word here is *implied*, it does not have to be expressed. These cases have involved employees who were successful in convincing a court that there was at least an implied contract that they would be kept on the job or at

least not fired without good cause. The usual fact pattern is that a new employee is hired (sometimes at a fairly high level) and then does not work out. The company fires the employee within a relatively short time, and the employee claims there was an implied contract. If the employee was induced to leave a fairly secure job and perhaps sell a house and purchase another one in a new location, the implied contract theory takes on even more credence. Why would the employee do that if there wasn't some implied agreement that he or she would have reasonable job security in the new position? Those types of arguments are very persuasive with a jury.

4. The discharge violated some actual contract. Employees have been able to convince courts that actual contracts arose out of such things as promises made during the recruitment process and statements in personnel manuals. The promises made during recruiting are often such things as "jobs are really secure here—you'll never get fired as long as you stay out of .trouble." Promises in personnel manuals often involve the procedure for discharge. They may say such things as no employee will be discharged without a reasonable opportunity to present the case to management or that employees will be discharged only for good cause. Today, it is incumbent upon all companies to closely examine their personnel manuals to make sure that nothing in them amounts to a promise like that, unless, of course, the company is prepared to keep whatever promises it makes. Most personnel manuals today have disclaimers to the general effect that they are not intended to be contracts. Those disclaimers are put in the personnel manuals because of cases that have allowed employees to recover based upon language in the personnel manual that sounded like a promise, a commitment, or a contract of some type.

5. The discharge was basically unfair. This is the catchall category, and there have been a lot of cases. Employees generally complain about two types of things: the basic unfairness of the discharge itself and the procedure used in the discharge.

In terms of basic unfairness, the most successful complaints were made by long-term employees who may have been discharged shortly before their pensions vested. Successful plaintiffs have argued that all contracts, including the employer-employee contract, imply the obligation of good faith. This means that the employee is entitled to bring into court evidence of everything the employer did and let the judge or jury decide whether the company was acting in good faith or not.

On the procedural side, plaintiffs have been successful with claims based on tort concepts such as intentional infliction of emotional distress. The idea here is that it is one thing to fire someone, but is is another to do so in a demeaning or hostile way and to publicize the discharge more than is necessary. Today, lawyers recommend reasonable sensitivity and common courtesy in any discharge situation.

The damages in these cases have been phenomenal. A recent study in California showed that the average verdict of a successful plaintiff was in excess of $600,000. Often those large verdicts are a combination of actual damages and punitive damages. Also, the plaintiff is entitled to a jury trial. Juries have sometimes reacted very severely when it appeared that the company was apting in a highhanded or unfair manner in one of these discharges.

Smokers in the Workplace

Another workplace legal issue of the 1980s involves the rights of smokers, nonsmokers, and employers relating to smoking in the workplace. Controversy between smokers and nonsmokers is certainly not new, but it has now reached the point that it cannot always be handled simply by negotiation. There are legal issues.

First, many states and localities now have one form or another of Clean Indoor Air Acts. Some of these laws are limited to public places but some extend into the private workplace. The first thing you need to know is whether or not your state or locality has any law that will restrict your ability to make whatever management decisions you think appropriate in terms of smoking in your workplace.

No general federal laws restrict your ability to make management decisions relating to smoking in the workplace, although some have implications for those decisions. Here is a brief rundown.

Safe and Healthy Workplace

There is a common law rule in some jurisdictions that employers must provide their employees with a reasonably safe and healthy workplace. That, of course, is also one of the basic tenets of the occupational Safety and Health Act. Some cases indicate that if a person is particularly susceptible to smoke, and the employer does not provide them an environment where they can be free from the smoking of others, the employer has not satisfied this duty. As of late 1990, there is no OSHA rule expressly on this subject, but several have been talked about. The basic idea is that employees have a right to be free from the so-called side stream smoke of their co-workers. At this point, only a few cases have related to sidestream smoke, and they have all involved people who were unusually susceptible to it. The conclusion, however, is that employers are no longer able to ignore complaints from nonsmokers about the environment caused by their smoking coworkers.

Retaliatory Discharge

There is at least one case where a worker alleged that he was fired for his persistent complaints about the smoking of his co-workers. The court held that, if he could prove it, that would be a case for recovery under the so-called retaliatory discharge or unjust dismissal theories currently used in most jurisdictions.

Handicap Laws

As indicated, many of these smoking-related cases are brought by people who are very sensitive to smoke. In some litigation under state laws, it has been held that people that were that sensitive to smoke were handicapped, and the company had a duty to make reasonable accommodation to their needs. With the enactment of the Americans with Disabilities Act imposing the reasonable accommodation duty on all employers, this concept of accommodating those who may be especially sensitive to sidestream smoke would appear to be even more important.

Benefits

In some cases, people either who quit because of exposure to a smoking environment or who were fired for excessive absences caused by that problem have been able to collect workers' compensation, unemployment compensation, and disability benefits.

What about a Total Nonsmoking Policy?

Some company policies totally prohibit smoking on company property at any time. To the best of our knowledge, these have not yet been challenged. Of course, such a policy would have to be enforced fairly and reasonably and certainly without any discrimination against any of the protected groups.

In summary, then, smoking in the workplace has become a legal issue. While it appears that management is free to adopt an absolute no-smoking policy, it does not appear that management is entirely free to ignore the problem and let anyone smoke who wants to. First, there may be local laws that restrict smoking, and, second, the rights of non-smokers in the workplace have achieved at least a certain degree of legal recognition. The bottom line appears to be that if you do not want to adopt a total no-smoking policy, you must use your best efforts to be fair and reasonable with everyone in adopting a compromise policy that allows some people to smoke in some locations, but that also provides smoke-free environments for those who want or need them.

The Legal Aspects of AIDS

One of the highly unwelcome visitors of the eighties was AIDS. In addition to the many social and economic problems it has caused, there are legal issues we need to keep in mind when dealing with AIDS in the workplace.

As indicated in the brief discussion of the Americans with Disabilities Act, AIDS is defined as a handicap, so you cannot refuse to hire people who test positive for the AIDS antibodies.

There is a tremendous amount of misunderstanding about AIDS, and at least to some degree an AIDS hysteria exists. This may very well mean that if your employees find that one of their co-workers has AIDS, you will be under pressure to discharge that employee or at least remove the employee from the work environment. While the issue is not entirely free from doubt, the overwhelming majority of counselors today feel that such an action would not only be inappropriate but perhaps illegal. The only way you could justify firing or reassigning someone with AIDS is if the person were in a position where he or she could reasonably be expected to transmit the disease, such as in a hospital, a medical environment, or perhaps a food handling job. Our recommendation is that no person should be discharged or reassigned on account of AIDS without a careful discussion with Your legal counsel.

Benefits

The Employee Retirement Income Security Act (ERISA) makes it illegal to discharge employees for making claims against their benefits. Thus, you could not discharge someone who has a positive AIDS test because you are afraid that he or she will require very expensive medical care.

OSHA

The Occupational Safety and Health Act requires us to provide a safe and healthy place for employment and one that is free of "recognized hazards." However, given the medical evidence to date, it is highly unlikely that the simple presence in the workforce of someone who has AIDS would make that workplace hazardous.

Right to Privacy

Almost all state laws recognize that everyone has a right to privacy, although the parameters of this rule are unclear. The obvious problem with AIDS is that, because of both normal and hysterical concerns, disclosing the results of an AIDS test could cause the affected person serious hardship. If the test results are kept in the employer's files and were to leak out to the wrong person, a serious invasion of privacy claim might result.

Unjust Dismissal

The new trend towards basic fairness or unjust dismissal lawsuits could very well be applied in the AIDS context. If someone were to be discharged because of AIDS, that person might very well have a good unjust dismissal case.

Antidiscrimination Laws

The antidiscrimination laws do not expressly list sexual preference or homosexuality as items for protection. In addition, AIDS is not strictly a homosexual disease, although it certainly appears to have a disproportionate impact on homosexual males. One could, therefore, structure an argument that a policy of not retaining people who test positive for the AIDS virus would be discrimination against males, and that would be just as illegal as a policy that turned out to be discriminatory against females.

Summary and Conclusions

The basic legal issues surrounding the AIDS problem relate to the refusal to hire people with AIDS, the testing of applicants and/or employees for AIDS, dealing with co-worker pressures, and the question of what types of reasonable accommodations one might have to make to all AIDS sufferers. Advance planning would seem to be appropriate because the extent of AIDS almost assures that at some time in the future you will be placed in the position of having to deal with an employee who has AIDS. We should all remember that there are legal implications to the AIDS problem and, at least when the occasion arises, we should discuss what actions we think might be appropriate to take with our legal counsel. AIDS, like smoking and drug testing, is no longer an issue left entirely to management's discretion.

Substance Abuse

While drug abuse certainly existed when we wrote the first edition of our book, its importance has mushroomed during the 1980s. Several legal issues now relate to substance abuse in the workplace.

One of the most important is the issue of drug testing and whether or not you must, or should, test applicants or employees for substance abuse. The law on this subject varies a great deal depending on whether you are solely a private employer or whether you have government contracts. For purposes of this brief discussion, I will eliminate the government contractor questions, but you should be aware that there is a separate law called the Drug Free Workplace Act of 1988 that provides for a more stringent set of rules. We will also eliminate companies in the transportation business since that industry also has a separate set of rules.

Should you test for drugs? One of the problems with this question is that to some extent there is no good answer. If you test for drugs, you are likely to run into some of the legal problems about to be discussed. If you elect not to test for drugs, you may also have problems stemming from what is sometimes called the *negligent hiring* theory. This theory says that if a company negligently hires someone and that person then causes an injury to a third party, the company who negligently hired the person, at least if the person was hired into a job where the injury to the third party was foreseeable, is liable to that third party. The example usually given is that the company hires someone who is going to be granted access to people's houses or who is going to be driving a car. The employee rapes someone in the house to which he is granted access (perhaps for repair purposes) or causes an injury on the highway. It is later ascertained that the employee was a known drug abuser and, in fact, was on drugs when the rape or the accident occurred. There have been several cases in which companies have been found liable to the injured person on the basis of the negligent hiring theory. The basic idea is that the company should have done a better job of screening so that it did not hire people with these types of propensities.

Because of this possibility, it is useful to divide your employees into two categories.

1. First is the category where the danger to third parties, either in people's homes or on highways, is a realistic possibility. For this category

of employee it would seem only prudent to have suitable screening and testing procedures to be sure that you didn't hire someone who, through employment with your company, would be in a position to harm others. This would include not only drug testing but, if he or she was going to be operating a motor vehicle, such things as examining the person's driving record. Searching for a possible history of criminal convictions for violent offenses, or for theft if the person was going to be in a position where he or she would be admitted into people's homes, would also be in order.

2. The other category of employee includes those for whom injury to third parties, at least during working hours, is not a realistic possibility. For these employees, the issue of whether or not to have a drug testing program is often subjective. No law requires you to have such a program. On the other hand, no law prohibits you from having a program, although there are certain limitations and legal risks that you should know about.

The lowest exposure for drug testing is when you test only applicants. Here you would simply make the offer of employment conditional on the applicant's passing a post-hiring physical examination, and you would make it clear that a drug screening test would be part of the physical examination. The applicant then would be free to chose whether to pursue a position with your company, and be subjected to the drug test, or to seek employment elsewhere. Even if your drug testing program is limited only to applicants, you should be aware of these things.

1. Some states have laws that restrict the use of preemployment drug screening tests.

2. If you use a drug screening test, you must be careful first to do it properly and second to handle the results carefully. In many drug testing cases, the initial drug screening was found to be inaccurate. We must all live with the fact that these drug testing procedures are less than 100-percent reliable. Further, the inexpensive tests (the ones you would want to use for preliminary screenings) are the least reliable. Correspondingly, the more accurate tests are more expensive. Many counselors recommend that an inexpensive preliminary drug screen not be used by itself to screen out an employee or applicant. In other words, you can use the cheaper test first, but if the results turn out to be positive, you should have it confirmed by a more expensive kind before actually refusing to hire someone. This procedure adds a little cost to your program, but even if it should save only one lawsuit, it would be money well spent.

Another factor to consider is the basic invasion of privacy problems. If you do a drug screen it is important to handle the results carefully. If those results are disseminated beyond the group of people who have an actual need to know about them, you could have an invasion of privacy claim. The invasion of privacy problem is minimized if you test only applicants.

Testing Current Employees

Testing current employees increases the legal stakes. First, the right of privacy problem is greater. Second, you can easily have a defamation problem if you circulate the drug test results too broadly.

Any drug testing program must also take into account the Americans with Disabilities Act. That law allows a drug testing program and allows you to discharge workers who are current drug abusers. It does not, however, allow you to discriminate against handicapped people and former drug users. Included among those identified as handicapped are those who may have abused drugs in the past but who have undertaken rehabilitation programs. You should also know that some state laws are a little different from the federal handicap laws. Under some state laws, for example, if you generally provide leaves of absence for people who are ill, you must also provide leaves of absence for drug abusers who want to attend rehabilitation programs. The theory would be that failure to provide such leaves would be discrimination against people who are handicapped by a drug problem.

Still another issue in testing current employees is whether you can test all employees, whether you can have random drug testing, or whether you can or should test people when there has been a specific occurrence, such as an accident, that would seem to indicate a test might be appropriate. There are no hard and fast legal rules on these questions.

If your workforce is unionized, the unions generally take the position that drug testing is a bargainable subject, and if you want to start testing, you have to negotiate with the union first.

Note. Drug testing is different from having a substance abuse policy. You can implement a substance abuse policy without much legal concern. It is almost always recommended that you have a "substance abuse policy" rather than simply a "drug" policy. The idea is that it is just as harmful to our business environment for people to abuse alcohol during working hours as it is for them to abuse drugs. There is no legal restriction at all against your having a policy that absolutely forbids drug or alcohol possession on any company property and also forbids anyone from coming to work under the influence of either drugs or alcohol.

Summary

Drug testing and substance abuse in the workplace are problems we are going to have to live with for the foreseeable future. Having a substance abuse policy is probably a step in the right direction and presents few, if any, legal difficulties, as long as you follow it in a reasonable, nondiscriminatory way.

The subject of drug testing, however, is legally much more complex. Our conclusion would be that no small businessperson is well advised to institute a drug testing procedure without advance consultation with legal counsel. First, even at the federal level, there are enough laws on the books to provide many different legal exposures. Second, many states are adopting laws relating to drug testing since it is a politically sensitive subject. Accordingly, you would need advice not only about the relevant federal laws but also about whatever state or local laws might be relevant.

Age Discrimination

The Age Discrimination in Employment Act protects workers over the age of 40. If you fire someone because he or she is old, that person may sue you and collect a lot of money. If age is even one factor in your determination to dismiss a person, that is enough to cause a violation of the act.

In my experience, problems under the age discrimination law will come about when adverse economic situations cause you to reduce your work force. If you have 20 people and have to let two go, it may be very tempting for you to lay off two older workers who may not be as productive, aggressive, or energetic as the younger ones. On the other hand, the following factors may complicate this decision.

1. Older workers may have more seniority than the younger workers, so that you will have that going against you. While seniority is not legally binding except in the case of a labor contract, it does color a case. If a judge finds that you have dismissed a worker who has 10 years' experience and kept one with only two or three years of experience, you will need more evidence as to the business reasons for dismissal.

2. It may be extremely difficult for you to objectively show that a person is less energetic or less productive. If the employee in question is selling, working on piecework, or doing some other job in which you can measure his or her output by a certain number of dollars or pieces, you can probably do it. In most jobs, however, productivity and the

quality of performance are very subjective, and it may be difficult or impossible to prove your argument.

3. Another problem that I frequently encountered in age cases is that management is careless in how they handle the dismissal. They may even mention the person's age, or there may even be a document that mentions retiring the older workers to make room for the younger ones. Such carelessness will make the plaintiff's case. Whenever you terminate someone, either by firing him or her for cause, by layoff for lack of work, or for any other reason, you must be very careful about the documents you create and what you tell the employee.

I am not suggesting that you lie to anybody, but I do counsel against making unnecessarily self-incriminating statements. I know it is difficult to tell someone that you are firing him or her because he or she is not as productive as the rest of the people in the company. It is hard to say that you have 10 workers, you have to lay the worst one off, and this person qualifies. On the other hand, if you try to smooth that over by some remark which is less offensive, you may cause yourself legal difficulties. For example, if you terminate someone over 65 because that person gets social security whereas the younger workers cannot, that is a clear violation. You may be a nice person, and you may not have hurt the worker's feelings quite as much as if you had told the truth, but you also may have a lawsuit, and you are probably going to lose it.

There is, of course, room for some subjectivity in determining whom you lay off during a work reduction. The key factor is to make sure that age (or race or sex or other minority status) plays absolutely no part in your determination. As a practical matter, the only way you can be sure of that is to have some legitimate business reason for taking the termination action.

What About Statistics?

There are books written about the importance of statistics in employment discrimination cases. Basically, however, common sense is the rule. If you operate in a big city and have 50 people working for you, all of whom are white males, and you get a discrimination complaint from a female or a black who made an application to your company and was not hired, you are going to have a difficult time defending that case. You can talk all you want about qualifications, experience, and the like, but you are going to have to settle that case. Keep in mind, however, that statistics have two important parts: One of them is the number of minorities that you have working for you, and the other is the availability of those minorities in the workforce. In areas in which it is very difficult to find qualified applicants who are not white males, an all-white male work force might not be a problem.

The Economics of Title VII Litigation

Employment discrimination cases brought by individual plaintiffs are not particularly attractive deals either for the plaintiff or for the plaintiff's lawyer. Let us say that an applicant who makes $12,000 a year applies to your company for a job. You do not hire the person; the person institutes a lawsuit claiming discrimination and wins. It turns out that the person is out of work for 6 months. That is $6,000 in damages, and you may have to pay it. Also, attorneys' fees can be recovered in this kind of a situation. Further, what if the employee, after having applied at your place for a job and being turned down, goes down the street to a large company and gets a job for $15,000 a year? There may not be any damages at all.

Further, Title VII litigation has a 180-day limitation. Someone who believes he or she has been discriminated against must file a charge with the appropriate state or federal agency within 180 days of the alleged discrimination. For example, if you have discriminated against everybody for the past 10 years and you clean up your act during the next 180 days, you do not have any realistic exposure as long as nobody files a charge within that 180-day period. For these reasons, single-plaintiff Title VII cases are not really attractive to many lawyers.

Further, the EEOC is not much interested in these either. It is more interested in the larger cases, where it can allocate its limited resources to provide more openings and opportunities for more people. If the EEOC spends a lot of time negotiating with you concerning a 10-employee plant at which the turnover is only 10 percent a year, there is not much benefit for minorities as a whole. If it spends the same amount of time with a very large company that has a lot of job opportunities every year, it benefits minorities more, and that is the approach it has taken.

Thus, as a practical matter, EEO exposure for smaller companies is much less than it is for larger ones. EEO exposure for large companies is so severe that almost all have full-time staffs of many people, including lawyers and EEO specialists, to deal with this problem. For a small company, that is not necessary. However, the same rules apply, and, for a small company, a $10,000 backpay award can be just as damaging as a multimillion dollar award is to a larger one. On the other hand, as small business people, we do have to allocate our "worry resources" among a wide variety of things, and it seems to me that employment discrimination is something that you do not have to be too worried about as long as you have the proper attitude and do not in fact discriminate.

However, let us assume that someone does file a charge against you. At this point, I recommend legal counsel. You are starting here to build a record for subsequent actions. It may very well be that you can dispose of a discrimination charge at a hearing with your federal or state civil rights agency without much trouble yourself. However, what if you cannot? You have built a record, and if you do not have a lawyer involved in the process, it might be a bad record. Private EEO cases by single plaintiffs are very easy to settle, and I recommend that you settle them promptly. On the other hand, I do not recommend that you try to settle them all by yourself without your lawyer.

Under current procedures, if someone files a charge of discrimination against you, the first round of problems will come from the state civil rights agency. Almost all states, except the southern states, have state civil rights agencies. The state's civil rights agency will try to negotiate a mutually agreeable settlement. If that fails, the federal government (that is, the EEOC) will step in and try to settle the matter. If that fails, the aggrieved person will be issued a stalled right to sue letter by which the government says, in effect, that it has tried to reach a settlement but cannot, and the person can get his or her own lawyer and sue you.

These hearings or conferences are relatively informal, and you do not absolutely need a lawyer to go along with you. It is not like going to court. There are no technical rules of evidence to worry about or technical procedures to cause you trouble. You simply go and tell your side of the story. On the other hand, you do need a lawyer in the background to make sure that you are taking the proper steps to keep a relatively small matter from developing into a large one. I definitely recommend that you consult counsel whenever a discrimination charge is filed, but the question of what role the lawyer should play is a little more complex and depends mostly on your personal predispositions.

I generally recommend that you be the one who goes to the fact-finding conference and tries to make the settlement. However, this depends on your personality and desires. You should send your lawyer if you feel that you might get steamrolled by the EEOC representative (who may be a lawyer and who will definitely have considerably more experience in this sort of thing than you), or if you are so emotionally involved with the situation that you think you may get upset and be unable to reach a settlement even if a reasonable one is proposed.

The key thing to remember is that the decision you make should be based on these kinds of considerations and not the fear of intricate legal maneuvering or strategy which only your lawyer can cope with. Approach this as you would any other kind of hard bargaining session. Get your entire story in order, including a clear statement of all the facts involved. Then make the decision as to who should present that story on the basis of the best person for that job. It may be you, your personnel person, or your lawyer. However, if you do send your lawyer, keep in mind that it might be an expensive deal. The lawyer will have to spend considerable time becoming familiar with all the facts of the situation, including how you have treated similar situations.

I have seen many people try to stand on principle at these early stages and refuse to consider even a modest settlement if they believe the case has no merit. The typical pattern is that someone will file a charge and the employer will feel that he or she is being blackmailed — "millions for defense but not one penny for tribute." The practical wisdom of this is highly doubtful. To be blunt, you may have to throw a few hundred dollars into the pot even in a situation where the plaintiff really does not have any case at all, to keep things from getting out of hand. This may make you angry, but it will save you a lot of money. Normally, the argument against this is that if you do it for one person, it is a blank check for every other minority or female in the community to institute a similar action. Theoretically, this argument has some appeal, but as a practical matter, it has not happened. Those companies that have settled cases at the early stages have generally avoided the monumental battles that can come about later in litigation. Also, they have not been subjected to multiple unfounded allegations of discrimination. On the other hand, I have seen quite a few situations, where relatively simple charges that could have been settled very economically at an early stage, excalate into very expensive and drawn-out legal battles because the employer wanted to stand on principle.

State Agencies and State Laws

In addition to the federal laws and the federal enforcement agencies, almost all states, have state agencies and state antidiscrimination laws. For example, at the federal level there is no prohibition against discrimination on account of marital status; you can have the so-called "no spouse" rules as long as you enforce them fairly. on the other hand, some states add marital status to the list of things that you cannot use to discriminate against your employees. As in most of the areas discussed in this book, you always have to supplement the general federal rules with whatever additional rules may be imposed by state governments.

Summary and Conclusions

The following list of rules will help you stay out of legal troubles with your employees.

1. Make sure all of your documents are legally clean. This means making sure that your employment application does not ask for any discriminatory information and that your personnel manuals do not contain any promises that you do not always keep, such as a statement that people will be discharged only for good cause or only after a warning.

2. Make sure everyone in your company that is involved in the employment or interviewing process has at least some training. This is very important since many cases involve unfortunate things that were said either during the interview process or during a discharge conversation. Interviews with applicants should be fairly well structured so that you are sure your people will only ask legally permissible questions.

3. Make sure that your performance reviews and evaluations are honest, accurate, and fairly recorded in your files. Nothing is more difficult than defending a case where the company claims that the employee was discharged for poor work performance—and then finding in the file only glowing performance reviews for the past several years along with substantial raises. This is not unusual because, when times are good, no one wants to rock the boat, say unpleasant things, or fire marginal employees. It's only when the economic conditions turn down a little that these harder decisions must be made, and in that context you are often saddled with the record that you created during a better economic environment.

4. Obviously, the most sensitive point of the whole process is the termination. Make sure you do at least two things:

One is to handle the termination in a sensible, diplomatic and gracious way. There should be no exceptions to this rule. Even if you discharge someone for theft, there is no reason why that discharge cannot be done in a businesslike manner.

Second, always prepare for the possibility that you may have to explain your discharge to a jury. This is probably the single most important item on the list of things that can prevent lawsuits. If you handle the matter in a way that would not be embarrassing to explain in open court, you will probably be successful in avoiding most litigation. Acting in a highhanded manner or making decisions arbitrarily without any particular need or business basis are, in today's legal climate, likely to be very costly things to do.

5. Periodically evaluate your pay scales between the men and the women. I often hear people say that they are absolutely sure they don't have any equal pay problems. On the other hand, an examination of actual pay practices, pay scales and job titles, practically always results in some serious questions as to whether people are really getting equal pay for equal work.

6. Before imposing discipline on anyone, make sure you ask yourself if you are treating all similarly situated employees the same. Courts look to the effect of what you do, not whether the practice looks acceptable on its face. A rule that says that people get fired if they miss more than three unexcused absences in a certain period looks good on paper, but if in fact you make an exception for your secretary, who happens to be white, and not for the secretary in the accounting department, who happens to be black, you could have a problem.

7. Be alert to clusters of minorities in lower paying jobs. If you have such a situation make sure that it is not the result of discrimination against these protected groups. Even if the discrimination was unintentional, it is still illegal.

8. If you use any written tests except for obvious job-related things like typing for a secretary, make sure that each test will satisfy the tough rules of the EEOC on testing.

9. Do not use arbitrary requirements in your hiring decisions. For example, do not require your secretary to have a college degree or your sales representative to have a certain level of education simply because you think it would be nice. If you need those requirements, it is fine to have them. But if you impose them just because you feel it's the right thing to do, you may find that they operate in a discriminatory fashion and are therefore illegal. Remember the basic rule: You must measure the person for the job, not the person in the abstract.

10. Last, but not least, be sure you contact your lawyer upon the receipt of any discrimination complaint, even if it's only with a state agency or with the EEOC. You can probably handle that yourself; indeed, it's often best to appear at these things without your lawyer. However, you should obtain legal counsel because you are building a legal record which may become important in subsequent court cases.

Help from the Government

In this area, the help that you can get from the government is likely to be limited to written documents that might help you in your compliance efforts. Many state agencies have helpful pamphlets that explain antidiscrimination rules and that list questions that you may and may not ask in job interviews. If the state has its own antidiscrimination laws and regulations, there may be pamphlets explaining those.

At the federal level, the EEOC has issued very helpful guidelines on many things. We recommend that business owners have either copies of the EEOC guidelines on the various discrimination subjects or equivalent explanatory material from books, their own lawyers, or trade associations. The EEOC guidelines that you should have, at a minimum, are:

Guidelines on Discrimination Because of Religion

Guidelines on Pregnancy Discrimination

Guidelines on Sexual Harassment

Guidelines on Discrimination on Account of National Origin

Guidelines and Rules and Interpretations under the Equal Pay Act

Guidelines on Preemployment Inquiries

You should also have a copy of the Immigration and Naturalization Service Compliance booklet on the Immigration Reform and Control Act of 1986.

We suggest you contact the local EEOC office for explanatory material relating to discrimination as well as the local INS office for the immigration booklet.

Protection of Veterans

The recent call up of our reserves to deal with the Iraq invasion of Kuwait serves as a reminder that, even in peace time, we should know about the laws protecting veterans' job rights. Essentially the law is that you have to do two things:

1. You must hold a job open for someone who is called into military service. In general this requirement applies whether the person is called up as the result of a reserve obligation or simply enlists.

2. When the employees come back to work, you have to put them back into the same position they would have been in had they not gone

into the military. This is the so called "escalator" provision. The basic idea is that the veteran is supposed to escalate up the seniority ladder to the same extent as those who remained on the job.

This is another area where the government has done a good job of explaining the rights and obligations of both employers and service people. To get a package of useful material, contact either the Office of Veterans Reemployment Rights in Washington, D.C. or the local office in your city, and ask for literature on veterans' reemployment rights. It should include publications called "Key Answers about Job Rights" and "Facts about Veterans' Job Rights," as well as copies of the relevant laws and regulations.

Insurance Note

Refer to Chap. 14, "Your Lawyer and Your Insurance," for a brief discussion of the possibility that some employment law exposures may be covered by your comprehensive general liability insurance policies.

9
Labor Law

This is gong to be a relatively short chapter, because I believe that labor law is an area where you need expert help. I would divide the expert help into two categories:

1. How should you operate your business in order to avoid a union organization attempt?
2. If there is a union organization attempt, what should you do?

Of course, if your business is already unionized, you will undoubtedly know everything I am going to say in this chapter and will already have a labor law advisor.

What Are the Implications of Having a Union?

The reason I believe you should try to avoid union organization is that operating a small business is hard enough without the additional complications and restrictions on your flexibility which will be involved if you have a union and a union contract to contend with. I should add, however, that unionization is not all bad. It simply represents a way of running a business which, in my judgment, is not conducive to the success of a small business. There is too much "us-versus-them" atmosphere in a union shop. That may work all right in a large company, but in my experience, it has not done much to help small business.

On the plus side, if management is not one of your strong points, there is some merit in having a set of hard-and-fast rules for the workers to work by. In some cases, union people may be paid more than nonunion people, but this is not universally true. In fact, the opposite can be the case if you happen to be the generous type that likes to share the wealth with your employees and if your business has been successful. Also, in a union shop, you have a rather standard set of procedures for grievances, work rules, etc., and while these can be more rigid than in a nonunion shop, they do simplify things considerably if you are the type of person that has trouble saying no to employees' requests and therefore feel that you may be taken advantage of. For example, if you are having trouble with your employees coming in late and leaving early, and if you feel that you cannot deal effectively with this problem in an informal way, it may be very nice to have a union contract which says that the workday starts at a certain time and ends at a certain time and includes certain lunches and coffee breaks, so you do not have to impose this discipline informally.

Nevertheless, on balance, I believe small businesses are better off operating without a union because there will be more of a team spirit and because the inherent uncertainties involved in so many small businesses do not coincide very well with the fixed work rules and hours that typically become imposed on a company with a union contract.

In summary, then, the following are the implications of having a union.

1. There will be a written contract setting forth all the obligations of each party. Everything will be done by the book.

2. There may be an elaborate and formal grievance procedure which culminates in binding arbitration. You may wind up with some third party telling you how to operate your business in important respects.

3. Promotion practices are based almost entirely on seniority. It is much more difficult to fire poor performers, and it is very difficult to reward good performers.

4. The direct costs of bargaining are very substantial. Bargaining sessions can consume 20 to 50 hours of table negotiations, and there are many hours of homework and planning for each hour of actual negotiation.

5. The quality of work may decrease because the union protects inferior workers and there is little incentive for good workers.

Why Employees Organize

If you know the reasons why employees would like to have a union instead of negotiating with you personally, you will be quite far down the road to avoiding the problem. There is usually no single reason why employees want a union. The reasons are a combination of the following factors.

1. As the organization gets larger, communications do not develop, and the employees feel that they are not important and not being listened to. The union comes along, listens to the employees, and tells them that the union can communicate with management better than they can on an individual basis, and this is a very appealing argument.

2. There may be substandard working conditions or facilities, and the union can look at them and tell the employees that they can improve them through negotiations with management. Note that we are talking here about working conditions and facilities, not necessarily just low pay.

3. There may be no regard for seniority, with promotions being strictly on a merit basis. Seniority is generally appealing to workers because it gives them a sense of security. While nonunionized organizations emphasize merit, unions emphasize seniority. In fact, the union will emphasize seniority to the point where it is almost the sole factor in considering promotion and raises. Of course, this argument cuts both ways—your highly motivated and aggressive employees may not want to wait around for the requisite seniority to get raises and promotions. Nevertheless, seniority is a factor which unions use to appeal to the majority of workers, and it usually works.

4. There may be no grievance procedure or even any informal way for the employees to make their complaints known to management and get a fair hearing. This promotes frustration and is also something which the union can seize upon, because a union is, of course, able to provide a rather formal and fairly efficient grievance procedure.

5. Unequal treatment of employees is a very aggravating factor which unions sometimes seize upon. The union can insist upon equal treatment—based largely on seniority. Problems of inequitable discipline, lack of uniformity in work rules and discipline, favoritism, or discrimination are all things which the union can and does seize upon. Usually these factors are present when management has tried to respond constructively to its best employees. The union will generally protect the inferior employees, and there are usually more of the latter than of the former. Accordingly, even though it is rather basic human nature to reward the better employees and to bend the rules in their favor, such treatment can contribute to unionization or at least problems with the

morale of all other employees. (See also Chap. 8, "Employment Practices.")

6. Union promises are a big factor. Unions are a business, and their business is to sell memberships. They are very good at it.

There are a number of signs that indicate a union organization attempt (or at least thinking about unions) might be present in an organization. These are the kinds of things you might want to be on the lookout for, and, if it seems appropriate, you may want to conduct a self-analysis to see why the employees might be unhappy. Some of the more common indications of thinking about a union rule are the following.

1. Technical questions from employees about their benefit plans or their pension plans. These can sometimes be prompted by union promises which tell employees that the union will be able to get them better benefits or pensions.

2. A more than normal amount of informal group meetings.

3. Rumors regarding unionism.

4. Union handbilling.

How to Remain Nonunion

The key to remaining nonunion is sound personnel practices. Much of what the experts have to say in this area is simply common sense. Following is a list of some of the areas which are important.

1. A safe and healthy working environment.

2. A direct and efficient resolution of employee complaints. This does not mean that you have to do everything the employees say you should; it merely means you have to deal effectively with their complaints. If you cannot do something employees think you should, you should be able to articulate a reason why.

Do not be afraid to use personal preference as a reason. After all, it is your business. If an employee makes a proposal or suggestion which has merit but which you just do not want to implement for some reason, there is nothing wrong with saying that. Simply state that the proposal or suggestion is a good one and has merit. However, there are some other considerations which go the other way. Sometimes judgments come down to personal preference, and your personal preference is not to implement the suggestion. If you are constructive and do not abuse this argument, employees will understand it. The key thing is a fair hearing and discussion and your indication of appreciation of suggestions and ideas.

3. Provide meaningful and interesting work for employees. The difference between actual work and expectations is important. For example, in the case of secretaries or administrative assistants where, realistically, there may be a very limited career path, it would be a mistake to raise high expectations with glowing talk of unrealistic opportunities for promotion. Meaningful and interesting work is a very personal thing which depends upon each individual. So long as the employees are happy and feel that their work is meaningful to the company and that their legitimate expectations have been properly described, there should not be any problem.

4. There should be incentive for good performance.

5. There should be opportunities for growth.

6. There should be respect for each employee as an individual.

7. There should be consistent administration of discipline and critism.

8. There should be up-to-date personnel policies.

9. There should be competitive salaries and benefits.

The above list is summarized from a wide variety of professional sources, and it is interesting to know that in the overwhelming majority of cases, the competitive salaries and benefits are placed last on this list. *You do not have to pay employees more than they are worth or more than the market value of their services in the community in order to avoid a union.*

A Fault and Need Analysis

One useful exercise is to look at a company in terms of possible faults and needs for improvement. Following are some of the areas that might be important.

1. The personnel administration and the staff. Do they function in a competent and efficient manner?

2. Is the supervisory staff good? Is the recruitment good? Is there

training and involvement of the maximum number of employees in the decision-making process?

3. Look at the employment process itself. Are there good job descriptions? Do you have interview guidelines? Is there an orientation program? Do you have a probationary period and use it properly?

4. Do you have transfer and promotion policies which are based on merit and which are understood by the employees?

5. Do you get the maximum benefit you can out of a termination situation? For example, do you have an exit interview where an employee who is no longer with the company can tell you what he or she feels the problems with the company are? Do you know what your turnover statistics are, and do they show that any particular department has an abnormally high turnover rate or that your turnover statistics are worse than others in the same industry?

The Union Organization Drive

In my judgment, everything I have recommended up to this point you can and should do by yourself with the help of written materials. Except in unusual circumstances or if you have a lot of money to burn, I do not think that professional help is needed. The opposite is true in a union organization drive. It is a highly technical process, and you need a good labor lawyer *immediately*. There are, however, some things you should know so that you don't do something disadvantageous before you have the opportunity to talk to a labor lawyer.

What Do You Do When the Union Comes and Says That It Wants to Represent the Employees?

It is possible that the first you will know of a union organization attempt will be when the union comes to you and says that they have authorization cards from your employees, and they want to negotiate a collective bargaining agreement. Do not look at these cards. Simply have your secretary seal them in an envelope and put them in a safe place. Respond that you have a good-faith doubt as to whether a majority of employees want the union, and request an election. At this point, you must seek professional help. These first things, however, are very important, and if you are surprised, it would be very easy to do the wrong thing. Looking at the authorization cards would be a mistake, because after you do so, you might be accused of discriminating against employees who have signed union authorization cards. Also, asking for an election buys you time to explain why your company and the employees are better off without a union than with one.

The law says that you can request an election only if you have a good-faith doubt about whether the union does in fact represent a majority of the workers. The union may say it has cards from more than 50 percent of your workers, and therefore, your doubt is not "good-faith." Do not pay any attention to that argument. The law also says that it is illegal to bargain with a union which does not represent a majority of the workers, and the only way to be sure is to have an election. Further, there are many complicating factors, including the definition of the appropriate bargaining unit. In fact, in many union contests, that definition is the *key*. A single union can represent only persons with a reasonably common interest. You need professional help to determine what kind of appropriate bargaining units you may have in your company.

Current union representation elections are running about 60 to 65 percent in *favor of employers*. If you do a good job of explaining to your employees why they are better off without a union than with one, you have a good chance of winning a representation election. Of course, you must take a realistic look at your situation. If there are simply too many problems to explain away, and if you know that the union has already obtained authorization cards from almost 100 percent of your employees, you will have an uphill battle. Nevertheless, you are entitled to request an election, and I suggest that you do so for the reasons mentioned above.

Labor Law Practicalities and Theoretical Rules

Labor law is a very difficult area, because the practical, real-life world does not always coincide with the reported cases. Specifically, what you can and cannot do during a union organization drive is very difficult to ascertain, because it depends on your motives as well as the views of the labor lawyer you are talking to. Some labor law firms are very aggressive. Some recent legal periodicals have featured such law firms because they not only counsel employers as to how to avoid a union but also, if there is a union organization drive, give very aggressive counsel on what actions the company can take to tell its side of the story. Other law firms are much more conservative. They read the many cases—both of the court and the National Labor Relations Board—and point out to corporate management that almost anything they do has some chance of being characterized as coercive, threatening, or inflammatory, and therefore, an unfair labor practice.

The problem is that the law says that an employer cannot coerce its employees against joining the union. This coercion concept, however, is much more subtle than just physical coercion. For example, if you tell the employees that if they join the union, you will not pay Christmas bonuses anymore, or that if they join the union, you will go out of business or move your plant to another city, those would be "threats" and would be an unfair labor practice. If you engaged in these activities and then you won the election, the union would be able to petition the National Labor Relations Board to have a second election because of these unfair labor practices. Thus, the union would get two chances instead of one. That is the danger. If you go so far in telling your side of the story that someone could later say that you coerced the employees, there can be a charge filed with the National Labor Relations Board, and it can order a new election. The union is entitled, as you are, to a fair election without any coercion. Of course, the rules are the same on the other side. The union cannot coerce employees either. In the context of an initial organization drive, however, union coercion really only takes the form of physical coercion, and while it is not unheard of, it does not appear to be widespread.

Another complicating factor is that you have to judge the totality of your conduct as well as the totality of the union's conduct. To take some extreme cases, if the union were to conduct its organizational drive in a manner which was absolutely beyond reproach, it would take very little in the nature of strong words from you to convince the National Labor Relations Board or a court that you had engaged in coercion, threats, or unfair labor practices. On the other hand, if the matter became somewhat heated and both sides exchanged strong views, that would also be taken into consideration. Of course, you do not just look at any single sentence, word, or speech; you must look at the conduct as a whole. If you do that, and it looks as if you are coercing the employees rather than simply informing them of your side of the story, it is possible that if you win the election, it will be set aside and the union will be entitled to another one.

Absent some unfair labor practice (on the part of either the union or the employer), an election will be binding for 12 months. Thus, after an election, you are assured of 12 months' peace.

With these general cautions, I think it is useful to set forth a checklist of certain do's and don'ts which represent things that are generally agreed to be permissible or not in an organization drive. Keep in mind, however, that we are dealing with a complex area where professional judgment plays a large part. I do not recommend that you substitute this checklist for good, solid, experienced labor counsel. I do recommend that you cross-examine your labor lawyer to make sure that you and he or she are on the same wavelength as far as the proper approach goes. There is nothing inherently good or bad about either conservative or aggressive advice. However, you should know which you are receiving. If your labor lawyer is telling you that if you follow his or her advice, you are going to be practically assured that there will not be a successful unfair labor practice charge filed, he or she will be giving you very conservative advice. Thus, you may not do a very effective job of telling your side of the story, and you may lose the election. On the other hand, if your lawyer tells you that he or she is giving very aggressive advice which extends to the limit the things you can and cannot do, and that you are running some risk of having an unfair labor practice charge successfully filed against you, you will probably be able to do a very good job of telling your side of the union-nonunion story, and you will have a much better chance of winning the election. The trade-off, of course, is that you will probably do some things which at least give rise to the filing of an unfair labor practice charge, and then you will have to defend these actions and run the risk that the board will overturn your successful election. I must confess that I do not have any good answers to this dilemma, but I do feel that it is extremely important that you and your lawyer discuss it so that both of you are operating on the same set of guidelines.

I have also included a brief description of the things you can expect a union to do if they want to organize your plant. As you can see, this list covers essentially the same considerations we mentioned before in our discussion of how to remain nonunion: Can the union offer the employees anything they don't have now? Can the union solve any of the employees' problems? Can the union offer better job security?

Checklists

The following checklists will do more than any narration I can give you to provide a flavor of what a union organization drive might involve.

Things You May Do

1. Tell employees what your negotiating position will be if they elect a union.
2. Make sure employees understand the benefits they have already.

3. Inform employees that the signing of a union authorization card does not mean they must vote for the union if there is an election.
4. Inform employees of the disadvantage of belonging to the union, such as the possibility of strikes, serving in a picket line, dues, fines, and assessments.
5. Inform employees that you prefer to deal with them rather than have the union or any other outsider settle employee grievances.
6. Inform employees what you think about unions and about union policies.
7. Inform employees about any prior experience you have had with unions and whatever you know about the union officials trying to organize them.
8. Inform employees that no union can obtain more than you as an employer are able to give.
9. Inform employees how their wages and benefits compare with unionized or nonunionized concerns.
10. Inform employees that the local union may be dominated by the international union, and that they, the members, will have little to say in its operation.
11. Inform employees of any untrue or misleading statements made by the organizers. You may give employees the correct facts.
12. Give opinions on unions and union leaders, even in derogatory terms.
13. Give your legal position on labor-management matters.
14. Reply to union attacks on company policies or practices.
15. Advise employees of their legal rights, provided that you do not encourage or finance an employee suit or proceeding.
16. Declare a fixed policy in opposition to compulsory union membership contracts.
17. Campaign against the union seeking to represent the employees.
18. Insist that any solicitation of membership or discussion of union affairs be conducted outside of working time.
19. Tell employees, if they ask, that they are free to join or not to join any organization so far as their status with the company is concerned. During a union organization drive you *must*:
    a. Administer discipline, layoffs, grievance, etc., without regard to union membership or nonmembership, or the employees involved.
    b. Treat both union and nonunion employees alike in making assignments of preferred work, desired overtime, etc.
    c. Enforce rules impartially, regardless of the employee's membership activity in a union.

Things You May Not Do

1. Attend any union meetings, spy upon employees, or engage in any undercover activity which would indicate that the employees are being kept under surveillance to determine who is and who is not participating in the union program.

2. Tell employees that the company will fire or punish them if they engage in union activity.

3. Lay off or discharge any employee for union activity.

4. Grant employees wage increases or special concessions in order to keep the union out.

5. Bar employee union representatives from soliciting employee memberships during *non*-working hours.

6. Ask employees about confidential union matters, meetings, etc. (Some employees may, of their own accord, walk up and tell of such matters. It is not an unfair practice to listen, but you must not ask questions to obtain additional information.)

7. Ask employees what they think about the union or a union representative.

8. Ask employees how they intend to vote.

9. Threaten employees with economic reprisal for participating in union activities. For example, you cannot threaten to move the plant, close the business, curtail operations, or reduce employee benefits.

10. Promise benefits to employees if they reject the union.

11. Give financial support or other assistance to a union or to employees, regardless of whether or not they are supporting or opposing the union.

12. Announce that you will not deal with a union.

13. Ask employees whether or not they belong to a union or have signed up for a union.

14. Ask an employee, during the interview when you are hiring him or her, about his or her affiliation with a labor organization.

15. Make antiunion statements or actions that might show your preference for nonunion employees.

16. Make distinctions between union and nonunion employees when assigning overtime work or desirable work.

17. Purposely team up nonunion employees and keep them apart from those you think may belong to the labor organization.

18. Transfer workers on the basis of union affiliation or activity.

19. Choose employees to be laid off on the basis of weakening the union's strength or discouraging membership in it.

20. Discriminate against union people when disciplining employees.

21. By the nature of work assignments, indicate that you would like to get rid of an employee because of his or her union activity.

22. Discipline union employees for a particular action and permit non-union employees to go unpunished for the same action.

23. Deviate from company policy for the purpose of getting rid of a union employee.

24. Take actions that adversely affect an employee's job or any pay rate because of union activity.

25. Become involved in arguments that may lead to a physical encounter with an employee over the union question.

26. Threaten a union member through a third party.

27. Threaten your workers or coerce them in an attempt to influence their vote.

28. Promise employees a reward or any future benefits if they decide against the union.

29. Tell employees overtime work (and premium pay) will be discontinued if they unionize.

30. Say unionization will take away vacations, or other benefits and privileges presently enjoyed.

31. Promise employees promotions, raises, or other benefits if they get out of the union or refrain from joining it.

32. Start a petition or circular against the union or encourage or take part in its circulation if started by employees.

33. Urge employees to try to induce others to oppose the union or keep out of it.

34. Visit the homes of employees to urge them to reject the union.

Things a Union May and May Not Do During an Organizing Drive

The union may:

1. Verbally attack the company, its supervisors, and all its practices.

2. Promise improved wages and benefits, including specific amounts if elected.

3. Threaten that the company will take away benefits, reduce wages, lay off employees, or close the plant if the union is not selected.

4. Ask employees about their union views or how they intend to vote.

5. Give assistance to employees in supporting the union.

6. Visit employees in their homes.

7. Give free dues to those who join the union early.

8. Promise that there will not be a strike if it is selected.

The union may not:

1. Harm or threaten to harm employees or their property.

2. Threaten employees who do not support it with economic reprisal if it is selected.

Union Organizers Who Are Not Employees In connection with impromptu visits by union representatives, your supervisors should be under instructions not to permit any strangers or visitors in the plant. They have no right there and can be told to leave and/or escorted out. The union can handbill at plant entrances on public property.

Employees who support or oppose the union must be treated equally. But you do not have to allow anyone to solicit during working hours, and you do not have to allow anyone to distribute literature in work areas, though anyone must be permitted to do so in nonwork areas of the plant during nonworking hours.

Union Organization Checklist Following is a checklist of the things the union will do if it wants to undertake a substantial organization drive. A single union will rarely do all of these things, and for a small company, the entire organizational effort may simply consist of a union representative who stops at the entrance after work and asks the employees if they want to join the union. Nevertheless, I think it is useful to go through this checklist so you can see the kinds of things which are important. Keep in mind that they are equally important even if the factors exist only in the employees' minds and are not raised by the union.

1. *Planning*: Be assured that the union will have thoroughly planned any substantial organizational efforts. They will have accumulated a lot of information about your plant location, its physical structure, starting and quitting times, the products you make, public transpor-

tation near the plant, and the eating and drinking establishments near the plant. They will also know about the labor history of the plant.

2. *Fact-finding*: After the preliminary planning, the union will get right down to the employees and their problems. They will try to find the key individuals in the plant who have leadership influence, or who have personalities which naturally draw people to them. At the same time, the union will want to find out all it can about working conditions, job descriptions, how complaints and grievances are handled, and what complaints the employees have. The union will get complete information about seniority practices, overtime, paid holidays, benefit programs, and the attitude of foremen and supervisors to employees.

3. *The plant organizational committee*: After the union has made several key contacts and has gotten all the necessary background material, they will want to build a core of union support within the plant. They will, of course, want a cross section of ages, races, and sexes.

4. *The first meeting*: After the "quiet" stages described above, there will be a first meeting which all the employees are invited to attend to listen to the union's pitch. Here the union will start to reap the dividends from the investment in time to gather all the background information. They will talk in detail about your plant, your practices, and indeed, even about your individual foreman and supervisors — by name. They will make a lot of promises, but the responsible unions won't make unreasonable or wild promises. They will sound very believable and convincing. Remember, selling memberships is their business and they are very good at it.

After the first meeting, everything should be out in the open, and you will want to start considering the things listed before in our checklist for union organization drives. At this point, you should have expert help available.

10
Commercial Transactions

This chapter is devoted to the proper preparation and use of three important commercial forms, alternative dispute resolution techniques, and a brief discussion of fair credit laws. The forms are the purchase order form, the sales order form, and the standard warranty form. These three forms are important to your business and have a high degree of legal content. Alternative dispute resolution is becoming increasingly popular as a way to avoid going to court, and there are some technical rules on granting credit you should know about.

Your Purchase and Sale Order Terms and Conditions

No matter what your business, it is very likely that the overwhelming majority of all your business transactions are going to be sales of your product or service, or purchases of other products or services. Large companies have purchase order forms and sales forms which they use for this purpose. Small companies should also—though many do not devote sufficient attention to this subject.

Preparation of good purchase orders and sales forms is easy. They can be looked at in two parts. The first part is the *substantive* or business aspects of the deal. The second part is the terms and conditions, or, as they are sometimes called, the *boilerplate*. Mechanically, the process works out conveniently to drafting the front and back of your forms.

The front of your forms must, of course, satisfy your business requirements. There is certainly no shortage of purchase order and sale forms which you can look at to get ideas. Note, however, that it is not necessary to have elaborately printed multipart forms. *Forms prepared by typewriter and duplicated on standard duplicating machines are perfectly adequate.*

The back of the forms can be a complicated and technical subject. However, if you take a look at some terms and conditions from other companies, plus the ones reproduced in this chapter, you ought to be able to come up with a set which is right for your products or services.

Why Bother?

You have never bothered to read the fine print on the back of these forms—and you suspect others don't either. That is true. However, if you do take a look at this boilerplate, you can see that some fairly important things are covered. I think that devising a set of terms and conditions for your business is worth the effort, does not necessarily require a lot of legal time and expense, and will give you the following benefits.

1. The most important benefit is simply the discipline of thinking about the terms and conditions on which you are willing to do business. When you sell your product, when do you want to get paid? Cash on delivery, net 10 days? 2 percent, 10 days? etc. Is the normal transaction to be FOB your plant with freight to the seller's place of business added, or do you want to use a delivered price system?

2. By setting forth the terms and conditions of your sales, and hopefully some of your purchases, you can work towards a better deal in all these transactions. Remember that price is only *one* of the aspects of a deal. The others include most of the things on these forms, such as warranties, obligations to replace and repair, time to present claims, etc.

3. *Last*, but certainly not least, if you do get into a dispute with a customer or supplier, your terms and conditions may help you negotiate a better settlement.

What About the "Battle of the Forms"?

You may say, "Okay, I see that if I put good terms and conditions which are favorable to me on my forms, I may get some advantages. But will my vendors and customers stand still for this? Won't they have terms and conditions which are favorable to them on their forms?"

First of all, the customers and vendors are going to read your terms and conditions just about as frequently and carefully as you are going to read theirs—hardly ever, and then only the portion which deals with a specific problem.

Second, if your vendors or customers have terms and conditions which are favorable to them, and you have no terms and conditions favorable to you, you will be doing business on *their* terms. If, on the other hand, you *both* do a good job with your forms, the inconsistent portions of the forms will cancel each other out, and you will both be left with the *general law*. Since the general law has been developed over the years to be fair to both purchasers and sellers, that is not too bad a result.

You may wonder, "If a vendor puts a burdensome or harsh clause in that fine, hard-to-read print on the back of his or her forms, could I be bound by it even if I never read it?"

That could happen. Courts will generally, at least in commercial transactions, give full effect to printed forms even if the print is fine and on the back of the form. Of course, you will run across an occasional case where a court will refuse to give effect to extremely fine print on the back of a form but those cases are the exception. In commercial transactions we have to assume that all of the fine print on both sides of the form is going to be looked at by the court.

If you're designing forms for use with a consumer, you do have to be much more careful about the readability of the form. In consumer cases courts will pay a little more attention to that.

What Is Meant by the "Battle of the Forms"?   Most commercial contracts are accomplished through exchanges of forms, with neither party reading the fine print on the other's forms until a dispute or problem arises. If both companies do a good job of drafting their forms to protect their interests, it is very likely that the forms will have different or conflicting terms on some fairly important points. However, this does not alter the fact that both parties intended there to be a contract; it just means that they did not agree on all the fine points.

What should the law do? The old law said that a contract was formed by an offer and an acceptance. The first person to issue a form was making an offer. That could be accepted by the other party only by an acceptance which was a mirror *image* of the offer. If the other party proposed different or additional terms, that was not an acceptance but a counteroffer. Therefore, in most commercial transactions there was no contract at all based on the exchange of forms. Usually this presented no problem because both parties performed. However, if a dispute arose before performance, business people were often surprised to find out from their lawyers that even though they thought they had made a contract, they really hadn't because no one had supplied an acceptance which was a mirror image of the other's offer.

In approximately 1960, the commercial laws were rewritten by a special group of lawyers and law professors in a Uniform Commercial Code. This has now been enacted in all states except Louisiana. The UCC says that the old law was bad on this subject, that business people intended to make a deal when they exchanged these forms even if the boilerplate on the back was different. It therefore wrote into the law a provision which deals with the exchange of conflicting forms. This provision creates somewhat of a lawyer's paradise, because if one party is on his or her toes and/or the other is asleep at the switch, an extremely advantageous (or disadvantageous) contract can be created merely by the exchange of appropriate forms without either party having negotiated or even thought about most of the terms.

The Legalistics This situation is created by the following provisions of the Uniform Commercial Code, which are worth reading carefully.

Section 2-207. Additional Terms in Acceptance of Confirmation

1. A definite and seasonable expression of acceptance or a written confirmation which is sent within a reasonable time operates as an acceptance even though it states terms additional to or different from those offered or agreed upon, unless acceptance is expressly made conditional on assent to the additional or different terms.
2. The additional terms are to be construed as proposals for addition to the contract. Between merchants such terms become part of the contract unless:
   a. the offer expressly limits acceptance to the terms of the offer;
   b. they materially alter it; or
   c. notification of objection to them has already been given or is given within a reasonable time after notice of them is received.
3. Conduct by both parties which recognizes the existence of a contract is sufficient to establish a contract for sale although the writings of the parties do not otherwise establish a contract. In such case, the terms of the particular contract consist of those terms on which the writings of the parties agree, together with any supplementary terms incorporated under any other provisions of this Act.

Basically, this provision was designed to accomplish two objectives. The first was to make certain that there was in fact an enforceable contract when normal business procedures were intended to create an enforceable contract. The provision was necessary to change the old mirror-image rule. The second objective was to establish certain ground rules to determine precisely what the terms of the deal were where the documentation was inconsistent.

Generally, the effect of this provision is that the additional terms contained in a response to an offer (whether to sell or to buy) become part of the contract. This happens *automatically* unless

1. the offer *expressly limits acceptance* to the terms of the offer,

2. the additional terms *materially alter* the offer, or

3. the offeree *objects* to those terms.

Naturally, a busy purchaser or seller cannot possibly read, evaluate, and make necessary objections to every form that comes across his or her desk. However, unless he or she does so, the result will very likely be a contract which is most unfavorable to his or her company. The "materially alter" language is not very useful for planning purposes because of its uncertainty. Here is where the forms come in. You want to *expressly limit* your offer to your terms. If the company personnel have an adequate arsenal of appropriate forms and a knowledge of their importance and how to use them, this problem can be minimized and, in many cases, turned into a distinct advantage for the company. Following is a brief discussion of a suggested technique to achieve this corporate advantage.

Forms.   Forms are the basic weapon in this battle. Naturally, anyone participating in the fight must have ammunition. Following are the four basic forms which every corporate purchaser or seller should have:

Purchaser	Seller
Request for quotation	Quotation
Purchase order	Sales form

What Should the Forms Contain?   The object of the forms is to make sure the contract is on your terms, not the other party's. Therefore, you must use a form which establishes that the only deal is the deal you propose, and that if the other party proposes additions or changes, those additions or changes are of no effect and your form governs. Following are two suggested clauses which will usually accomplish the desired objective.

Terms for Buyer's Documents.   Vendor's commencement of work on the goods described herein or shipment of such goods, whichever occurs first, shall be deemed an effective mode of acceptance of purchaser's offer to purchase contained in this purchase order. Any acceptance of this purchase order is limited to acceptance of the express terms of the offer contained on the face and back hereof. Any proposal for additional or different terms or any attempt by vendor to vary, in any degree, any of the terms of this offer in vendor's acceptance shall not operate as a rejection of this offer, unless such variance is in the terms of the description, quantity, price, or delivery schedule of the goods, but shall be deemed a material alteration thereof, which is hereby objected to by purchaser, and this offer shall be deemed accepted by vendor without said additional or different terms. If this purchase order shall be deemed an acceptance of a prior offer by vendor, such acceptance is expressly conditional on vendor's assent to any additional or different terms contained herein.

Terms for Seller's Documents.   Any acceptance of the offer to sell contained herein is limited to acceptance of the express terms of such offer contained on the face and back hereof. Any proposal for additional or different terms or any attempt by buyer to vary, in any degree, any of the terms in buyer's acceptance by purchase order or otherwise shall not operate as a rejection of this offer to sell unless such variance is in the terms of the description, quantity, price, or delivery schedule of the goods, but shall be deemed a material alteration thereof, which is hereby objected to by the seller, and this offer shall be deemed accepted by buyer without said additional or different terms. If this document shall be deemed an acceptance of a prior offer by buyer, such acceptance is expressly conditional on buyer's assent to any additional or different terms contained herein.

When Do You Use the Form?   An analysis of Section 2-207 reveals that the statute gives a very slight potential advantage to the first party to submit an offer (of either purchase or sale). This is so because it is the terms of the first piece of paper which are used to base all further adjustments. If the second piece of paper has terms which are materially inconsistent with the first offer, those terms will have no force or effect if the first document contained the magic language, but there probably will still be a contract. However, if the first document did not contain the magic language, any additional terms in the second document will become a part of the deal unless they materially alter the original proposal or they are objected to within a reasonable time. Furthermore, in many situations, the offeree will do one of the following two things:

1. Expressly accept the offer or accept by a course of conduct (like starting work)
2. Send a confirmation document which does not have the magic language

If either of these occurs, the first offeror has his or her way entirely.

If the offeree is on his or her toes and sends you an acceptance which has the magic language making the acceptance expressly conditional on your acceptance of his or her additional terms, you have a square conflict. Then what happens? Generally, the rule is that the inconsistent terms simply cancel each other out, and the parties are left with:

1. the terms which they agree upon or which are not inconsistent, and
2. such other terms as are generally imposed by law.

Therefore, if you play the game right, you may wind up with your desires entirely, and the worst that can happen is that you wind up with as many of your terms as are not inconsistent with the other party's terms, and the remainder of the contract is governed according to general principles of law. If you either do not play the game at all or play it wrong, you may wind up with a contract almost entirely on the terms of the other party.

Warranties

Warranties are an important subject worth some of your thought and time. There are two sides to the coin:

1. Make sure you focus on warranties whenever you are buying anything important for your business.
2. Make sure you clearly decide what warranties you are going to give on the products you sell.

On the first question of warranties on products you purchase, I would simply like to refer you back to the previous section, "Purchase Order Terms and Conditions." Naturally, you should specifically negotiate warranties on important products if your bargaining position allows you to do so. Remember that your warranty protection is a cost item. If you buy something with good warranty protection, it is worth more than that same product with less significant protection.

The same principle—only with much more importance—extends to the products you sell. In today's litigious climate, you simply must build the cost of warranties into your price. Also, it is important for you to remember that, if you do nothing you will automatically provide fairly good warranty protection by operation of law. If you want to disclaim warranty responsibility, you must do so in clear and specific legally approved language. Since warranties are potentially so important, I recommend you seek specific legal advice concerning the warranties you give—or do not give. *The key is to make sure you understand what warranties you are giving for your products.* The lawyer can make sure the right legalese is used—but you have to make the business judgment and build the cost of that warranty into the product. I would like to offer you the following thoughts and guidelines on warranties which should help you assess the magnitude of this problem in your situation and discuss some appropriate solutions with your lawyer.

Do You Sell a Consumer Product?

If you sell a consumer product to consumers you must comply with the Magnuson Moss Warranty Act. This statute was enacted in 1976 to provide a relatively uniform system of providing warranties throughout the nation and to make those warranties honest. Essentially, the law says the following:

- You do not have to give any warranty at all.
- If you do give any warranty, it must be either a full warranty or a limited warranty. A *full warranty* is a rather good warranty which must satisfy strict legal requirements. You must know what those are for your product. A *limited warranty* is essentially any kind of warranty you want to give which does not measure up to the standards of a full warranty. The legal requirements for a limited warranty involve disclosure. The warranty must be worded correctly, and your lawyer can help you.
- You still must consider the UCC. The Magnuson Moss Warranty Act did *not* supersede many important Uniform Commercial Code requirements. Many companies, including some large ones, have either elected to ignore this problem or done a legally inadequate job of drafting their warranties.
- Because of this problem, you cannot be sure that warranties you see from other companies do the job they seem to be intended to do. I

have seen some which offer a limited warranty under the Magnuson Moss Warranty Act but do not adequately disclaim the UCC-implied warranties. Thus, a purchaser has both sets of warranties—and this may not have been intended.

In summary, then, if you sell a consumer product to a consumer, my advice is to seek legal advice on your warranty, because you are in a highly technical area.

Do You Sell a Product Which Could Injure Someone?

Essentially, the rule here is that you cannot disclaim responsibility for a defective product which causes a personal injury—no matter what. Warranties are good only to grant or limit commercial rights. They don't serve many useful purpose in limiting product liability exposure— in fact, the contrary is the case. If you give a warranty, and a breach of that warranty causes personal injury, that is one of the theories the injured person can use to recover damages from you.

What About the Commercial Situation?

If you sell products which are not consumer products or if you sell consumer products but do not give any warranty to the consumer, you don't have to deal with the Magnuson Moss Warranty Act, but you still must consider the UCC warranty provisions.

What Are the UCC Warranty Provisions?

The Uniform Commercial Code starts off with a key principle—almost absolute freedom of contract. The UCC does not require you to give any warranty whatsoever. However, certain warranties are implied unless you disclaim them. Further, you have to disclaim them by certain legally prescribed language. Here is a brief rundown of the UCC warranty provisions.

- Unless disclaimed, you warrant that the product does not infringe anyone else's patent and that you have title to it. Usually this presents no problem.

- Any statement you make about the product is an express warranty. Again, there is no problem so long as you say what you mean and mean what you say. If you sell a "3-foot square table," there is an express warranty that the table is 3 feet. If you sell a "1-horsepower motor," there is an express warranty that the product is a motor and generates "1 horsepower." Anything said about the product, any picture, any descriptive literature or brochure, or any samples create an express warranty.

- Unless disclaimed, two additional warranties are implied by the UCC: the implied warranty of merchantability and the implied warranty of fitness for particular purpose. The implied warranty of merchantability provides that the product is fit for the general use to which products of that kind are usually put; the implied warranty of fitness for particular purpose provides that if there is a specific purpose for which the product is going to be used the product will be suitable for that purpose.

- In order to disclaim these warranties, you must follow certain technicalities. To disclaim the implied warranty of merchantability, you must use the word "merchantability." To disclaim the implied warranty of fitness for particular purposes, you must use clear language, although no precise words are required. In both cases, the disclaimers must be conspicuous — which means that they must be in larger type than the remainder of the document. (For an example of how to disclaim these warranties, see the sample terms and conditions of sale.)

- You can limit warranty exposure to the cost of the product. This is a very important provision, because, normally, a breach of warranty will allow the buyer of the product to recover not only the cost of the product, but all other damages which flowed from that breach. Example: Absent any disclaimer, if you bought defective film for your photographic trip to Europe, the manufacturer of the film could be liable not only to replace the film but also to give you another trip to Europe. With the proper disclaimer, they are liable only to replace the film.

For these reasons, I strongly suggest that you carefully consider drafting forms which disclaim the implied warranties, and *limit* a purchaser's remedy under any breach of warranty claim to replacement of the product. Of course, this is subject to the requirements of the marketplace. However, remember that without some limits, a very small sale can give rise to a very large liability.

Example

You sell gaskets. You provide some defective gaskets to a motor maker. The motor maker puts the defective gaskets into his motors and sells them before he finds out they were defective. There must be an expensive recall to fix the motors. With a disclaimer and limitation on warranties, you are liable to provide new gaskets. Without the limitations, you may be liable for the cost of the entire recall campaign.

The subject of warranties is very closely related to that of product liability, so if this kind of problem is present in your business, I suggest you read Chap. 12 in conjunction with this one.

Following are samples which illustrate these points:

- Purchase order terms and conditions
- Terms and conditions of sale
- Sample – Full warranty
- Sample – Limited warranty

TERMS AND CONDITIONS OF PURCHASE

---

1. ACCEPTANCE

   This order must be accepted as written and it must be accepted by Vendor by written acknowledgment mailed to Buyer, or by commencement of performance, within ten (10) days of the order's date. After acceptance, this order, with any attachments, will constitute the entire agreement of the parties. Any addition to, change in, modification of, revision of, or waiver of this order will be invalid and rejected unless specifically agreed to in writing by Buyer.

2. PRICES

   Buyer will not be billed at prices higher than those stated on the front of this order unless other prices are specifically agreed to in writing by both parties. Such prices will include all charges for packing, hauling, storage and transportation to the point of delivery. Vendor will pay delivery charges in excess of those that Buyer has agreed to pay. The prices stated will include all taxes except those which Vendor is required by law to collect from Buyer. Such taxes, if any, will be separately stated in Vendor's invoice and will be paid by Buyer unless an exemption is available. Vendor agrees that any price reduction made with respect to the items covered by this order subsequent to its placement but prior to payment will be applicable to this order.

---

3. DELIVERY

Time is of the essence in this order and substitutions will not be accepted. The entire order must be shipped by the date requested, but it may not be shipped more than one week in advance of the time(s) specified herein without Buyer's prior approval. If Vendor's shipments fail to meet the delivery schedule, Buyer, without limiting any other rights or remedies that it may have at law or in equity, may direct expedited routing of such shipments and any excess costs incurred as a result thereof will be debited to Vendor's account. When more than one shipment is made against any order, the invoice and shipping papers accompanying the last shipment must indicate that it is the final shipment. Buyer will not be obligated to accept untimely, excess or under shipments, and such shipments in whole or in part may, at Buyer's option, be returned to Vendor, or held for disposition at Vendor's expense and risk. Buyer will not be liable for Vendor's commitments or production arrangements in excess of the amount or in advance of the time necessary to meet Buyer's delivery schedule.

4. RISK OF LOSS

Vendor will bear all risk of loss of all merchandise covered by this order until such merchandise has been delivered to the designated location.

5. MODIFICATION OF ORDER

Buyer may modify this order at any time by submitting a written notice of new order to Vendor. If such modification affects the cost or time of performance and if Vendor makes a written claim for an equitable adjustment within thirty (30) days after receipt of notification of change, an equitable adjustment will be made by Buyer.

6. INSPECTION AND TESTS

All goods ordered hereunder will be subject to inspection and testing by Buyer at all reasonable times and places, including the period of manufacture, and in any event prior to acceptance. Vendor agrees to permit access to its facilities at all reasonable times for inspection of goods by Buyer's agents or employees and will provide all tools, facilities and assistance necessary for such inspection at no additional cost to Buyer. It is expressly agreed that inspections and/or payments prior to delivery will not constitute final acceptance and that all goods will be subject to final inspection after delivery to Buyer. If the goods delivered do not meet the specifications or otherwise do not conform to the requirements of this order, Buyer will have the right to reject them. Goods which have been delivered and rejected in whole or in part may at Buyer's option, be returned to Vendor for reimbursement, credit or replacement, or may be held for disposition at Vendor's expense and risk.

7. WARRANTIES

Vendor warrants that all goods and services furnished hereunder will *conform to applicable specifications, instructions, drawings, data* and *samples, will be merchantable* of *good material and workmanship* and *free from defects, will be fit and sufficient for the purposes intended by Buyer*, and *will be free from all liens and encumbrances.* These warranties will be in addition to all other warranties, express, implied or statutory. *All warranties will survive acceptance of and payment for any and all goods ordered pursuant hereto and will run to Buyer and its customers.*

8. DRAWINGS AND SPECIFICATION REVIEW

   If during the term of this order, Buyer's representatives review drawings, specifications or other data developed by Vendor in connection with the order and make suggestions or comments or approve such documents and data, such actions are only expressions of opinion by Buyer and will not serve to relieve Vendor of any of its responsibilities or obligations under this order.

9. USE OF INFORMATION

   Vendor agrees that all information furnished or disclosed to Buyer by Vendor in connection with this order is furnished or disclosed as a part of the consideration for this order, that such information is not, unless otherwise agreed to by Buyer in writing, to be treated as confidential or proprietary, and that Vendor will assert no claims (other than for patent infringement) by reason of the disclosure, reproduction or use of such information by Buyer, its agents, its assigns or its customers.

10. TOOLING

    Unless otherwise specified in this order, all tooling and/or all other articles required for the performance hereof will be furnished by Vendor, will be maintained in good condition and will be replaced when necessary at Vendor's expense.

11. ADVERTISEMENTS

    Vendor will not in any manner advertise or publish the fact that it has furnished, or contracted to furnish, the goods or services included herein without the prior written consent of Buyer. Vendor will not disclose the existence of or any information about this order to any party without the prior written consent of Buyer.

12. SUBCONTRACTING

    Vendor agrees to obtain Buyer's prior written consent before subcontracting this order or any substantial portion hereof, provided, however, that this limitation will not apply to the purchase of standard commercial supplies or raw materials.

13. BUYER'S PROPERTY

    Title to and the right to immediate possession of any property, including patterns, tools, jigs, dies and any other equipment or material, furnished to Vendor or paid for by Buyer will remain in Buyer. No articles made therefrom will be furnished by Vendor to any other party without Buyer's prior written consent. Vendor will keep adequate records of such property which will be made available to Buyer upon request, and will store, protect, preserve, repair and maintain such property in accordance with sound industrial practice, all at Vendor's expense. Unless otherwise agreed to in writing by Buyer, Vendor will insure Buyer's interest in such property against loss or damage by reason of fire (including extended coverage), riot or civil commotion. Copies or certificates of such insurance will be furnished to Buyer on demand.

In the event that Buyer's property becomes lost or damaged to any extent from any cause, including faulty workmanship and/or negligent acts by Vendor, its agents, or its employees, while in Vendor's possession, Vendor agrees to indemnify Buyer or replace such property, at Vendor's expense, in accordance with Buyer's request. At the completion of the goods requested by Buyer in this order for which Buyer's property was required, Vendor will request disposition instructions for all such property, or the remainder thereof, whether in its original form or in semi-processed form. Vendor agrees to make such property available to Buyer at Buyer's request, in the manner requested by Buyer, including preparation, packing and shipping as directed. Expenses for preparation for shipment will be for Vendor's account and shipment will be made F.O.B. Vendor's plant.

14. DRAWINGS AND DATA

Vendor will keep confidential all information, including designs, drawings, specifications and data, furnished by Buyer, or prepared by Vendor specifically in connection with the performance of this order, and will not divulge or use such information for the benefit of any other party. Except as required for the efficient performance of this order, Vendor will not make copies or permit copies of such information to be made without the prior written consent of Buyer. Vendor will not use, either directly or indirectly, any such information or any data derived therefrom for any purpose other than to perform this order without obtaining Buyer's written consent. Vendor will return all such data and information to Buyer upon completion by Vendor of its obligations under this order, or upon demand.

15. TERMINATION

Buyer may terminate the performance of work under this order in whole or in part at any time(s), by written notice to Vendor. Upon receipt of such notice, Vendor will, unless the notice directs otherwise, immediately discontinue all work and the placing of all orders for materials, facilities and supplies in connection with the performance of this order and will promptly cancel all existing orders and terminate all subcontracts insofar as such orders or subcontracts are chargeable to this order. Upon the termination of work under this order, full and complete settlement of all claims of Vendor with respect to the terminated work will be made as follows:

(i) As compensation to Vendor for such termination, unless such termination results from the default of Vendor, Buyer will pay to Vendor the percentage of the total order price corresponding to the proportion of the amount of work completed on the date of termination to the total work to be done as Vendor's full compensation for the work completed under this order; and

(ii) Upon Buyer's payment to Vendor in accordance with this paragraph, title to all equipment, materials, work-in-progress, finished products, plans, drawings, specifications, information, special tooling and other things for which Buyer has paid will automatically vest in Buyer.

Nothing contained in this paragraph will be construed to limit or affect any remedies which Buyer may have as a result of a default by Vendor.

16. DEFAULT-CANCELLATION

Buyer reserves the right, by written notice of default, to cancel this order, without liability to Buyer, in the event of any default on the part of the Vendor, the discontinuance of business by Vendor, or the sale by Vendor of the bulk of its assets other than in the usual course of business. If Vendor fails to perform as specified herein, or if Vendor breaches any of the terms hereof, Vendor will be liable to Buyer for all damages, losses and liability incurred by Buyer directly or indirectly as a result of Vendor's breach, and Buyer reserves the right, without liability to Buyer, upon written notice to Vendor, to cancel this order in whole or in part and/or to obtain the goods ordered herein from another source with any excess cost resulting therefrom to be chargeable to Vendor. The remedies provided in this paragraph will be cumulative and in addition to any other remedies provided at law or in equity.

17. FORCE MAJEURE

Neither party hereto will be liable for defaults or delays due to Acts of God, or the public enemy, acts or demands of any government or governmental agency, strikes, fires, floods, accidents, or other unforeseeable causes beyond its control and not due to its fault or negligence. Each party will notify the other in writing of the cause of any such delay within five (5) days after the beginning thereof.

18. COMPLIANCE WITH LAWS

Vendor agrees to fully observe and comply with all applicable Federal, State and local laws, rules, regulations and orders pertaining to the production and sale of the goods ordered, and, upon request, Vendor will furnish Buyer certificates of compliance with such laws, rules, regulations and orders.

19. EQUAL OPPORTUNITY

Executive Order No. 11246, as amended, relative to Equal Employment Opportunity and all other applicable laws, rules and regulations, including Title VII of the Civil Rights Act of 1964, are incorporated herein by this specific reference. In addition, if this purchase is, or is deemed, to be issued under a government contractor, all applicable laws, rules and regulations relating to the hiring of disabled veterans and veterans of the Vietnam era and to the hiring of individuals with physical or mental handicaps are incorporated herein by this specific reference.

20. GOVERNMENT CONTRACTS

If this order is placed, directly or indirectly, under a contract of the United States Government or any State or other governmental authority, then all terms and conditions required by law, regulations or by the Government Contract with respect to this order are incorporated herein by reference. To the extent that the terms and conditions of this order are inconsistent with any such required terms and conditions, the required terms and conditions will prevail and be binding on both Buyer and Vendor. Vendor agrees, upon request, to furnish Buyer with a certificate or certificates in such form as Buyer may require certifying that Vendor is in compliance with all such terms and conditions as well as any applicable law or regulation. Upon request, Buyer will make available to Vendor copies of all pertinent terms and conditions required by any such Government Contract.

21. NOTICE OF LABOR DISPUTES

Whenever Vendor has knowledge that any actual or potential labor dispute is delaying or threatens to delay the timely performance of this order, Vendor will immediately give written notice thereof, including all relevant information with respect thereto, to Buyer.

22. INDEMNIFICATION

Vendor agrees to indemnify and hold harmless Buyer, its successors, assigns, customers and users of its products, against all suits at law or in equity and from all damages, claims and demands arising out of the death or injury of any person or damage to any property alleged to have resulted from the goods hereby ordered, and/or resulting from any act or omission of Vendor, its agents or employees, and, upon the tendering of any suit or claim to Vendor, to defend the same at Vendor's expense as to all costs, fees and damages. The foregoing indemnification will apply whether Vendor or Buyer defends such suit or claims and whether the death, injury or property damage is caused by the sole or concurrent negligence of Vendor or otherwise.

To the extent that Vendor's agents, employees or subcontractors enter upon premises occupied by or under the control of Buyer, or any of its customers, or suppliers in the course of the performance of this order, Vendor will take all necessary precautions to prevent the occurrence of any injury (including death) to any persons, or of any damage to any property, arising out of acts or omissions of such agents, employees, or subcontractors, and except to the extent that any such injury or damage is due solely and directly to Buyer's negligence, will indemnify, defend and hold Buyer, its officers, employees and agents, harmless from any and all costs, losses, expenses, damages, claims, suits, or any liability whatsoever, including attorney's fees arising out of any act or omission of Vendor, its agents, employees or subcontractors. Vendor will maintain and require its subcontractors to maintain (1) public liability and property damage insurance including contractual liability (both general and vehicle) in amounts sufficient to cover obligations set forth above, and (2) worker's compensation and employer's liability insurance covering all employees engaged in the performance of this order for claims arising under any applicable Worker's Compensation and Occupation Disease Acts. Vendor will furnish certificates evidencing such insurance which expressly provide that no expiration, termination or modification will take place without thirty (30) days prior written notice to Buyer.

23. PATENT INDEMNIFICATION

Vendor will indemnify and hold harmless Buyer, its successors, assigns, customers and users of its products, against all suits at law or in equity and all loss, liability and damage, including costs and expenses, resulting from any claim that the manufacture, use, sale or resale of any goods supplied under this order infringe any patent or patent rights, and Vendor will when notified, defend any action or claim of such infringement at its own expense.

24. ASSIGNMENT

Neither this order nor any rights or obligations herein may be assigned by Vendor nor may Vendor delegate the performance of any of its duties hereunder without, in either case, Buyer's prior written consent.

25. CONTROLLING LAW

All questions concerning the validity and operation of this order and the performance of the obligations imposed on the parties under this order will be governed by the laws of the State of _____, U.S.A.

26. REMEDIES

The remedies provided herein will be cumulative and in addition to any other remedies provided by law or in equity. A waiver of a breach of any provision hereof will not constitute a waiver of any other breach hereof.

27. LANGUAGE

All correspondence pertaining to this order, or to any of the terms and conditions covered by this order, will be in the English language.

STANDARD CONDITIONS OF SALE

1. DELIVERY

Unless otherwise specified on the reverse side hereof, Seller will deliver all products to Buyer F.O.B. Seller's factory. Seller reserves the right to make partial deliveries and to ship products as they become available. Delivery dates are approximate and will be calculated from the date that Seller has received all information necessary to permit Seller to proceed with work immediately and without interruption.

Seller reserves the right to supply the products and/or services ordered by Buyer from any of its world-wide manufacturing facilities.

If any or all products are not delivered when ready due to the request of Buyer or cannot be delivered when ready due to any cause referred to in the "Delays" Article hereof, Seller reserves the right to invoice Buyer at any time thereafter and to place such products in storage. In such event, (1) Seller's delivery obligations will be deemed fulfilled and title and all risk of loss or damage will thereupon pass to Buyer, (2) any amount otherwise payable to Seller upon delivery will be due and payable upon presentation of Seller's invoices and its certification as to such cause, and (3) all expenses incurred by Seller such as for preparation for and placement into storage, handling, storage, inspection, preservation, and insurance will be due and payable by Buyer upon submission of Seller's invoices.

If Buyer wishes to pick up products from Seller's designated manufacturing facility, such pickup must be made within three (3) working days after Buyer has received notice from Seller that such products are ready to be picked up. If Buyer fails to pick up the products within the three (3) day period after receiving the notice from Seller, Seller may deliver the products to Buyer at Buyer's expense.

2. PRICES

The sales price(s) for products will be the list or posted price(s) of Seller in effect at the time of delivery, and will include the cost of Seller's usual factory tests and inspections. The cost of packing and crating in accordance with the standards of Seller is an additional charge and will be added to the sales price(s).

Uness otherwise agreed to by Seller and Buyer in writing, prices applied to this order are firm for the duration of the order.

3. TAXES

All prices are exclusive of any applicable U.S.A. federal, state or local sales, use, excise or other similar taxes. All such taxes will be for Buyer's account and will be paid by Buyer to Seller upon submission of Seller's invoices. If Buyer is exempt from any applicable sales tax but fails to notify Seller of such exemption or fails to furnish its Sales Tax Exemption Number to Seller in a timely manner and Seller is required to pay such tax, the amount of any such payment made by Seller will be reimbursed by Buyer to Seller upon submission of Seller's invoices.

Any taxes (including income, stamp and turnover taxes), duties, fees, charges, or assessments of any nature levied by any governmental authority other than of the U.S.A. in connection with this transaction, whether levied against Buyer, against Seller or its employees, or against any of Seller's subcontractors or their employees, or otherwise, will be for Buyer's account and will be paid directly by Buyer to the governmental authority concerned. If Seller is required by law or otherwise to pay any such levy and/or fines, penalties, or assessments in the first instance, or as a result of Buyer's failure to comply with any applicable laws or regulations governing the payment of such levies by Buyer, the amount of any payments so made by Seller will be reimbursed by Buyer to Seller upon submission of Seller's invoices.

4. PAYMENT

Unless Buyer and Seller otherwise agree to terms other than those specified herein, payment will be made in U.S. Dollars at _____ as follows:

(i) On orders by shipment to countries other than the U.S.A., payment on all sales over five thousand U.S. Dollars (U.S. $5,000) will be made through the medium of a Letter of Credit to be established by the Buyer at its expense including any bank confirmation charges. All Letters of Credit will be in favor of and acceptable to Seller, will be maintained in sufficient amounts for the period necessary to meet all payment obligations, will be irrevocable and issued, or confirmed, by a bank in _____ satisfactory to Seller within fifteen (15) days after acceptance of any order, will permit partial deliveries and will provide for prorata payments upon presentation of Seller's invoices and Seller's certificate of delivery F.O.B. Seller's factory, or of delivery into storage with certification of cause therefore, and for the payment of any termination charges.

(ii) On all other orders payment will be made within thirty (30) days after the actual date of Seller's invoice(s).

(iii) A monthly interest charge at the rate of one and one-half percent (1½%) or the maximum legal rate, whichever is less, will be assessed on all past due payments.

If Buyer fails to fulfill any condition of this Article, Seller may suspend performance and any costs incurred by Seller as a result thereof will be paid by Buyer. Seller will be entitled to an extension of time for performance of its obligations equal to the period of Buyer's non-fulfillment whether or not Seller elects to suspend performance. If such non-fulfillment is not rectified by Buyer promptly upon notice thereof, Seller may terminate performance and Buyer will pay Seller its termination charges upon submission of Seller's invoices.

5. RISK OF LOSS AND TITLE

For non-export sales, risk of loss and title to products will pass to Buyer at the time of delivery specified in Article 1 hereof. Buyer will pay, or reimburse Seller for, all freight and in-transit insurance costs from time of delivery.

For export sales, Seller reserves the right to request that the Buyer agree that title to, beneficial ownership of, right of possession to, risk of loss on, and all property rights in products will remain with Seller and pass to Buyer at the port of entry of the ultimate country of destination (but prior to unloading or customs inspection at such port) specified on Buyer's order and/or declared as a country of ultimate destination on Seller's invoices.

Neither (i) the time, method, place or medium of payment provided for herein, or any combination of the foregoing, nor (ii) the manner of consignment provided for, whether to, or to the order of, the Buyer or its agent, will in any way limit or modify the rights of Seller, as the owner of the products, to have control over and the right to possession of the products until the title thereto passes to Buyer as provided for above. The term F.O.B. (Free on Board) or other commercial abbreviations, if used on any documents related to the transaction contemplated herein, will not be deemed to relate to the time when or the place where the ownership of and responsibility for the products is transferred from Seller to Buyer.

Buyer will pay all freight and insurance costs from the point of delivery specified in Article 1. In-transit insurance to the point that title passes to Buyer as provided above will be purchased for Seller's account and will be in an amount in U.S. Dollars not less than the aggregate prices of products delivered hereunder. Any insurance proceeds collected by Buyer for Seller's account will be promptly remitted to Seller in U.S. Dollars. The insurance policies purchased by Buyer will be for the benefit of Seller, whether or not Seller is named as an insured in such policies, until title and risk of loss to products passed to Buyer pursuant to this Article 5. Where possible the policies will provide that they are for the benefit of Seller and/or Buyer "as their interests may appear." Seller agrees that any insurance proceeds which Seller may receive in excess of amounts payable by Buyer for the products will be promptly remitted to Buyer.

6. EXPORTS

Seller reserves the right, with respect to any and all goods purchased for export pursuant to these Standard Conditions of Sale, from time to time, to request and obtain from Buyer a written statement or statements certifying that such goods were in fact exported within one (1) year of the date of Seller's invoice(s) therefore.

7. TESTING AND ACCEPTANCE

Prior to the delivery of any products, Seller will perform its standard factory acceptance test applicable to such products, and, upon request by Buyer, Seller will certify in writing that the products have satisfied the requirements of such test. Such certification will be in the form of Seller's standard quality control stickers or stamps. Buyer will be deemed to have accepted the products upon satisfactory testing, and title thereto, will pass to Buyer in accordance with the terms of Article 5 hereof.

8. LIMITED WARRANTY

Seller warrants that products manufactured by Seller, when properly installed, used, and maintained, will be free from defects in material and workmanship. Seller's obligations under this warranty will be limited to repairing or replacing, at Seller's option, the part or parts of the products which prove defective in material or workmanship within one (1) year from the date of delivery, provided that Buyer gives Seller prompt notice of any defect or failure and satisfactory proof thereof. Products may be returned by Buyer only after written authorization has been obtained from Seller, and Buyer will prepay all freight charges to return any products to Seller's factory, or any other repair facility designated by Seller. Seller will deliver replacements for detective products to Buyer freight prepaid to the destination provided for in the original order. Products returned to Seller under this warranty will become the property of Seller. With respect to any product or part thereof not manufactured by Seller, only the warranty, if any, given by the manufacturer thereof, will apply. Seller's obligations under this warranty will not apply to any product which (1) is normally consumed in operation, or (2) has a normal life inherently shorter than the warranty period stated herein. **THE FOREGOING WARRANTIES ARE IN LIEU OF ALL OTHER WARRANTIES, WHETHER ORAL, WRITTEN, EXPRESS, IMPLIED OR STATUTORY. IMPLIED WARRANTIES OF MERCHANTABILITY AND FITNESS FOR A PARTICULAR PURPOSE WILL NOT APPLY. SELLER'S WARRANTY OBLIGATIONS AND BUYER'S REMEDIES HEREUNDER ARE SOLELY AND EXCLUSIVELY AS STATED HEREIN.**

With respect to products purchased by consumers in the United States for personal use, the implied warranties, including but not limited to the warranties of merchantability and fitness for a particular purpose, are limited to twelve (12) months from the date of delivery.

In those states which do not allow limitations on the duration of an implied warranty the above limitation will not apply. Similarly, in those states which do not allow the exclusion or limitation of consequential damages, the above limitation or exclusion will not apply. This limited warranty gives consumers specified legal rights and they also will have all other rights provided by law.

9. PATENTS

If Buyer receives a claim that any product or part thereof manufactured by Seller infringes a United States patent, Buyer will notify Seller promptly in writing and give Seller all necessary information and assistance and the exclusive authority to evaluate, defend and settle such claim. Seller, at its own expense and option, will then (i) settle or defend against such claim, or (ii) procure for Buyer the right to use such product, or (iii) replace or modify the product to avoid infringement, or (iv) remove it and refund the purchase price less a reasonable amount for depreciation. Provided such timely notice has been given by Buyer, should any court of competent jurisdiction hold such product to constitute infringement, Seller will pay any costs and damages finally awarded on account of such infringement and, if the use of such product is enjoined, Seller will take, at its option, one or more of the actions described in (ii), (iii) or (iv) above. With respect to any product or part thereof not manufactured by Seller, only the patent indemnity, if any, given by the manufacturer thereof will apply. The foregoing indemnity will not apply to any product made to the specification or design of Buyer. The rights and obligations of the parties with respect to patents and all other industrial property rights are solely and exclusively as stated herein.

10. LIMITATION OF LIABILITY

The total liability of Seller (including its subcontractor) on any claim, whether in contract, tort (including negligence) or otherwise, arising out of, connected with, or resulting from the manufacture, sale, delivery, resale, repair, replacement or use of any product will not exceed the price allocable to the product or part thereof which gives rise to the claim. In no event will Seller be liable for any incidental or consequential damages including, but not limited to, damages for loss of revenue, cost of capital, claims of customers for service interruptions or failure of supply, and costs and expenses incurred in connection with labor, overhead, transportation, installation or removal of products or substitute facilities or supply sources.

11. INDEMNIFICATION

Buyer will indemnify Seller and hold Seller harmless from and against any liability, damage, loss, expense, claim or judgment arising from injury (including death) to any person (whether an employee of Buyer or any other person) or damage to any property, however caused, whether by Seller's sole or concurrent negligence or otherwise, arising from the sale, resale, repair, replacement or use of any products delivered pursuant to this order.

If requested by Seller, Buyer, at its own expense, will defend any claim, suit or action which is brought against Seller and is within the indemnification set out in the preceding paragraph provided that Seller promptly gives Buyer notice of such claim, suit or action, furnishes a copy of all documents and instruments served upon Seller in connection therewith and reasonably cooperates with Buyer in such defense. Seller, at its own expense, will have the right to be represented in such defense by advisory counsel of Seller's selection. If Seller does not request Buyer to defend any such claim, suit or action, Seller, at its own expense, will undertake the defense thereof and Buyer, at its own expense, will have the right to be represented in such defense by advisory counsel of Buyer's selection.

Buyer will pay any judgment finally awarded in any claim, suit or action which is brought against Seller and is within the indemnification set out hereinabove, whether Seller or Buyer directs the defense thereof, and Buyer agrees to pay any amounts payable in settlement or compromise of any such claim, suit or action, provided that Buyer agrees in writing to the settlement or compromise amount and to the terms of settlement or compromise.

12. NUCLEAR USE

Buyer and third parties will not use any product or part thereof in connection with any activity or process involving nuclear fission or fusion or use or handling of any nuclear by-product material, as those materials are defined in the U.S. Atomic Energy Act of 1954 (as amended), unless Seller's written consent has been obtained prior to such use, and until such time as Buyer, at no expense to Seller, will have arranged for insurance coverage, indemnities and waivers of liability, recourse and subrogation, all acceptable to Seller, and all fully adequate in the opinion of Seller, to protect Seller (and its subcontractors and suppliers) against liability of any kind whatsoever whether in contract, tort (including negligence) or otherwise.

Seller will not be obligated to deliver the products until such indemnities, insurance and waivers have been procured and are legally operative in Seller's favor, failing which Seller may rescind the sale without liability for damages of any nature.

13. DELAYS

The date on which Seller's obligations are to be fulfilled will be extended for a period equal to the time lost by reason of any delay arising directly or indirectly from (1) acts of God, unforeseeable circumstances, acts (including delay or failure to act) of any governmental authority (de jure or de facto), war (declared or undeclared), riot, revolution, priorities, fires, floods, strikes, labor disputes, sabotage or epidemics, (2) inability due to causes beyond Seller's reasonable control to timely obtain instructions or information from Buyer, necessary and proper labor, materials, components, facilities, or transportation, or (3) any other cause beyond Seller's reasonable control.

The foregoing extension will apply even though such cause(s) may occur after Seller's performance of its obligations has been delayed for other causes.

If delay resulting from any of the foregoing causes extends for more than sixty (60) days and the parties have not agreed upon a revised basis for continuing the work at the end of the delay, including adjustment of the price, then either party, upon thirty (30) days written notice, may terminate the order with respect to the unexecuted portion of the work whereupon Buyer will pay Seller its termination charges.

14. GOVERNMENTAL AUTHORIZATIONS

Buyer will be responsible for the timely obtaining of all required authorizations, including Export Licenses, Import Licenses, Exchange Permits and all other governmental authorizations, even though such authorizations may be applied for by Seller. Buyer and Seller will assist each other in every manner reasonably possible in securing such authorizations as may be required. Seller will not be liable if any authorization is delayed, denied, revoked, restricted or not renewed and Buyer will not be relieved thereby of its obligations to pay Seller for its work.

All sales hereunder will at all times be subject to the export control laws and regulations of the United States Government and any amendments thereof. Buyer agrees that it will not make any disposition, by way of trans-shipment, re-export, diversion or otherwise, except as said laws and regulations may expressly permit, of U.S. origin goods purchased from Seller, other than in and to the ultimate country of destination specified on Buyer's order and/or declared as the country of ultimate destination on Seller's invoices.

15. DEFAULT-CANCELLATION

Seller reserves the right, by written notice of default, to cancel this order, without liability to Seller, in the event of any default on the part of the Buyer, the discontinuance of business by Buyer, or the sale by Buyer of the bulk of its assets other than in the usual course of business.

16. GENERAL

(i) Any order resulting herefrom will in all respects be construed and be given legal affect in conformity with the laws of the State of _____, U.S.A.

(ii) These Standard Conditions of Sale supersede all prior discussions and writings and constitute the entire agreement between Buyer and Seller with respect to the terms and conditions governing all orders. No waiver or modification of these Conditions will be binding upon Seller unless made in writing and signed by a duly authorized representative of Seller.

(iii) Seller's obligation hereunder will be dependent upon Seller's ability to obtain the necessary raw materials.

(iv) The remedies provided herein will be cumulative and in addition to any other remedies provided by law or equity. A waiver of a breach of any provision hereof will not constitute a waiver of any other breach hereof.

(v) All correspondence pertaining to this order, or to any of the terms and conditions covered by this order, will be in the English language.

(vi) All prices are subject to change without notice and may be subject to any increase which may be in effect on the date of shipment.

(vii) Any provisions in any purchase order, quotation, acknowledgment, or other forms or contract documents applicable to sales of Seller's products which are inconsistent, or in conflict, with any of the provisions herein are hereby objected to and will be deemed to be inapplicable to such sales.

Sample Warranties

Warranties are a technical subject which require legal counsel. You can help your lawyer by thinking about your situation and suggesting approaches. You can also help by gathering form warranties from other companies/products.

The same product can have a rather complex series of warranties. For example, a lawn mower may have a 2-year warranty, but for the first year, the engine would be protected by a 1-year warranty from the engine maker. Similarly, an appliance may have a full warranty on some parts and only a limited warranty on others. A tool might have a full warranty for a relatively short period and then a limited warranty thereafter. A product which must be installed might have a full warranty on the installation but only a limited warranty on the product itself. There is considerable flexibility in structuring your warranties, and the following are only two relatively simple examples. If you are alert to the problem, you can collect a fairly good sample of other companies' warranties by merely saving them from your normal household purchases.

Example of a Full Warranty

Caution

There are many restrictions imposed by the Federal Trade Commission on limitations which can be placed in a full warranty. At this time, those are only in proposed form. Warranties are a very technical subject which requires legal counsel — especially where consumer products are involved.

Your (well-known vacuum cleaner) is warranted in normal household use, in accordance with the instruction book, against original defects in workmanship for a period of one year from date of purchase. In commercial or rental use, the period of warranty is ninety days. This warranty provides, at no cost to you, all labor and parts to place this appliance in correct operating condition during the warranty period.

Warranty service can only be obtained by presenting the appliance to one of the following authorized warranty service outlets.

(Factory Service Centers)

(Authorized Warranty Service Dealers)

This warranty does not cover pickup, delivery, or house calls; however, if you mail your appliance to a factory service center for warranty service, transportation will be paid one way under this warranty.

While this warranty gives you specific legal rights, you may have other rights which vary from state to state.

It there are any questions concerning this warranty or the availability of warranty service outlets, write or phone.

Example of a Limited Warranty

Note that a limited warranty is used where you do not want to satisfy the technical requirements for a full warranty. Because you are limiting your warranties, it is essential to consider both the UCC and the Magnuson Moss Warranty Act. Otherwise, you may find that you have limited your obligations under the Magnuson Moss Warranty Act, but the buyer still has remedies under the express or implied warranty provisions of the UCC. We have seen many "limited warranties" which do not appear to take this into consideration. Following is one which seems to do a good job.

We warrant this (instrument) to be free from defects in workmanship or material for a period of one year from date of purchase. During the warranty period, such defects will be repaired or the defective instrument will be replaced, at our option, without charge. This warranty does not cover damage through accident or misuse.

ALL IMPLIED WARRANTIES, INCLUDING BUT NOT LIMITED TO WARRANTIES OF FITNESS AND MERCHANTABILITY, ARE HEREBY LIMITED IN DURATION TO A PERIOD ENDING ONE YEAR FROM DATE OF PURCHASE.

Some states do not allow limitations on how long an implied warranty lasts, so the above limitation may not apply to you. This warranty gives you specific legal rights, and you may also have other rights which vary from state to state.

Repair or replacement will be made at our option if this instrument is returned postpaid to:

Fair Credit Laws

The 1970s saw the development of a vast body of law relating to consumer credit. Keep in mind that this is *consumer* credit. It only applies if you are giving credit to a consumer. If you are in another type of business that operates in a commercial atmosphere—such as wholesaling or manufacturers who sell to wholesalers or retailers—these credit rules do not apply.

I have some very simple advice for any small business which desires to sell to consumers on credit. *Don't.* The plain fact of the matter is that the government has made this just too complicated and risky for a small business. Should you desire to do so anyway, the second piece of advice is to make sure you see a good consumer credit lawyer. These laws and regulations are just ungodly complex and technical. They are so technical that they prescribe the exact words you must use to state your interest charges and the exact size and kind of type in which certain words and numbers must appear. Further, if you extend credit to someone and he or she does not pay you, and you have the audacity to try to collect, there is another law called the Fair Debt Collection Practices Act which says in effect that you have to be gracious about it. Otherwise the deadbeat who did not pay you has a cause of action against you instead of vice versa.

All the credit laws are enforced by the Federal Trade Commission, and, should you desire more explanation of what they provide, you can call your local FTC office and they will send you not only copies of the statute but also relatively good and understandable brochures as to what those statutes say. The relevant statutes, in case you want to ask for material by name, are the following.

1. The *Truth in Lending Act*, which contains all the provisions about how you have to compute the annual percentage rate and spell it out in the documents in certain prescribed ways.

2. The *Equal Credit Opportunity Act*, which was designed to assure females equal access to credit regardless of their martial status.

3. The *Fair Credit Billing Act*, which tells you how you have to deal with complaints about bills that you send your customer.

4. The *Fair Debt Collection Practices Act*, which restricts the techniques you can use to collect from people who do not pay you.

5. The *Fair Credit Reporting Act*, which gives consumers the right to see their credit files and correct any erroneous information which might cause them to have credit denied in the future.

Keep in mind that all of these apply only if *you* are issuing the credit. The reason I suggest you not bother is that there are so many alternative ways of granting people credit. For example, if you honor a credit card, that credit company is extending the credit, and you are completely off the hook on all these laws. Thus, you can grant consumers credit by honoring Visa, Master Charge, American Express, Diners' Club, or other credit cards without any concern whatsoever for these laws—they are the credit card company's problem. True, it is going to cost you a little money, but, on the other hand, running a credit department yourself is going to cost you money also.

In summary, then, the bottom line is very clear. Steer clear of granting consumers credit yourself. If you have to grant consumers credit in your business, do so either by bank cards or by some other credit card system. If you must grant consumers credit and if you cannot use someone else's system, be prepared to spend a rather substantial amount of money in legal fees for complying with the numerous federal requirements on extension of consumer credit.

Alternative Dispute Resolution Techniques

The 1980s saw an increased interest in ways to resolve disputes other than through our traditional judicial court system. Some of the techniques are new, and some are old. They all, however, have as their common objective the resolution of commercial disputes in less time, at less cost, and with less emotional turmoil and hostility than result from litigation. Following is a rundown of some basic techniques that are available. You may find that some will be appropriate for a number of your small business transactions.

Arbitration

This is one of the oldest and most traditional of the alternative methods currently available. There are many who perceive arbitration as having many shortcomings, and this is one of the reasons for the development of the other techniques on this list. However, some of those perceived shortcomings can be avoided, and to some extent arbitration may have been overly maligned in the past.

Traditional arbitration is binding. This characteristic distinguishes arbitration from most other alternatives. Under traditional arbitration rules, if you have an agreement by both sides to submit the matter to binding arbitration, the decision of the arbitrator is final. Neither party can appeal it to the courts. In other words, you give up one of the rights that Americans hold so near and dear to their hearts—to have your day in court no matter what the cost or how long it may take. That, however, is not the case in every arbitration. In all alternative dispute resolution techniques, the key is flexibility. Since they are outside the court system, they are not subject to any of the legal rules that apply there. You can make your own rules. One of these rules could be to have an advisory (rather than binding) arbitration hearing.

One of the raps against arbitration is the perceived tendency of arbitrators to "split the baby" (i.e. render compromise judgments). However, you can avoid this by simply telling the arbitrator that you do not want a compromised judgment. Some people call this "baseball arbitration" because it is used in resolving baseball club disputes with the players (others call it "high/low" arbitration). In a baseball arbitration, the arbitrator has only two available options: in favor of the player for the salary he wants, or in favor of the ball club for the amount it wants to pay. The idea is that the arbitrator has only two choices—one position or the other—and has no authority to render his or her own independent judgment as to the real value of the ball player. You can easily arrange that same type of result in a commercial dispute.

In summary, arbitration is a valuable means of resolving a dispute and some of the reasons for its not being appropriate in a given situation can easily be resolved.

When is arbitration appropriate? There are two points at which you and the other side can decide if you want arbitration. The first (and the one we think most productive) is when drawing up the contract itself. You simply put a clause into the contract saying that any dispute under the contract will be settled by binding arbitration. If you want to use a standard form promulgated by the American Arbitration Association you can do that. It reads as follows:

> Any controversy or claim arising out of or relating to the contract, or the breach thereof, shall be settled by arbitration in accordance with the commercial rules of the American Arbitration Association, and judgment upon the award rendered by the arbitrators may be entered in any court having jurisdiction thereof.

The second opportunity for going to arbitration is when your contract does not have an arbitration clause and a dispute arises. That, however, is likely to be a little harder to negotiate because once you know what the dispute is about, arbitration is likely to favor one party or the other.

The Escalation Clause

By inserting an escalation clause into a contract, the parties agree that before either sues the other, the party will "escalate" the negotiations to more senior company officials. This is intended to accomplish the basic objective of getting the matter resolved by people who do not have a personal stake in it.

The Cooling-Off Period

Another alternative to litigation is a simple cooling-off period. The contract can state that neither party will institute any legal action against the other unless there has been notice of an intent to do so in a 30- to 60-day cooling-off period, during which there shall be at least two meetings of responsible company officers in an attempt to settle the dispute.

The Least Favored Choice of Form Clause

This technique is aimed at making it hard for one party to sue the other by saying that the party filing suit must go to the other's home jurisdiction to do so. For example, suppose there is a contract between an Ohio company and a California company, with a clause saying that if the Ohio company wants to sue the California company, it has to do so in California, and vice versa. The idea is to slow the process and discourage the parties from automatically filing suit when they might be able to resolve the matter by negotiation or compromise.

Mediation

Mediation is also a type of ADR. We are as familiar with this in labor disputes, and mediation in a commercial case is very similar. The parties select a respected neutral party who might be able to engage in a little "shuttle diplomacy" to bring the parties to a settlement. The key to the success of mediation is the mediator. The person chosen must have the absolute confidence of both sides.

Legal Dispute Consulting

This is something like getting a legal second opinion. If you are thinking of suing someone, or if you have been sued and are in a defensive
struggle, you might want to get another lawyer to take an independent
look at the situation. That second opinion may give you some insights
that your first lawyer—who is probably very close to the transaction—
does not have. Even if the second opinion doesn't help, it is still helpful
in planning your strategy.

Rent-a-Judge

The rent-a-judge system is used a lot in California, largely because of
state laws that make it attractive. You simply hire someone as a private
judge, usually a retired judge, but not necessarily. The reason the practice is so successful in California is that state laws make the decision of a
rented judge as legally binding and effective as the decision of a regular
courtroom judge. Other states are looking at this system, and it may be
that in your state something along these lines is possible. Its advantage is
usually speed. In some states, such as California, the courts are crowded
and it may take you years to get a trial date. The rented judge system
can be moved along much faster.

Negotiation

Negotiation is, of course, the oldest form of alternative dispute resolution. What is new is that it has been elevated to somewhat of a science or
perhaps a pseudoscience. There are dozens of books on negotiation,
courses in law school to teach lawyers how to negotiate, and even entire
programs at major universities, such as the highly publicized one at
Harvard, which study the dynamics of negotiation.

All other alternative dispute resolution techniques involve negotiation. In today's business world, there is a premium on having access to
professional negotiators, who need not actually be retained professionals, although they can be. They also need not be lawyers, although many
lawyers have increased their own training in negotiation and are very
good at it.

11
OSHA and the Environment

One of the important reasons for a second edition of this book is the growth in the importance of OSHA and the environmental laws for all businesses, including smaller ones. In the first edition, we discussed OSHA, but the emphasis was on handling the OSHA inspection. That discussion, still relevant, is retained in the second edition. However, some very important things have happened:

1. Today, one of the most important OSHA requirement is that we must have a *Hazard Comminucation Program*. This is a program to make sure all our employees know about the chemicals they work with and what they can do to handle them safely.

2. Now environmental laws can, in some cases, be the single most important factor in deciding how you run your business or even if you can go into certain businesses. Concern with our environment today is very high. The laws say essentially that if you cannot afford to respect the environment, you should not be in business at all.

The remainder of our chapter discusses some of the basic things all of us know about OSHA and the environmental laws.

OSHA Requirements

In general, the Occupational Safety and Health Act (usually simply called OSHA) requires us to provide a safe and healthy place for our

employees. In particular, most small businesses need to meet OSHA requirements in the following areas.

Record-keeping

The system of record-keeping for OSHA is rather simple but important. There are basically only two required forms. The first is OSHA
Form 200, which is simply a log and summary of occupational injuries
and illnesses. The second is a supplement Form 101, which describes
each incident in more detail. Form 101 asks for essentially the same
kind of information that the state Workers' Compensation laws require,
and many companies use forms that satisfy both requirements. The law
requires an annual posting of the summary of all occupational injuries
and illnesses. OSHA publishes a very helpful booklet containing all the
forms you need and an explanation of how to fill them out. You should
have this. It is available from OSHA or any local OSHA office.

Notification of OSHA in the Event of
a Serious Accident

While there is no general requirement to file any forms with OSHA, if
there is a serious accident resulting in either a death or hospitalization
of five or more employees, you have to notify OSHA promptly. Failure
to do so would be viewed as a very serious violation by OSHA.

Discrimination and Employee
Discipline

It is illegal to discharge or discipline employees for refusing to do work
that they reasonably believe exposes them to an immediate and serious
risk of harm. It is also illegal to discriminate against any employee because they may have complained to OSHA about safety violations.
These are also viewed very seriously by OSHA.

Employers also have to make a reasonable effort to make sure employees actually observe the safety rules, including wearing appropriate
personal protective equipment. It is not enough to just provide equipment and issue safety rules. Supervision, training, and discipline for
those who fail to use the equipment or follow the rules are required.

Criminal Penalties

There are criminal penalties under OSHA if someone is killed at work
because of a willful violation of a safety standard. In addition, local

prosecutors have shown a propensity to bring these cases. They can be brought either against the corporation itself or against the responsible officers of the corporation.

What should you do if a worker refuses to do a job because of an alleged safety problem? This depends on the magnitude of the safety problem. The general rule is that the worker is supposed to do the work, and if the worker feels there is a safety problem, he or she can complain to management, OSHA, or both later. However, if there is a risk of serious bodily harm, the worker has the right to refuse the work. It is very risky to order a worker to go ahead with a job that the worker feels presents a risk of serious injury. That could lead to OSHA problems, possibly including criminal exposure if, in fact, there is an accident and the worker is killed. There have been several cases on essentially those facts, and company management and those who ordered the workers to proceed make attractive targets for local prosecutors.

The OSHA Hazard Communication Rule

The newest, and perhaps most important aspect of OSHA for many companies, is compliance with the so-called hazard communication rule. Essentially, this rule says that any company using any hazardous chemicals in the workplace must have an adequate program for informing the workers of the nature of those chemicals, their possible effects, and safe ways of handling them. Here are some things you should know about this rule.

Who Is Covered.   All companies are covered. When the rule was originally promulgated, only manufacturing companies were covered. It has since been amended, however, to include all companies. Even companies that have only office workers are covered.

Which part of the standard applies to you depends on what type of a company you are. Chemical companies and companies who import or sell chemicals are covered by more parts of the rule than companies that simply use the chemicals in the workplace. This discussion is limited to the latter category. If you manufacture, import, or sell chemicals, you need a much more detailed discussion.

There is no minimum number of employees required for an employer to be covered, but the program itself will not necessarily include every employee in your company. Only those employees who may be exposed to hazardous chemicals under normal operating conditions or foreseeable emergencies are covered. This is almost certainly going to cover production workers, line supervisors, and maintenance workers.

It may, however, even include office workers who may use chemicals in duplicators, grounds-keepers who may use fertilizers or other maintenance chemicals, and security guards who may be stationed near places where chemicals are used or stored. Even temporary help will be covered if their job fits this description.

What Is Covered.   The standard says that all chemicals in the workplace must be evaluated to see whether or not they are potentially hazardous. Many chemicals are automatically listed as hazardous. If all you do is purchase and use chemicals, you are entitled to rely on the information supplied by the manufacturer of the chemical. This information is generally contained in a document called a Material Safety Data Sheet (MSDS). As a practical matter, compliance for most companies with this portion of the program means:

Being sure you get the MSDS for each chemical you buy.

Keeping an up-to-date notebook of those MSDSs where all of your employees can examine them.

The Hazard Communication Program.   The Hazard Communication Program you need consists of the following:

1. *A written program*: Don't forget this, the OSHA inspector will want to see it. There is no prescribed form. It can be any length or style, but it must describe how you are going to meet the labeling, MSDS, and training requirements. It must also list all the hazardous chemicals in the workplace. Generally, this will simply be a list of all the chemicals for which you keep and MSDS.

2. *A program for labeling all chemicals in the workplace*: This program is aimed at informing workers of the nature of the chemicals and the possible effects on their health or safety. Chemical suppliers are required to provide these labels on the containers they ship. In most cases, that will be enough. However, if your practice is, for example, to purchase chemicals in large containers, and then transfer them into smaller containers for use throughout the plant, you will have to be sure the smaller containers are properly labeled.

3. *The MSDSs*: These are perhaps the key documents for most of us.

4. *A program of information and training*: This is for the employees to make sure you carefully and completely explain all the chemicals, their dangers, safe handling, etc.

Help from the Government.   This is one place where the government has done us a considerable service. They have, in essence, put together a very good "how to do it" booklet. It is called OSHA Publication 3104, *Hazard Communication — A Compliance Kit*, and it is available from the Superintendent of Documents, U.S. Government Printing Office, Washington, D.C. 20402, (202) 783-3238, GPO Order No. 929-022-000009 for $18.00. In our view, it is a must have publication for all companies.

Other publications which you should probably have can generally be obtained free from OSHA field offices or the OSHA Publications Office, Room N3101 Washington, D. C. 20210 (202) 523-9667. These include:

OSHA-2056   All About OSHA

OSHA-2098   OSHA Inspections

OSHA-3021   Employee Workplace Rights

OSHA-3084   Chemical Hazard Communication

OSHA-3047   Consultation Services for the Employer

OSHA-3088   How to Prepare for Workplace Emergencies

OSHA-3071   Job Hazard Analysis

OSHA-3077   Personal Protective Equipment

OSHA-3079   Respiratory Protection

OSHA-3085   OSHA Computerized Information System (This contains chemical information on about 750 workplace chemicals.)

The actual text of the OSHA Hazard Communication Standard Title 29 of the Code of Federal Regulations part 1901.1200

Worker's Compensation Issues

The general rule is that, if a worker is injured on the job, the worker's sole claim against the company is under the applicable worker's compensation statutes. Generally, the worker cannot sue the company for negligence. However, there is an important and growing exception. That is for "willful and intentional" conduct. Virtually all worker's compensation laws contain such an exception to the general rule. The usual example given is that if a doctor hired a nurse and then raped the nurse, the doctor could not claim that the nurse's sole right against the doctor was worker's compensation. The rape would be an intentional act.

While we would all agree with that example, some cases have extended that broad exception for intentional acts to other less obvious things. For example, if a company knows about the existence of hazardous chemicals in the workplace and forces the workers to go into those hazardous areas anyway, there could be a possible suit by the workers against the company outside the workers compensation law. Another example is a company that knows its vehicles are unsafe, but has the drivers continue using them anyway. If there is an accident, the injured driver may have a suit against the company which could be maintained outside the workers compensation umbrella.

Some lawyers have called this the "erosion of the worker's compensation shield" and that is a descriptive phrase for what is happening. The extent of the erosion varies from state to state. However, no discussion of employee safety would be complete without mentioning it. We can no longer assume that worker's compensation will protect us against suits from our employees if those suits allege that we knowingly and willfully exposed them to injury.

Inspections

I would like now to turn to OSHA inspections. The Occupational Safety and Health Act allows occupational safety and health inspectors to enter your plant, without notice and without any warrant, and conduct a "wall-to-wall" inspection. This is one of the most controversial features of the law. These unannounced inspections were thought to be unconstitutional. Certainly, it would be unconstitutional to allow the police to come into your home unannounced and conduct a search unless they had a search warrant or unless you consented. Employers thought that the same thing should apply to the business location. Federal inspectors should not have carte blanche access just because they feel like coming in and snooping around.

After a number of cases, the Supreme Court did decide that this was, in fact, the rule. Occupational Safety and Health Act inspectors do not have the authority to enter your premises unless they have a search warrant or unless you voluntary grant them permission to do so. This has given rise to considerable disagreement among lawyers as to whether it is more desirable to force OSHA inspectors to get a warrant or to cooperate voluntarily. Generally, OSHA can get a warrant to enter your premises; it is only a matter of delay. To be sure, there are exceptions— OSHA must apply to the nearest federal district court. There are hundreds of federal district courts and even more federal district court judges. Each has his or her own ideas as to when a search warrant should be issued. In some cases, federal district courts have refused to issue the warrant because OSHA has failed to show any probable cause for thinking that there was a violation. In other cases, OSHA inspectors have been denied access to a plant and never gone to court to get the warrant. In other cases, OSHA has gotten the warrant, but not come back to inspect the plant. It appears from discussing this matter with many different lawyers that these situations are in the minority — but it is a significant minority. Most of the time, OSHA will ask for and receive a warrant if it is denied access to the plant. In most of these situations, OSHA inspectors will in fact come back and inspect the plant. Thus, it is possible that if you ask them to get a warrant, the only thing you will do is delay the inspection a few days and cause them to be very mad when they come back.

The overwhelming majority of large companies seem to be granting OSHA inspectors access to their plant voluntarily without insisting on a warrant. However, in the case of small business, I just do not know what the statistics show. Certainly, there are many lawyers representing small companies who take the position that their clients should not allow an OSHA inspector into the plant unless the inspector has a warrant. Other lawyers think this is a waste of time and energy and simply counsel their companies to do a good job on employee safety and let OSHA conduct its inspections. My advice is between the two extremes.

1. I do not think you should welcome the OSHA inspector with open arms and invite him or her into your plant to issue you citations.
2. I do not think that, unless there are special circumstances, you should automatically declare legal war on OSHA if one of their inspectors arrives at your plant.
3. I do think you should understand the extent to which OSHA applies to your plant, and if it is substantial, have an OSHA lawyer available. Since you will need an OSHA lawyer available to respond to emergencies, you might as well ask that lawyer for his or her views on inspections and warrants. Keep in mind, however, that the decision is for you, and the best legal answer might not be the best business answer. After all, you have public relations and employee relations to consider also.
4. Remember that you do not need a definite and unalterable action plan before the OSHA inspector arrives. You can wait until the inspector arrives and then discuss the matter with the inspector. Here are some questions to ask *before* you grant access to the plant.
   a. Why is the inspector there?
   b. Has any employee filed a complaint? (You do not want the name of the employee that filed a complaint, you just want to know if a complaint has been filed.)
   c. What parts of the plant does the inspector want to see?
   After you know these facts, you can make a much better judgment of

what to do than simply deciding beforehand without knowing the circumstances. For example, if the inspector said that an employee had filed a complaint about a particular machine and all the inspector wanted to do was inspect that machine, you have a very different situation from one where the inspector says he or she has no particular reason for wanting to inspect your facility—your name just came up, and he or she wants to go through the whole facility on a wall-to-wall inspection which he or she estimates will take three days.

Also, remember that you do not have to make any decision right then. You can call your OSHA lawyer. If your OSHA lawyer is not available, you can ask the OSHA inspector to either wait or come back later. You can even ask for two or three days to discuss the matter with your lawyer. The OSHA inspector will almost always go along with this, because it will take that long to get the warrant anyway. However, if a serious employee complaint is involved, the inspector may say that you can have your two or three days, but he or she must get a warrant so that when he or she does come back, you will have to let him or her in.

Of course, these couple of days have secondary benefits. Not only can you go through your plant and remedy possible safety problems before the inspector comes back and cites you for them, but you can also make sure that your forms and records are up to date, that the plant is generally in good order from a housekeeping standpoint, and that appropriate people in the plant know about the forthcoming inspection.

I do not recommend asking OSHA inspectors to get warrants unless you are willing to get your lawyer involved in the inspection. When you start to get technical like this, you definitely need good legal advice at every stage of the inspection.

Your Rights During the Inspection

Once you grant the inspector permission to enter your facility without getting a warrant, that does not mean you cannot change your mind. Of course, everything that the inspector sees while on your premises with your permission and everything the inspector sees while he or she is being escorted out the door after you have changed your mind are possible subjects where citations can be issued. The only time you would want to change your mind is if you granted an inspector access to your facility and he or she started what you believe to be an extremely burdensome and nit-picking investigation, and you wanted to get your lawyer involved. Most of the time, OSHA inspectors are not this way. In the overwhelming majority of cases, an OSHA inspection will not be too much of a problem to you. He or she may find a few safety violations, and there may even be a citation and some penalties. These, however, will be rather modest. OSHA penalties are generally not large—on the order of hundreds of dollars rather than thousands. Many cases involve penalties of less than $100. Of course, there may be many violations, and in total the amount of penalties may drift into the low four-figure range, but that is the exception rather than the rule. Imminently hazardous situations can, however, generate substantial penalties.

During the inspection, the following ground rules apply:

1. Technically, the inspector is a guest in your plant (unless he or she has a warrant). You have the right to stop the inspector from doing anything you object to. This, however, is somewhat akin to asking for a warrant—a strict insistence on all your legal rights at every stage. I do not recommend this unless you have previously consulted your lawyer and have a clear set of ground rules and procedures.

2. In most cases, you will not elect to insist on your legal rights in this manner and will allow the inspector certain liberties, which might include talking to your employees in private or taking pictures.

3. If the inspector arrives with a warrant, his or her authority will be spelled out in the warrant. You should read it, and I think you should get legal counsel promptly. If the inspector has gone to the trouble of getting a warrant without first asking you to grant access to the plant voluntarily, you can be sure OSHA thinks there are serious problems.

4. In many cases, the OSHA inspector will want to take air samples or make measurements of the noise levels in your plant. If this occurs, you should take exactly the same measurements at exactly the same time. If you have these kinds of situations, you are getting into a more technical set of problems, and expert legal and industrial hygiene help is probably called for.

5. The inspection will always begin with an "opening conference," at which time the OSHA inspector will want to see your records. These will include the OSHA forms discussed above as well as any other required forms or records relating to one of the many chemicals which OSHA regulates. The inspector will also want to see your written Hazard Communication Plan. Medical records of your employees might also be requested but this is rare. The OSHA inspector will inform you of your basic legal rights, and will ask for an employee representative to accompany him or her. If your shop is unionized, or if you have a safety committee, you probably have such a person. If not, the inspector will simply talk with employees during the inspection.

6. The inspection will usually concentrate on either safety problems

or health problems, depending on your particular operation, Most inspectors will be generally knowledgeable about all safety and health matters, but particularly knowledgeable about either safety (things like machine guards) or health (things like air contamination or noise or chemicals). OSHA will probably know quite a bit about your business before they send an inspector and will, therefore, be able to make a decision as to which type of inspector would be most appropriate.

7. After the walk-through inspection, there will be a closing conference where the inspector will tell you informally about any problems that were observed. If the inspector his observed a serious hazard which is severe enough to ask for immediate corrective action, he or she may ask you to shut down a particular operation until the problem is corrected. On the other extreme, if there are minor problems which can be corrected easily (such as housekeeping violations), he or she may also ask you to correct them immediately and not write them up at all. In between these two extremes are the kinds of violations which are not too serious, but which do take some time to correct. In occupational safety and health jargon, this is called the abatement period.

One of the most productive things you can do during the closing conference is to try to negotiate a reasonable abatement period. Keep in mind that the OSHA inspection process is basically a negotiation process, and to some extent at least, you can persuade the inspector to give you enough time to fix a violation so that you do not have to contest a citation merely for that purpose. Also, there may be problems that you know about that the inspector does not. For example, the inspector might have noticed a particular machine guard which he or she feels is inadequate, and you may have already spent considerable time and effort trying to design a better one. In such a case, you should certainly tell that to the inspector so he or she can take this into consideration. Perhaps the machine guarding question is a little more difficult than the inspector had thought, and he or she will allow you more time for abatement.

8. After the inspector leaves, he or she will go back to the OSHA office and discuss this matter with his or her immediate superiors. Within a month or so, OSHA will issue you any citations which they feel are justified. Once you receive a citation, you have only 15 days to object to it. Otherwise, it becomes final and you can no longer object. Thus, it is very important to examine that citation immediately and determine whether or not you want to make any objections. If you do, you have to do so very promptly, and I strongly suggest consultation with your lawyer at this point. I am not saying that you should have your lawyer handle the entire process, because it is something that you or your employees can probably do. On the other hand, it may be more efficient for

your lawyer to do it, and in any event, your lawyer should review the work. Remember that contesting an OSHA citation is just like any other administrative proceeding. It is rather technical, and you are building a very important record. These are the kinds of things which your lawyer can help you with.

The On-Site Consultation Program

In the late 1970s, OSHA instituted a program where their inspectors would voluntarily go through your plant without a formal inspection. Before that time the only way an OSHA inspector could help you was by a formal inspection. This meant that if the inspector saw a violation, he or she was required by law to issue you a citation. There was no such thing as informal consultations or informal help. However, in response to widespread criticism, principally from small businesses, OSHA changed their rules, and this is no longer the case. OSHA can, and is indeed happy to, have an inspector visit your plant and have a mock OSHA inspection. If the inspector sees a violation, he or she will just tell you about it, but will not issue you any citations or make you pay penalties. Further, the whole thing is confidential. No records are kept or follow-up inspections made to see that you have, in fact, corrected any problems. Further, if you have a " regular" inspection later on, there is no connection between that and the informal one. In short, there is nothing to lose.

There is one very minor hitch. If the inspector sees something which is imminently hazardous, he or she will ask you to correct that problem immediately. In that situation, he or she may even issue you a citation and, if the problem is serious enough, may ask you to shut down the operation until the problem is corrected. Except, however, in the case of one of these imminently hazardous problems—which I assume you could spot yourself—there is no downside risk of having one of these voluntary OSHA on-site consultations. They are performed by OSHA without any cost to you whatsoever.

When the voluntary on-site consultation program was first announced, there was some uneasiness about it. Admittedly, the concept of calling up a federal inspector and asking him or her to come out and go through your plant seemed like unnecessarily asking for trouble. However, experience has not proved out these first fears. I know of no complaint that OSHA has misused this on-site consultation program. The OSHA on-site consultation program may not be necessary or appropriate for everyone, but I do think it is useful in some cases and worth your careful consideration. It is certainly an inexpensive and efficient way to obtain expert technical advice on safety problems.

Help from the Government

OSHA is one of the most helpful government agencies. They not only have the on-site consultation program mentioned above, but do an excellent job of preparing useful brochures which explain to you and your employees exactly what your rights and obligations are. Of course, OSHA will also give you copies of the law, the regulations, and the standards. I suggest you take advantage of this service and ask for this material. Following is a list of things I would ask for at this time, but keep in mind that OSHA is always generating new pamphlets and revising existing ones. A personal visit or a telephone call to your local OSHA office will provide you quite a bit of free and useful information.

The publications on the list are all free. Many of them would be useful in training or safety sessions and could probably be obtained from OSHA in quantity for this purpose. Usually, your local OSHA office is the best place to get them. (There are more OSHA publications you should have relating to the Hazard Communication Rule which are listed in that section of this chapter.)

OSHA Handbook for Small Businesses. Publication No. 2209, 1979, 51 pages. Good discussion, applicable to both small businesses and individual facilities of larger companies. Contains general discussion of procedures for compliance plus good, understandable checklists.

Record Keeping Requirements Under the Occupational Safety and Health Act of 1970. Contains the relevant record-keeping forms and instructions. Forms are Form 200, Log and Summary of Occupational Injuries and Illnesses; and Form 101, Supplementary Record of Occupational Injuries and Illnesses.

OSHA Inspections: How You Can Help—A workbook and guide. Publication No. 3023, 1979. Booklet is meant for employees to help OSHA inspector, but is also useful information for employers.

OSHA Health Inspections: How You Can Help—A workbook and guide. Publication No. 3024. Same as above, except concentrates on health inspections instead of safety inspections.

The following are good pamphlets averaging about 30 pages in a 3 × 7 inch format. They are typically meant for employees, but provide useful information for employers—especially for safety sessions or training programs.

Job Safety and Health: OSHA Inspections Are Only the Beginning. Publication *3029.*

You Have a Right to Protect Your Life on the Job; That Right Is Called ELEVEN-C. Publication *3032.*

Job Safety and Health: Answers to Some Common Questions. Publication *3024.*

Health and Safety Committees: A Good Way to Protect Workers. Publication *3035.*

The Target Health Hazards. Publication *2051.*

General Industry OSHA Safety and Health Standards Digest. Publication *2201.* A short and small (4 × 5 inches, 50 pages) digest of most important general industry standards.

Construction Industry OSHA Safety and Health Standards Digest. Same as above for construction industry.

Environmental Law

In the first edition, we did not even cover environmental law. That is not to say it was not important. We had the Clean Air and Clean Water Laws which were sometimes difficult and costly to comply with. However, they are both "permit driven." In other words, the key concept is that any company covered must get a permit to discharge into the air or water, and exactly what you can and cannot do is covered in detail by the permit. That is still the case. These laws are very important. However, if you do not discharge anything into the air or water, they are simply inapplicable to you.

We now, however, have some new environmental laws that are very important for all business. In fact, any corporate lawyer today, must also be an environmental lawyer. Virtually all corporate transactions must take into account the enormous exposures inherent in these environmental laws.

In addition, new environmental laws, deal with the disposal or handling of hazardous substances, have substantially changed the business landscape. All you need to do is drive down the road and see how many independent or mom and pop gas stations you see to understand the effects of the rules on underground storage tanks. In essence, the government has made a policy decision that if you cannot afford to handle underground storage of petroleum properly, you should not be in business. Since this costs more than many small companies could afford, the operation of gas stations is basically limited to fairly large companies with the resources to remove and reinstall underground storage tanks in accordance with these new rules.

Similarly, dry cleaning establishments and print shops (those using printing presses rather than photocopy duplicators) are much different undertakings today than a few years ago.

Here is a very brief rundown of the new breed of environmental laws, and what they can mean to you.

Superfund

This is perhaps the most important and pervasive of the new laws. It started out innocently enough. The idea was simply to clean up hazardous waste sites. A new tax on petroleum and chemical companies was supposed to pay for some of the clean-up, and for the rest the responsible parties—those who put the hazardous waste in the ground—were going to have to pay.

Then, however, things mushroomed. First, there were a lot more hazardous waste sites than people thought. Second, it cost a lot more to clean them up than originally anticipated. These two developments made the total bill many billions of dollars.

The law developed too. The key part of the law affecting us as smaller companies is the so-called joint and several liability provision. This says that the liability for the clean-up rested on the companies who put the waste in the site to begin with, and that liability was joint and several. Thus a company that contributed only a small amount of waste—say one barrel—to a site that was going to cost many millions of dollars to clean up was potentially responsible for the whole bill, not just its proportionate share. The average cost of clean-up for a dump site today can easily get to $50,000,000. This is largely because the clean-up standards are so strict that just about the only way to satisfy them is to incinerate all the material at the site—a very costly process.

Here are a few samplings of the situation as we face it today.

1. Say you sent one barrel of waste to a site where it was disposed of completely in accordance with the laws and regulations at the time. Now, because of the stricter standards, that site has to be cleaned up under superfund at a cost of $50,000,000. You are one of the parties who gets a notice from the EPA saying that you are responsible for the clean-up. You have the potential of being responsible for the entire $50,000,000. True, most of the time this will not happen. In most cases there can be a settlement where you pay something bearing a reason-

able relationship to the volume of waste you contributed. However, you can depend on a substantial bill for both the cleanup cost and attorney's fees to handle the problem for you. You will need a lawyer. With exposures like that, this isn't the place to try to handle it yourself.

Superfund Rule 1: When you get a notice from the Environmental Protection Agency concerning your potential responsibility for a cleanup bill, immediately contact your lawyer. Do not respond in any way until you do that.

Superfund Rule 2: If you receive any other information from any source (such as citizen complaints, newspaper articles, etc.) saying that a place where you may have sent waste may need to be cleaned up under superfund, contact legal counsel immediately. There may be some things you can do to minimize your exposure.

2. Say you have, in the past, disposed of waste improperly on your own property. You now face these very serious potential problems:

It may be necessary to clean up the problem. If the toxic substances you buried or dumped start leaching into the ground water or onto someone else's property, you may get a lawsuit from either the EPA, local officials, or neighbors. Remember there is no fault concept here. The fact that it was not illegal to dump waste on your private property when you did it makes no difference. You, as the landowner, are responsible for the clean-up, and you may be responsible for any damages to neighboring property or ground water.

When you sell the property, you can expect an environmental audit, which will disclose this problem. Further, if you do not disclose the problem to a subsequent purchaser, you could be liable for damages for fraud or concealment of the situation. You cannot get out of environmental responsibility for your property by selling it.

Superfund Rule 3: If you know about, or suspect, a problem of toxic waste on property you own, contact your legal counsel promptly. There may be some steps you can take to minimize your financial exposure. In general, the recommendation will be to do everything you can to remedy the problem yourself as soon as practical. That is almost always the lowest cost alternative. If you wait until, for example, you sell the property, the buyer will almost certainly discount the price it is willing to pay by more than your actual cost of remedying the problem. If you wait for a complaint from public officials or private parties, you will no longer be in control of the methods for dealing with the waste, and you can expect your costs to go up substantially.

3. Say you want to buy a piece of real property or acquire a business that has real property. If toxic wastes are buried on that property, you, as the current landowner, will more than likely be responsible for their cleanup. This cost would be many millions of dollars.

Superfund Rule 4: Never purchase any real property, or acquire any business that has real property (including occupying it as a lessee) without a thorough environmental audit. There are now many consultants in the field that do these audits. We suggest, however, that one of the people you call to get assistance is your lawyer, as the contract with the environmental consultant is itself an important legal document.

Superfund Rule 5: The financial institution will also more than likely want an environmental audit. You should encourage this, but in my judgment, not rely on it. It may be possible to save money by having one firm do the audit both for the financial institution and for you, but you should definitely have a contract with the auditing firm. The reasons for the environmental audit for the lender, and the standards they will use, are very similar to those you would use, but not identical. For example, if you are purchasing a piece of property for $1,000,000, and asking for a $600,000 loan, a lender may well feel that a $ 100,000 environmental problem is not too serious. Their security is still a piece of property worth, net of the environmental clean-up costs, $900,000. Obviously a prudent buyer would look at it much differently.

Superfund Rule 6: There is no such thing as a standard environmental audit. Like all audits, the environmental audit must be tailored to the situation. The environmental audit can be a fairly low-cost item that can be done quickly, or a high-cost item that takes several weeks, depending on the facts. Rule 6 is always to be sure you understand exactly what was done in an environmental audit or what will be done in one you ask for. These audits range from someone going on the property and looking around and perhaps checking publically available records for prior uses of the property, to someone actually boring holes in the soil to see if there are any buried waste. You should know what was done, and be comfortable with it, before buying any property. Do not just take a statement that "an environmental audit was done and no problems were found" to dispose of the problem.

4. Say you contract with a company to properly handle some waste you develop. You pay a premium price, and deal only with a company with all the permits and authorizations required. That company (the dump site operator) actually disposes of the waste in a way that is entirely in compliance with all existing rules. Alternatively, suppose they

do not—but rather dispose of the waste improperly. When that dump site has to be cleaned up, you will be one of the responsible parties—and therefore liable for some portion of the clean-up cost. The fact that you acted prudently yourself is not a defense.

Superfund Rule 7: Sites that are operating entirely within the law today may be subject to a superfund clean-up tomorrow. Some environment lawyers use the phrase "todays RCRA site, tomorrows superfund site." (RCRA is the solid waste law under which dump sites are permitted.) Rule 7 is therefore not to take anything for granted when you contract with people to dispose of your waste. A good investment may be of your time a little detective work to fund out where the wastes are going what is really being done with them, and how well the waste disposal facility is operating.

In summary then, the superfund law has become a very important part of running your business, and of buying or selling businesses or real estate. Our brief discussion touches only some of the high points. Most law firms today have environmental experts, and much of their time and effort is spent on superfund or superfund related problems. Any business owner needs to be aware of the fact that these problems are potentially very large. They cannot be taken lightly, and timely legal advice is always a good investment.

Solid Waste Disposal

The solid waste disposal law alluded to in our discussion of superfund is technically called the Resource Conservation and Recovery Act (hence RCRA). It is the law regulating companies dealing in the field of disposal of hazardous solid waste. Specifically, the law governs any company operating a disposal facility or any company operating a transport facility that hauls hazardous waste.

The heart of the law is the so-called manifest system. It works basically like this:

1. All companies in the industry must have a permit, and companies wanting to dispose of hazardous waste must deal only with permitted transporters or disposal facilities.
2. The permits are waste-specific. In other words, one facility may be permitted to handle one type of waste, while you will need to send another type of waste to another facility.
3. All companies generating waste are responsible for identifying the content of the waste, so that they can have it transported by and disposed of at the facilities permitted for that waste.

4. Once you identify your waste, and transporters and disposal companies who are authorized to handle it, you prepare a manifest for each shipment. The manifest is in four parts, and the system works substantially like this:

    a. You prepare the four-part form. You identify the waste, the permitted transporter, and the permitted dump site.

    b. You give the manifest to the transporter, retaining part 1.

    c. At the dump site, the transporter gives the manifest to the dump site operator, retaining part 2.

    d. The dump site operator retains the third copy and returns the fourth to you, thus closing the circle.

        If you do not get that fourth copy back within 35 days, you need to make inquiry. If you do not get it back within 45 days, you need to tell the EPA.

        The idea is a so-called cradle to grave system for the disposal of hazardous waste.

Here are some things to know.

1. If you intentionally misstate the composition of the waste, there are criminal penalties.

2. The word "intentionally" in this law is broader than deliberately making wrong entries in the form. It connotes also some degree of reasonable competence and conscientious effort. In other words, you can go to jail under this law even if you do not actually know about the problem, if the EPA and courts feel that you should have known about it.

3. Assuming the transporter or the dump site improperly disposes of the waste, you can still be liable—even criminally—if the EPA or courts feel that you should have known what was going on. One of the facts that sometimes may give this impression is if you get an unreasonably low price for either the transportation or the disposal of the hazardous waste.

Summary and Conclusions

All business owners should know the content and amount of their companies' wastes. There are some "small quantity exceptions" in the law, but under todays version of the rules, the exempted quantities are very, very small. In most cases, about one-third of a 55-gallon barrel per month will be enough to trigger this law, and the amounts are even smaller if the waste is very toxic.

After you ascertain the content and amount of waste you generate, you should be sure it is being disposed of properly. This means it is being transported by a permitted hauler to a permitted dump site. This may be expensive. You may need to factor this cost into your business operations. If you operate a print shop, for example, the waste ink and other chemicals used in the printing process must be disposed of properly, and this is an added item of cost. Just about any company that does some production work will have some type of hazardous waste that needs to be disposed of properly under this law.

There are also consultants in this field. A team approach, where you discuss the general compliance with your lawyer and consultants, help you to identify which wastes are hazardous, what your wastes contain, and the permitted transporters and disposal facilities you can use.

Insurance Note.   Please be sure to look at Chap. 14, "Your Lawyer and Your Insurance," for a brief discussion of the possibility that some of your environmental law exposures could be governed under your comprehensive general liability insurance contracts.

12
Product Liability

What Is the Problem?

The two kinds of companies that face the largest product liability problems are manufacturers of capital goods which are used by employees of other companies (lift trucks, metal working equipment, power presses, etc.) and manufacturers of consumer goods which have shown a high degree of hazard to the consumer (lawn mowers, hand power tools, bicycles, ladders, boats, etc.). These kinds of companies have had tremendous problems getting product liability insurance at any reasonable cost—even if their claims history has been 100-percent clear. The problem of product liability created quite a stir in the mid-to late 1970s—rising to the point of near-crisis. Largely, this was the result of a relatively small, but still significant number of horrible example-type cases, most of which involved a variation on one or more of the following themes.

1. A capital goods manufacturer would point to a case where someone was injured using a piece of equipment it had made many years ago and which might have been resold, rebuilt, and even misused by the employees. The employee who was injured on the machine could not sue the employer, because workers' compensation would preclude that. The injured employee could, however, sue the maker of the piece of equipment alleging that it was defective because it did not have proper guards, was not designed properly, etc. Many of these cases were successful—as they could well be today.

2. Small manufacturers of consumer goods which have proved to be frequent sources of injury to consumers have had their insurance canceled and been unable to obtain new insurance at any premium, or if insurance was offered, it was offered only at a high cost. Sometimes, an

insurance company would quote a premium which was one to one and a half times the coverage. In other words, for $50,000 of coverage the premium might be $80,000. The insurance company then would be assuming that there would be 1.6 losses of the maximum amount each year in order to justify this kind of premium. Some small companies never had any claims at all, and therefore questioned the rate-making processes of the insurers in setting these kinds of rates.

3. Very large companies which could afford self-insurance or could afford to establish captive insurance companies were not hurt as much as smaller companies. Lobbyists for small companies felt that Congress ought to enact laws which would reverse this trend.

4. Some insurance companies had been turning to a "claims made" basis. This means that the insurance applies on the date a claim is made, not necessarily on the date the injury was caused or the date the product was made or sold. Some insured companies had been surprised by this because it was not fully explained to them. They felt that it was unfair—especially when coupled with the insurance company's right to cancel the insurance. If a claim is made which looks like it might be the first of a series, the insurance company might cancel the insurance, and no new insurance would be obtainable. The insurance company that had previously accepted the premiums—perhaps for many years— would be off the hook except for the small number of claims which were instituted before the policy was canceled.

The law on product liability cases is extremely bad for defendants. Essentially, the courts in almost all jurisdictions have, under one theory or another, taken the view that an injured plaintiff ought to be able to recover from either the manufacturer or the seller of a defective product which caused the injury. Further, the meaning of "defect" has been expanded to include almost anything imaginable, including foreseeable misuse by the plaintiff, improper labeling or warning, or even claims made by the maker of a product that the product was "safe" when it was capable of causing an injury.

There are some other, social factors which have also made the picture bleak. Juries tend to award large amounts as damages when injured. Verdicts over a million dollars are becoming common. Another social factor is that Americans are becoming more litigious. When I graduated from law school in 1966, product liability suits were fairly common. Ten years before that they were rather rare, and 10 years after that, there was a virtual flood of them. Today, if a consumer is injured, the first thing he or she thinks about is whether he or she can sue someone for the injuries. Usually, a lawyer will be able to develop a claim against someone, and if the injury is real, there will almost always be a recovery. A person who comes into court with a lost arm, permanent disfigurement, or paralysis is going to leave with a lot of money. It's just that simple. Very few juries are going to send such a person home empty-handed when the defendant is an impersonal corporation which everyone on that jury is going to assume is covered by an even more impersonal insurance company.

Do You Have the Problem?

The first thing you have to do is understand if there is any circumstances whatsoever where your product could cause personal injury to others. Even if you are simply in a retail or wholesale operation, you still have to be concerned, because the plaintiff can sue *either* the person who sold the product or the company which made the product. For example, many cases involve suits against grocery stores alleging personal injury caused by the explosion of bottles of pop. The plaintiff can sue the grocery store, and the grocery store can, if it so desires, join the maker of the soft drink in question in the lawsuit. This does, however, place the burden on the grocery store, and you could envision a situation where a plaintiff would be able to recover from the grocery store but the grocery store would not be able to recover from the company that sold it the product in question. One of the basic principles of product liability law is that an injured consumer cannot have his or her rights cut off by any kind of contract. Thus, no matter what kind of contract, disclaimer, etc., is involved, if a consumer is injured, he or she is very likely to be able to recover. The rule is exactly the opposite, however, in a commercial situation. A store, being a business enterprise, is not a "consumer." If you buy things from a manufacturer pursuant to a contract which limits the manufacturer's liability *to you* in the event of a personal injury, that contract is certainly valid. The manufacturer cannot cut off its obligation to the consumer, but the consumer does not have any obligation to sue the manufacturer — the consumer can simply elect to sue you because you are handy and locally available. The first step, then, is to assess your level of risk. It would be a good idea to discuss this with your lawyer, because there are many legal implications in determining that risk.

I am sure you have all read newspaper accounts of persons injured by products which really do not seem hazardous. Such cases include the following:

■ Liability based on fingernail polish catching fire when a cigarette ignited the fumes.

- Liability based on clothing catching fire if the clothing was not coated with flame-retardant materials. Further, the major flame-retardant material was determined to be a potential carcinogen by the Consumer Product Safety Commission, causing many recalls of products which used it.

- Liability based on a lawn mower injury where the injured consumer was using the lawn mower to trim hedges.

- Liability for an oven based on an injured woman who fell when the oven door collapsed while she was standing on it to clean the kitchen.

- Liability for injuries caused when the roof of a car collapsed when the driver ran the car into a ravine, based on the theory that the roof should have been strong enough to stand up if the car rolled over in an accident.

- Liability for loss of an eye when an auto mechanic used a screwdriver for a chisel and when he hit it, a piece of metal broke off and went into his eye.

Remember that all these kinds of cases are very common. Would you have thought that a six-figure verdict could be rendered against you because of a screwdriver that you either made or sold? These examples show clearly that you must discuss this subject with your lawyer to assess your level of risk. You can also get useful information from your trade association and your insurance broker.

How Can You Minimize the Problem?

While you cannot eliminate the product liability problem, there are a number of things you can do to minimize it. Following are some examples — each of which is rather technical and should be discussed with your counsel.

Your Forms

Make sure, to the maximum extent possible, that transactions are governed by forms prepared by you, not the other company's forms. This brings into play the entire battle of the forms process discussed in Chap. 10. While you cannot cut off any consumer's rights by doing this, you may be able to cut off rights of intermediaries, or you may be able to give yourself additional rights against other people involved in the transaction — for example, your suppliers.

Express Warranties

Evaluate all express warranties. A breach of warranty is one of the theories that a plaintiff can use to bring a successful product liability claim. The kind of warranty you give, of course, is a mixture of legal, financial, and marketing considerations, but do not forget the product liability aspect. Also, do not forget that "warranties" is an extremely broad term—they include any promise you make about your product or, indeed, even a description of your product.

Your Written Materials

Consider your warnings, your instruction booklets, your advertisements, and any other written statements that go along with your product. Many lawsuits have been based not upon the product itself but on a failure to warn of a defect, or some misstatement or failure to describe a hazard in the literature that went along with the product.

Consider Insurance

You will have to consider your insurance coverage both with your lawyer and with your insurance advisor. Following are some suggestions.

1. Do not select an insurance carrier on the basis of cost alone. Make sure the carrier has a practice of ethical dealings with the public and has adequate claims—servicing facilities for your company—including expertise in the product or products you sell.

2. Participate actively in the discussion of any reserves. Review these at least quarterly.

3. Participate actively in all major claims, and discuss them with the insurance carrier. Do not just assume that once a claim is presented it is the insurance company's problem.

4. Make sure you get any available technical assistance from your insurance company. You are paying for it and might as well take advantage of it.

Records

Records are both a problem and an opportunity. If you have good records to show exactly how products were tested, how specific reports of injuries were evaluated, etc., that might help you. On the other hand, it might also hurt you, because it would show a prior knowledge of the hazard in question. The worst thing that you can have are documents which show that you knew about an alleged hazard and did nothing to correct it. The multimillion-dollar verdict in the case against a large auto-manufacturing company (involving an alleged defect in the design of one of its models, causing it to catch fire when hit from the rear) was based in large part on the fact that internal company documents disclosed a knowledge of this danger and, allegedly, a failure to make the relatively minor change which would have minimized the danger.

Get Legal Counsel

Make sure you have access to a good product liability lawyer. Chances are that if you are a small company, you will want to depend upon the insurance company's lawyers to actually handle the defense of any claims. On the other hand, that does not mean you should not have your own lawyer to monitor the cases and also to provide you with advice on how problems can be minimized.

Price

In my view, this is the most important aspect of product liability. Product liability exposure is a cost, and you should make sure you understand that cost and have built it into the price of your product. Further, rights against your suppliers, or indemnification from your suppliers, is valuable, and the reverse is also true. If your suppliers will not indemnify you from product liability claims based on their products, they are not entitled to the same price as companies who will. Do not get caught in the middle. Don't say that, from a marketing point of view, you simply cannot insist on disclaiming product liability responsibility from your commercial customers (remember that you cannot disclaim it as far as the consumer is concerned), but that you do not have the bargaining position to make your suppliers stand behind their products. That places *you* on the product liability hot seat, If you end up in this position, you simply must have adequate insurance, and you must price your products according to this risk. Remember, it is something which can strike from out of the blue. One day you look at your history and find that you never had a problem. The next day you get served with papers on a lawsuit where a person has been injured—perhaps in a bizarre type of accident-and wants damages in the millions of dollars.

Prevention

Of course, your first line of defense on the product liability front ought to be simply to make safe products. We all know this is a goal which is virtually unattainable—but that does not mean you should not strive to come as close as you can. Your lawyer can help you minimize your exposure, but cannot do very much in the area of helping your business operation, other than pointing out litigated cases involving your products or similar products and alerting you to dangers which have already caused injuries.

In summary, then, I recommend that the product liability question be placed on your agenda of things to discuss with your lawyer if you feel that it is even remotely a problem for you. Your insurance advisor should also be involved in this discussion. Unfortunately, unless the present situation changes, if you really do have a serious product liability problem, your insurance advisor may have difficulty in placing insurance which is cost-effective. Your lawyer can also be of only limited help, because while he or she can tell you how to minimize exposure, he or she cannot eliminate the exposure altogether, and in a small company even one lawsuit can literally wipe the business out.

I do not have any very good solution to this problem. It has been studied by numerous federal agencies and task forces of interested people and they have not figured out any solution either. It is an inherent problem of small business. That is the place where even a single catastrophe can put you out of business, where insurance coverage may not be available at a reasonable cost, and where self-insurance is not a viable alternative.

The Consumer Product Safety Act

The Consumer Product Safety Act was enacted in 1972 to establish an independent regulatory agency with extremely broad powers to protect consumers from unreasonable risk of injury from hazardous products. The agency has the authority to set safety standards for consumer products and to ban those products showing evidence of undue risk of injury. The Act covers consumer products, but defines a consumer product very broadly as "any article or component part thereof—whether American-made or imported—manufactured or distributed (1) for sale to a consumer for use in or around a permanent or temporary residence or a school, in recreation or otherwise; or (2) for the personal use, consumption, or enjoyment of a consumer in or around a permanent or temporary household or residence or a school, in recreation or otherwise." The reason I mention this law is to make small business owners aware of the following important things:

1. If you make or sell a consumer product, you simply must be aware of this law and know whether anything you sell is subject to any Consumer Product Safety Act standards. Your lawyer can help you — so can the Consumer Product Safety Commission in Washington.

2. The act contains a very important notification provision which provides that if you make or sell a consumer product which you think may cause a serious risk of injury, you must notify the Consumer Product Safety Commission. Failure to do so can cause serious civil penalties and, in extreme cases, criminal penalties.

The relevant provision of the Consumer Product Safety Act on the notification provision is as follows:

> Section 15(b). Every manufacturer of a consumer product distributed in commerce, and every distributor and retailer of such product, who obtains information which reasonably supports the conclusion that such product—
>   (1) fails to comply with an applicable consumer product safety rule, or
>   (2) contains a defect which could create a substantial product hazard as described in subsection (a)(2)
> shall immediately inform the Commission of such failure to comply or of such defect unless such manufacturer, distributor, or retailer has actual knowledge that the Commission has been adequately informed of such defect or failure to comply.

The definition of "substantial product hazard" in subsection (a)(2) referred to above is as follows:

> (2) a product defect which (because of the pattern of defect, the number of defective products distributed in commerce, the severity of risk, or otherwise) creates a substantial risk of injury to the public.

There are elaborate regulations under this provision, and I suggest that anyone involved in the manufacture or sale of consumer products obtain a copy from his or her lawyer and read and understand them. You simply cannot ignore this requirement. If someone sues you alleging that he or she has been seriously injured by one of your consumer products, or if a customer writes you and says that there was a "near miss" on a potentially serious injury caused by a defect, you must not only decide what your monetary risk might be and what you should do to minimize it, but also address this notification requirement. Again, the key thing is not to do anything foolish such as finding out about a serious problem and then sweeping it under the rug and hoping no one will ever find out. It is almost impossible to incur criminal penalties under the substantive provisions of the Consumer Product Safety Act. You have to fail to do something the commission tells you specifically to do. However, in cover-up cases, the prosecutions are not under the substantive law; they are under the other criminal laws which make obstruction of justice, conspiracy, and making false statements to the government a crime.

The bottom line on the Consumer Product Safety Act is this:

1. Make sure you know about it and what requirements apply to you.
2. Make sure that if the law applies, you appreciate the implications of the notification requirement and consult your lawyer any time you think it *might* be applicable.

13
Intellectual Property

Intellectual property includes patents, copyrights, trademarks, and trade secrets. These can be a very important part of your business, and your lawyers can both help you exploit them and prevent others from taking them away from you. This chapter will, give you a few of the basic principles and suggest some things that you should keep in mind and discuss with your lawyer.

The Intellectual Property Bar

In common parlance, intellectual property lawyers are sometimes called "patent lawyers," since much of their work is usually related to getting patents for you. In today's information society, however, the so-called "patent bar" now does much more work in the other areas of intellectual property (principally copyrights and trade secrets) than they did before. In general, your corporate attorney will probably know next to nothing about patent law, but may have some familiarity with copyright law and trade secret law. One of the first things you need to do if intellectual property is any part of your business is to be sure you are getting appropriate legal advice. If patents are important to your business you will certainly want a patent lawyer, and if you have one, the lawyer may be a better person to get advice on copyrights and trade secrets than your general practitioner. If patents are not an important part of your business, most general practitioners today, with a working knowledge of copyright and trade secret laws, will probably be able to handle matters. You should, however, keep in mind that this whole area of intellectual property is somewhat specialized and technical, and it is certainly a good idea to sit down with your corporate general lawyer and discuss his or her knowledge of these areas, as well as whether you need a specialist.

Patent Law

The best known of all intellectual property rights is the patent. Patent laws are federal; one United States patent law applies in all jurisdictions, and there are no state patent systems. There are, however, numerous foreign patent systems. If you transact business internationally you will have to obtain patent protection in any country in which you may want to try and exploit the patented product. This can be a very expensive process, but it is necessary. Your United States patent will protect you here, but there is no reason for a European company, for example, not to manufacture and sell the patented article in Europe unless you have some European patents to protect it. The cardinal rule on patents, therefore, is to be sure you have thought about your entire market and that, if it is international, you have discussed this with your patent counsel so that appropriate international protection can be obtained. This is likely to be rather expensive, so you do not want to simply get patent protection automatically. You would want to have some reasonable basis for believing that you can market your product internationally before doing that.

What Things Are Patentable

You can get a patent on either a product or a process. The major requirement is that your product or process be "substantially different" from the "prior art," which is simply patent jargon for what existed before your invention. There is, however, one rather important qualification—the so-called one-year rule. A patent can be granted for anything you invent within one year after it is "reduced to practice." So, for example, if you invent a new kind of machine, you have one year after you have finally perfected that new machine to get a patent. There are two obvious problems:

1. Exactly when you perfected the device (or reduced it to practice) is likely to be the subject of some debate.
2. If you use the device yourself for more than one year after you have

perfected it, you will not be able to get a patent at all. You will have precluded this method of coverage, and you will be restricted to trade secret protection.

Thus, the decision on whether you want to get a patent on something cannot be postponed indefinitely. You have to make the decision promptly because of those two factors. It is much better to be conservative and file your patent application early than chance some second guessing as to when you might actually have reduced your invention to practice, and how long you used it yourself before you filed the patent application.

Infringement

If you have a patent and someone else makes a product infringing that patent, you are entitled to both an injunction precluding them from continuing the infringement and damages. Similarly, if someone else has a patent on a product that you are making, that person is entitled to an injunction against you and damages. Note that there is no knowledge or intent requirement here. The beauty of a patent—if you have the patent—is that you do not need to show that anyone intentionally infringed the patent or even that they knew of the existence of your patent. All you have to show is that their product is covered by your patent. This has two obvious implications.

1. If you are making something that you do not have a patent on yourself, you want to be very sure that no one else has a patent on it either. A patent lawyer can generally search the patent records and come up with a fairly good, but usually not conclusive, opinion that some product either does or does not infringe patents already issued. The question of whether it is necessary to have a patent search is often subjective, but you certainly should be discussing it with your patent lawyer. The results of inadvertently infringing a patent can be very substantial. In well publicized litigation, the court found that Kodak had infringed one of Polaroid's patents and caused Kodak to go out of business in that particular product line; this is only one example of how serious these suits can be.

2. The second obvious implication is that, if you are successful in getting a patent on your products, you don't need to be very careful about safeguarding the specifications of the products to prevent others from manufacturing them. Further, if someone happens to independently in-

vent the product themselves, you can still prevent their manufacture or sale of it through enforcing your patent.

Licensing

The way that patents are generally exploited is through a license. Of course, you can also retain the patent yourself; there is no requirement that you license anyone else to use it. On the other hand, most of the time someone holding a valuable patent will find that it is in their best economic interest to license others to use it. In general, you can license people to use the patent in such a way so that your own market is protected. Similarly, you may very well be able to obtain valuable rights to manufacture important products by obtaining a license to use other people's patents.

Patent licenses tend to be rather long and complex documents. (They do not have to be; we have seen two- or three-page patent licenses that seem to work quite well.) If you feel that a patent of yours could be licensed, or if you want to license someone else's patent, you can assume that fairly substantial legal fees may be involved in drafting and negotiating the appropriate licenses. This should be done by your general corporate lawyer, your patent counsel, or both. I like to recommend both. The reason is that these patent licenses often raise issues, such as antitrust and tax issues, outside of patent law. Many patent lawyers tell me that it is wasteful to have a general corporate lawyer review these because the patent lawyers are fully capable of steering clear of antitrust, tax, and other problems in the patent licenses that they draw. Many of them are. Accordingly, it isn't a hard and fast rule that you absolutely need to have both your general corporate lawyer and your patent counsel involved in patent licensing matters, but I believe it is at least worth some discussion. Involving your general corporate lawyer should not be costly since you really want to ask the general corporate lawyer to briefly review the license and offer any legal comments that seem appropriate. If the license doesn't have any significant legal problems, a corporate lawyer ought to be able to do that in only a couple of hours. If legal problems need to be explored, obviously more time would be required. You are entitled, however, to be sure that your general corporate lawyer and your patent lawyer coordinate their efforts. You do not want both, for example, to research antitrust or tax questions that might be relevant to your license.

In my experience, most patent lawyers and corporate lawyers have established a good relationship and work quite well together. In fact, many patent lawyers will suggest that you have your general corporate lawyer review important licenses. Remember, however, that you are entitled to control that process, and you do not want to give your patent lawyer a blank check with your general corporate lawyer so that unnecessary time and money are spent in possibly duplicative efforts.

Patent Litigation

If you feel that you should institute a patent suit against someone for infringement, or if you feel you need to institute a suit against one of your licensees, you have in my opinion a very high-risk transaction. You should definitely have any patent litigation, even something as simple as a suit for a money judgment against a licensee who hasn't paid royalties, reviewed by both your patent lawyer and your general corporate lawyer. History and experience teach us that patent suits are almost always met with counterclaims or defenses, which can be very disadvantageous to you. For example, you may end up in a complicated antitrust suit where your licensee has alleged that you have engaged in some type of antitrust violation. If the licensee is successful, you may end up paying the licensee triple damages, as well as the licensee's attorney's fees, and having your patent declared unenforceable. That does not mean that you should be afraid to enforce your rights under a valid patent that is subject to a well drafted patent license agreement. It doesn't however, mean that your general corporate lawyer ought to be involved in those decisions.

Copyrights

Copyright law is in some ways similar to patent law. First, we have only one federal copyright law, no state copyright laws. Second, the way you exploit copyrights is either to produce the copyrighted material yourself, to license them to others, or obtain a license yourself. If you do want to license copyrights, either as the licensor or the licensee, everything said about the patent license would be appropriate. It probably should be at least in some measure a joint effort between your patent and intellectual property lawyers.

There are, however, some important differences and additional things that we ought to discuss relating to copyrights. Following is a very brief discussion of things we should all be aware of.

Obtaining a Copyright

Until recently, it was necessary to put a copyright notice on material in order to have it protected by a copyright. We have all seen these notices; they contain the word "Copyright" or the copyright symbol (©), the year, and then the copyright owner. That rule, however, has now changed and there is no longer any need for any copyright notice. Current law is that copyright protection arises automatically and even if you don't have any copyright notice on the work and even if you never bother registering it with the U.S. Copyright Office. There are, however, some very clear legal benefits in putting the copyright notice on your work and in registering copyrights. This means the following.

1. When you are looking at other people's documents — catalogs, software programs, documentation, instructional manuals, etc. — that you may want to copy, you cannot conclude that you are free to copy it if there is no copyright notice on the document. Indeed, the opposite is the case: Copyright protection exists automatically even in the absence of any copyright notice. Accordingly, you will have to get permission or a license to copy anything that would be protected by a copyright.

2. Correspondingly, since there are legal benefits from placing the copyright notice on the work and in registering it with the Copyright Office, you should carefully consider those options in anything that you create yourself. Putting the copyright notice on the item is easy, and you should probably do that as a matter of course. Registering the work with the U.S. Copyright Office is not difficult. Forms are available in almost all libraries and it is possible to do this yourself. It is also, however, at least somewhat of a hassle, and there are modest filing fees, so you don't want to bother unless the item in question has some potential economic value.

The Work Made for Hire Doctrine

Another unusual twist in copyright law has to do with the so-called work made for hire doctrine. Consultants' clients relied on this doctrine in consulting and other agreements to be sure that they owned the copyrights and things written by consultants, not the consultants. But the doctrine has been eroded to the point where we should no longer rely on it. Instead, all consulting and other similar agreements that might result in something copyrightable should have a copyright assignment clause. In some cases you might even want a separate copyright assignment form.

The basic law is that the copyright vests automatically in the creator of a work, not in the person who may be paying the bills. Therefore, if you hire a computer programmer to write a program, or a photographer to take pictures, or a technical expert to prepare some manuals for you, the person who creates those things is the owner of the copyright. Formerly, to vest the copyright in the company hiring those people, a clause was inserted into the contract stating that the things they create would be considered a work made for hire under the copyright laws. Recent-court decisions, however, have made it clear that this doctrine is much narrower than many had assumed. Accordingly, the only prudent thing to do is get those copyright assignment clauses and forms. One of the illustrative forms in this chapter is a simple consulting agreement which shows, in a very simple case, what the copyright assignment clause might say.

Software

Another legal issue to keep in mind is that packaged software is protected by copyright. This means that your word processing, data base, or spreadsheet programs are all protected by copyright. If you have three secretaries using a word processing program, you should have purchased/licensed three copies of that program. You should not simply get one copy and then have two additional ones made. In these days of proliferation of computers and programs, this sometimes can get complicated. Many large companies have sophisticated procedures for making sure that they do not inadvertently infringe software copyrights. Some, for example, require that every user of a computer maintain a list of programs that they are authorized to use, and there may even be some auditing of that. For example, if a company has purchased ten copies of a word processing program, and then adds another person and purchases another computer, there would be some auditing procedure to be pure that the eleventh person didn't simply copy a program from one of the first ten. Similarly, if the three of the ten word processors also worked on spreadsheets, there may be three spreadsheet programs. Again, there would be some auditing to be sure that, if you had purchased three copies of the spreadsheet program, you had only three people using it. In a small company you may not need such elaborate policing mechanisms, but you should at least remember that software is protected by copyright and you should purchase/license enough copies of the programs to avoid infringement.

What Constitutes Infringement

Actual copying, of course, constitutes infringement. But is it infringement to paraphrase or copy only a few portions of some copyrighted work? This issue is being litigated a lot today in the context of software. The basic rules are fairly easy to state.

1. If someone copies someone else's computer program, that is clearly copyright infringement.

2. If a computer programmer goes into a room, closes the door, and creates on his own initiative a complete computer program, which just happens to be very similar to someone else's computer program, there is no copyright infringement. Note that this is a rather important difference between copyright law and patent law. Copyright does protect against "copying," but it does not protect against someone independently coming up with essentially the same thing.

3. It's the middle ground that causes the difficulty. Computer programmers may use quite a bit of their own thoughts and ideas, but they may also take one or two thoughts and ideas from someone else's program. Is that infringement? The answer is that it depends on all of the facts, mostly whether the court feels that the person "copied" anything substantial. The legal point to keep in mind is that if you have occasion to use other people's copyrighted works in order to develop something for yourself, you want to discuss the extent of material that you take from the copyrighted work with legal counsel. The law is fairly restrictive: You can't take very much without running into infringement problems.

Example

Your company publishes a newspaper or a magazine and wants to excerpt only a few pages from a popular book of several hundred pages. Is this infringement? The answer is probably yes. The fact that you took only a few pages is immaterial.

Example

Your company distributes 500 different products, and you want to prepare a catalog. One of your competitors has prepared the kind of catalog you want. You copy the information from the competitor's catalog, including specifications, part numbers, etc., and use that as your own catalog. All of the information contained in the competitor's catalog is publicly available. Is this infringement? The answer is clearly yes. Even though the information is publicly available, and you could have gotten it yourself, you did not. You copied from your competitor's catalog and that is a violation of the copyright laws.

What Is Not Protectable by Copyrights

Some things cannot be copyrighted. The biggest example is ideas. The copyright protects only the expression of an idea, not the idea itself. Obviously, there can be some close cases as to where you have taken only an idea and where you have taken the expression of that idea, but the concept is quite clear.

Example

Lotus, a very popular spreadsheet program, can protect the precise way in which it operates, including the screen displays, all of the instructional manuals, and so on. Lotus, however, cannot claim any copyright protection in the idea of having a spreadsheet program. Competitors are free to write their own spreadsheet programs, which may accomplish precisely the same function in almost exactly the same way so long as they do not do so by copying any of the Lotus material.

United States Government publications, statutes, cases and generally anything created by our government is also free from copyright protection. Note, however, that the way in which the material is printed on a page can be protected by copyright. For example, a legal case is not copyrightable but if a publishing company goes to the expense of typesetting the case in a certain way in a book, that typesetting or the arrangement of the case in the book is protectable by copyright.

Trademarks and Trade Names

The federal trademark law is the Lanham Act, sometimes called the Trademark Act, which was adopted in 1946 and amended on several occasions. The legislation provides for a federal registration system of trademarks, and the federal registration gives the registered owner of the trademark certain procedural rights should the owner decide to sue another company for infringing the trademark or trade name.

One of the amendments to our trademark law involves the use of the trademark. Under the previous law, you obtained rights in a trademark by using the trademark, not by registering it. Indeed, the trademark registration process itself required that you show the Trademark Office exactly how you had used the mark. That created some problems for test marketing. How could you test a product without running the risk of someone stealing your trademark after you had used the mark but before you had got enough use to justify a trademark registration? Accordingly, the law was amended so that now you can register a trademark as long as you intend in good faith to use it in the reasonably near future.

When to Register Trademarks

Assuming your company has trademarks or trade names that you feel are valuable, ask yourself whether they should be registered to provide protection against others using the same or very similar names or marks. On the other hand, a trademark registration, while not terribly expensive, does cost something; so you wouldn't want to do it unless there was some benefit. The following examples show either where you should register the mark or where that might not be necessary.

1. Let us first consider the local store situation. This could be any store, but for purposes of illustration, let us assume that you have developed a way to manufacture inexpensive replicas of old spinning wheels and other antiques and want to sell them locally in a store under the trade name Oak Wheel Reproductions. You have your trade name Oak Wheel Reproductions set forth in a distinctive style of type. You have a die made, and you have it burned into all of your items. You also have a sign at the front of your store which displays this trademark. Should you bother to register the mark?

If you are going to sell the products locally, there would not appear to be any advantage in registering the mark. By using the mark and advertising it in your city, you will have obtained all the rights you need to stop anyone else from using that mark in your city to sell competitive goods. However, there would be nothing to prevent someone from selling competitive goods bearing that same mark in another city. The theory is that you have used your mark and thereby obtained rights in it in the area where you have actually used it, but you have not obtained any rights anywhere else.

2. Suppose we change our example from a store that you opened to sell things that you make yourself to a pilot program to sell the same things which you manufacture on a relatively large scale and hope to sell in a broader geographical area. Here you will be spending a substantial amount of money on advertising in the local area in hopes that you can sell your product in other locations in the future. If you do not register the mark, you may find that someone beat you to the punch in another city or another state. This, then, is the classic and most important situation where registration of your mark is necessary. It will prevent you from spending a lot of money only to allow someone else to capitalize on it before you do.

3. Pursuing our example, suppose that you are a national furniture company and want to establish a new line and introduce it nationwide. You are going to embark on a nationwide program of advertising Oak Wheel Reproductions in all major cities. Here there would be little to be gained by registering the mark because your actual use of the mark in all of the major markets would give you sufficient rights to prevent anyone else from selling competitive goods with that mark. On the other hand, a nationwide advertising campaign like this costs so much money that it tilts the scales in favor of registration. The registration fees are substantial when weighed against the revenues of a small local shop but insubstantial when weighed against the advertising costs and promotional expenses for a nationwide campaign. In this situation, almost all major companies will register the mark even though they know that the increased rights they get by registration are more procedural than substantive.

In summary, then, if your business is such that you are talking about a small local area and you are sure that you are going to use your trademark and trade name in your area and are not going to want to expand into other major cities or states, there is not much point in spending money for attorneys' fees and registration costs to register your trademark. By the same token, if it is a pilot program and you intend to expand it, it is almost imperative that you register the mark.

When Should You Conduct a Trademark Search?

The other side of the trademark registration coin is trademark infringement. If someone else registers your Oak Wheel Reproductions mark in another city, you still have the right to use that mark in your city. Again, use is much more important than registration. Since you will know who is advertising products similar to yours in your own city, you do not have to spend the money for a trademark search. On the other hand, if this is only a pilot program, you are going to want to know about other trademark registrations so that when you expand your product, you will not run into problems. That is where a trademark search becomes very important. For a relatively modest amount, you can have a professional trademark-search company search all of the registered marks for those which may be confusingly similar to yours. If you run across someone else who has used your Oak Wheel Reproductions mark in another city but has not used it nationally and has not registered it, you are not in too much trouble. Only one city is off limits to you. On the other hand, if someone has registered the mark nationally, you are going to be under some restriction in your future use. You can still use it in your own city because the other person has not acquired any rights by use. On the other hand, you are not going to be able to register your mark because of the other person's prior registration, so when you start expanding, you are likely to run into competition from the other person, and his or her rights on the mark are going to be superior to yours in the new areas. It is very important that you know this and weigh the risks involved before you spend a lot of money promoting a mark which you cannot register nationally.

In summary, then, if you are going to be using a trademark or a trade name, you want to ask yourself the question, Where am I going to want to use this mark? If the answer is, in a very small geographical area where you know the situation firsthand, there is no need to register the mark yourself or to conduct a trademark search. On the other hand, if there is a realistic possibility that you will expand your use of the mark into other areas, both a registration and a search would probably be justified. Assuming the matter does not get too complicated, you are talking about $2,000 to $2,500 for both the registration and the search.

Trade Secrets

A trade secret is anything which you use in your business, which gives you a commercial advantage, and which is not generally known. Commonly, trade secrets are thought of as secret formulas or top secret processes for manufacturing esoteric things. They are not limited to these things. A customer list, a mailing list, a list of qualified vendors, and a list of customers who pay their bills as opposed to those who do not are all extremely valuable trade secrets. Financial information can also be a valuable trade secret. The prices you pay for components in your products, the wages you pay your employees, the total cost of each product, your overhead expenses, and your capital resources are all things which competitors might like to know and which would help them hurt you. To the maximum extent possible, you want to prevent this from happening.

As we discussed in our patent section, one of the biggest potential trouble spots for losing trade secret information is employees leaving your company and either starting their own business or going with a competitor. Therefore, in addition to having employees sign an invention assignment form as we discussed in the patent chapter, I always recommend having the employee sign a confidentiality or nondisclosure agreement. I have included a sample drawn from a relatively large company which had extremely valuable trade secrets of this classic type. You may not need something this elaborate. On the other hand, it is easier to take things out of the form then to add them in, so I think you can use the form to some advantage. As in the case of all forms, it is much better if you can obtain specific legal advice from your own lawyer as to how the form might be tailored to your own circumstances.

Another way to inadvertently disclose your trade secrets is through supplying information to your vendors. In some cases, this is necessary, because you will have to give the vendor enough information for him or her to supply you with the proper kinds of products. In this situation, I recommend a nondisclosure agreement carefully spelling out exactly what kind of trade secret information you are supplying and exactly how it will be protected. I have included several forms which deal with this point from several angles so you can see the differences. One form is to use where you are giving your confidential information to the vendor, another is for cases where the vendor asks you to sign an agreement holding his or her information in confidence, and the third is for a joint exchange of confidential information. Obviously, these forms take different positions, and you must be careful to use the proper form in the proper circumstance. Of course, these examples are intended to facilitate working with your lawyer—not to be simply copied.

Note the specificity with which the nondisclosure form covering your information deals with the relevant considerations. Don't be bashful. Spell all these things out. You should know who in the vendor's company is going to have access to the information, how that access is going to be granted, etc. In my judgment, it is *entirely inadequate* to simply write a short cover letter stating that a package of confidential information is trade secret and you expect the vendor to treat it as such. That is much too vague. If the information is worth protecting at all, it is worth going those extra steps to make sure the vendor understands that he or she (and perhaps other named persons in the vendor's company) is the *only* one who is granted access to the information, that no copies should be made, that the copies should be returned to you, etc.

In short, unless you are going to do this right, I question whether it is worth bothering with at all. The reason for this approach is partly legal—if you do not do a good job, a court is likely to say that you didn't exercise enough care over the information to bring it up to the status of a legal trade secret. The major reason, however, is simply that most people honor agreements they sign. If you spell out everything in the agreement as to exactly what is going to happen with your information and how you are going to get it back, in the overwhelming majority of circumstances, it will turn out that way. On the other hand, if you leave the entire matter so vague that you cannot reasonably expect the other party to understand exactly what his or her responsibilities are, I do not think you are in much of a position to complain if the other party is careless with your data.

The other half of the trade secret problem is receiving information from other companies in confidence. There are two parts to this half. One is a commercial-type arrangement, and the other is receipt of unsolicited ideas. In the commercial setting, there is every reason to believe that you will get some benefit from the information, and the only question is how much trouble you should go to in order to protect the information. As you can see from the form, I have limited your obligations in this kind of situation to treating the information with the same degree of care as you treat your own information. If you undertake a higher degree of care, be sure to exercise that higher degree, because if you do not, you can be subject to many dollars of damages if you lose the other party's trade secret. These are usually negotiated documents—the other party has lawyers, too. The key thing to remember is that this is an important and sensitive area. Read all the documents and make sure you understand and abide by them. Essentially, the same thing is true for exchanges of information, except that here the obligations of both parties are in the same piece of paper. That makes it a little difficult to say that you want a low degree of care for you to exercise concerning the other party's information and the reverse for the other party in the case of your information. You must hit a politically acceptable medium, and I have tried to do that in the suggested form.

The last area I would like to discuss is the receipt of unsolicited ideas. The experience of most large companies has shown that unsolicited ideas are not very valuable. They either are something you already knew or are not worth doing. They can, however, be productive of litigation. Suppose, for example, someone gives you an idea which merely duplicates something you already have in process. When you finally come out with your new product using this idea, the person who submitted you the idea is going to think you stole it, and you are then going to have to prove that you thought of it first yourself. This can be costly and difficult. For that reason, most large companies either will not accept unsolicited ideas at all or will do so only pursuant to a letter agreement similar to the one I have included.

In summary, you are likely to be in one of two situations regarding industrial property. The subject may be very important to you, in which case a patent, trademark, and copyright lawyer is going to be a very important part of your team. The key thing here is to pick a good one who will provide you good, economical, and efficient service. Everything I talked about in Chap. 1 about selecting your general lawyer would, of course, be applicable, with one very important addition. Your patent, trademark, and copyright lawyer will have to work hand in hand with your general corporate lawyer, so they will have to get along well. In fact, the best way to find a good intellectual property lawyer is to have a good general corporate lawyer who will recommend one. If your business is not such that you need an intellectual property lawyer, the items that I discussed in this chapter probably will not cause you much of a problem if you keep in mind the precautions I have suggested.

Summary

To briefly review, ask yourself the following questions.

1. What is my patent situation? Do I have adequate protection for my own patents? Am I sure I am not infringing anybody else's?

2. What is my copyright situation? Do I have anything that I should copyright? If so, have I placed the copyright notice on it? Am I sure when I prepare my catalogs and other materials that I am not infringing someone else's copyright? Have I obtained permissions when I have copied things out of other people's catalogs, or do I have some exposure to the trap line problem?

3. Am I using a trademark, and should it be registered? Am I spending a lot of money to promote my mark in hopes that I can expand it in the future? If so, did I have a trademark search and register my mark so that I can do this without legal difficulties?

4. What is my trade secret situation? Do I have any (keeping in mind that customer lists and financial information can be considered trade secrets)? If so, have I taken the rudimentary steps necessary to protect them, including having my employees sign nondisclosure agreements, being careful about information I give to vendors, and using agreements with vendors and others whenever I do have to disclose proprietary information? Have I protected myself from the unsolicited idea trap by refusing to accept unsolicited ideas unless I have a protective letter absolving me from any responsibility?

Note. The following form covers *both inventions* and *confidential information*. The drafter can divide these into separate forms if it is thought appropriate. If the agreement is not signed at initial employment, be sure it is supported by consideration.

EMPLOYEE INVENTION AND CONFIDENTIAL INFORMATION AGREEMENT

[The Company Name]
XYZ, Inc.

XYZ's special competence in its various fields of endeavor is the secret of its growth, and provides the source of both career opportunities and security for employees throughout the Company. Career opportunities for XYZ people have been a Company tradition not only because of the generally high competence of XYZ personnel, but also because of Company growth. Such growth depends to a significant degree on the Company's possession of proprietary information—not generally known to others—more and better information than others have about research, development, production, marketing and management in XYZ's chosen fields.

To obtain such information and use it successfully, XYZ spends considerable sums of money in research and product development, product improvements, the development of marketing methods, and service to its customers. Many XYZ people make major contributions. This results in a pool of information which enables XYZ to conduct its business with unusual success, and thus with unusual potential for its employees. However, this potential exists only as long as this information is retained proprietary within XYZ. Once generally known, this information gives no advantages to XYZ, its employees or its stockholders.

In effect, all XYZ employees have a common interest and responsibility in seeing that no one employee accidentally or intentionally siphons off or distributes to non-XYZ people any part of this pool of information.

To help protect you, all other employees and the Company against such a possibility, this Employee Agreement has been prepared for your signature and the Company's so that we have a common understanding concerning our mutual responsibilities in this connection. Please read it carefully so that you may understand its importance.

_____   _____   _____

Employee's Last Name   First Name   Initial

Inventions

1. I will promptly disclose in writing to the Company all inventions, discoveries, developments, improvements, and innovations (herein called "Inventions") whether patentable or not, conceived or made by me, either solely or in concert with others during the period of my employment with the Company, including, but not limited to, any period prior to the date of this agreement, whether or not made or conceived during working hours which,
   (a) relate in any manner to the existing or contemplated business or research activities of the Company, or
   (b) are suggested by or result from my work at the Company, or
   (c) result from the use of the Company's time, materials, or facilities and that all such inventions shall be the exclusive property of the Company.

2. I hereby assign to the Company my entire right, title and interest to all such inventions which are the property of the company under the provisions of paragraph 1 of this Agreement and to all unpatented inventions which I now own except those specifically described in a statement which has been separately executed by a duly authorized officer of the Company and myself and attached hereto and I will, at the Company's request and expense, execute specific assignments to any such invention and execute, acknowledge and deliver such other documents and take such further action as may be considered necessary by the Company at any time during or subsequent to the period of my employment with the Company to obtain and defend letters patent in any and all countries and to vest title in such inventions in the Company or its assigns.

3. I agree that any invention disclosed by me to a third person or described in a patent application filed by me or in my behalf within six months following the period of my employment with the Company shall be presumed to have been conceived or made by me during the period of my employment with the Company unless proved to have been conceived and made by me following the termination of employment with the Company.

Confidentiality

1. I will not during or at any time after the termination of my employment with the Company use for myself or others or divulge or convey to others any secret or confidential information, knowledge or data of the Company or that of third parties obtained by me during the period of my employment with the Company and such information, knowledge or data includes but is not limited to secret or confidential matters,

   (a) of a technical nature such as but not limited to methods, know-how, formulae, compositions, processes, discoveries, machines, inventions, computer programs and similar items or research projects,

   (b) of a business nature such as but not limited to information about cost, purchasing, profits, market, sales or lists of customers, and

   (c) pertaining to future developments such as but not limited to research and development or future marketing or merchandising.

2. Upon termination of my employment with the Company, or at any other time at the Company's request, I agree to deliver promptly to the Company all drawings, blueprints, manuals, letters, notes, notebooks, reports, sketches, formulae, computer programs and similar items, memoranda, customer's lists and all other materials and all copies thereof relating in any way to the Company's business and in any way obtained by me during the period of my employment with the Company which are in my possession or under my control.

   I further agree that I will not make or retain any copies of any of the foregoing and will so represent to the company upon termination of my employment.

3. The Company may notify anyone employing me or evidencing an intention to employ me as to the existence and provisions of this Agreement.

4. The invalidity or unenforceability of any provision of this Agreement as applied to a particular occurrence or circumstance or otherwise shall not affect the validity and enforceability or applicability of any other provision of this Agreement.

5. This Agreement shall inure to the benefit of and may be enforced by the Company, its successors or assigns and shall be binding upon me, my executors, administrators, legatees, distributees and other successors in interest and may not be changed in whole or in part except in a writing signed by a duly authorized officer of the Company and myself.

I agree to comply with and do all things necessary for the Company to comply with provisions of contracts between it and any agency of the United States Government or contractors thereof. This includes but is not limited to all provisions relating to invention rights or to the safeguarding of information pertaining to the defense of the United States of America.

SAMPLE UNSOLICITED IDEA LETTER

Thank you for offering to show us your idea. As I am sure you must realize, our company receives many such suggestions, and experience has shown us that in most of these cases, the idea presented has already been considered by us. Accordingly, we are unable to accept your proposal unless you are willing to agree to the following conditions:

1. If appropriate, provide that samples cannot be returned to the submittor.

2. Provide that compensation will be paid only if the company, in its sole discretion, deems it appropriate, and only then in such amounts as the company, in its sole discretion, deems appropriate.

3. Provide that the company accepts no responsibility for holding any information in confidence.

FORM 1. CONFIDENTIALITY AGREEMENT WHERE YOU ARE GRANTING ANOTHER COMPANY ACCESS TO PROPRIETARY INFORMATION

This agreement shall evidence the terms and conditions on which _____ _____ shall be granted access to certain proprietary information of our company.

Whereas Clauses or Purpose Clauses

Whereas or purpose clauses are important. They should set forth the reasons why you are granting the information. It is impossible to think of every possible contingency, and a recitation of the basic purpose of the transaction gives both parties and the courts, if necessary, some framework within which to resolve any future problems. Do not, however, put important substantive or procedural provisions which you intend to rely on in the whereas clauses. Some courts do not consider this to be technically a part of the agreement.

Definition of Information

Be sure to describe carefully what information is being transferred. Be sure the definition includes two things:

1. A careful itemization of exactly what information is covered — including both written information and information which may be disclosed orally at certain meetings or when the other party goes through your plant.
2. A general definition of all other information which shall be disclosed in conjunction with the relationships between the parties regarding this aspect of business.

Do not limit the scope of the agreement to certain specific documents unless that is clearly appropriate.

Obligation of the Other Company

In consideration of our disclosing the above information to you, you agree that you will hold all such information in trust and confidence, that you will refrain from using it for any purpose except that which is expressly contemplated by this agreement. Further, you will abide by the following restrictions:
1. No copies will be made of any of the written information supplied.
2. Only the employees of your company listed below shall be granted access to this information, and each of them shall be required to sign a copy of this agreement.
3. At the conclusion of our discussions or upon demand by us, all the information shall be immediately returned, including any written notes which you may have made regarding the information.
4. This information shall not be disclosed to any consultant retained by you except upon our prior written approval, which shall be conditioned on such consultant's signing a copy of this agreement and agreeing to be bound by it.

Public Information

Your company shall have no obligation with respect to any item of information (1) known to your company prior to receipt from our company, or (2) generally known in the industry prior to such receipt or (3) after the same is published or becomes generally available in the industry through no act or failure on your part.

Termination

The termination clause affects only discussions between the parties, the project they are working on, etc., not the confidentiality provisions. Therefore, in some cases you will not want any termination clause at all. If you do, one like the following is suggested.

This agreement shall expire _____ from the date hereof, but may be terminated prior to expiration by either party giving 30 days prior written notice to the other party; provided, however, the obligations to protect the information shall survive such termination and shall continue forever.

Scope of Agreement

No rights or obligations other than those expressly recited herein are to be implied from this Agreement. No license is hereby granted, directly or indirectly, under any patent or for any of the information disclosed.

FORM 2. YOUR COMPANY IS ASSUMING CONFIDENTIAL
OBLIGATIONS

This agreement shall evidence the terms and conditions on which _____ shall be granted access to certain proprietary information of your company.

Whereas or Purpose Clauses

Whereas or purpose clauses are important. They should set forth the reasons you are granting the information. It is impossible to think of every possible contingency, and a recitation of the basic purpose of the transaction gives both parties and the courts, if necessary, some framework within which to resolve any future problems. Do not, however, put important substantive or procedural provisions which you intend to rely on in the whereas clauses. Some courts do not consider this to be technically a part of the agreement.

Definition of Information

When you are receiving information, make sure you undertake obligations only with respect to clearly identified and labeled information.

1. Identify specific documents or files by name and label each piece of information.

2. If meetings are involved, specify the meeting and who was there, etc.

3. Try *not* to put a catchall clause in this form.

Obligation of Our Company

For a period of _____ from the date hereof, we will refrain from using your information in connection with the manufacture or sale of products or services, and we will exercise the same degree of care for your information as we use for our similar information. However, you agree that we will not be liable for any unauthorized disclosure which may occur in spite of such care.

Public Information

We will have no obligation with respect to any information (1) known by us prior to receipt from you, or (2) generally known in the industry prior to such receipt, or (3) independently developed by us, or (4) after substantially the same information is published or becomes available to others without restriction through no act or failure to act on our part, or is received by us from a third party having no obligation to you with respect to the information.

Manner of Disclosure

Information subject to this agreement shall be disclosed to us in written form and marked with the legend (your company proprietary information) or an equivalent conspicuous legend. No sheet or page of any written material shall be so labeled which does not contain proprietary information. We will have no obligation with respect to any written material which is not so labeled, or any information disclosed orally unless a written summary of such oral disclosure is delivered to us within 15 days of the oral disclosure specifically identifying the items considered proprietary.

Duration

This agreement shall expire _____ but may be terminated prior to expiration by either party giving 30 days prior written notice to the other party; provided, however, the obligations to protect proprietary information in accordance with this agreement shall survive such termination.

Additional Rights

No rights or obligations other than those expressly recited herein are to be implied from this Agreement. No license is hereby granted, directly or indirectly, under any patent.

FORM 3. BOTH PARTIES HAVE CONFIDENTIAL OBLIGATIONS

This agreement shall evidence the terms and conditions on which your company and our company shall exchange certain confidential information.

Whereas or Purpose Clauses

Whereas or purpose clauses are important. They should set forth the reasons you are granting the information. It is impossible to think of every possible contingency, and a recitation of the basic purpose of the transaction gives both parties and the courts, if necessary, some framework within which to resolve any future problems. Do not, however, put important substantive or procedural provisions which you intend to rely on in the whereas clauses. Some courts do not consider this to be technically a part of the agreement.

Definition of Information

The information subject to this agreement shall be information dealing with _____. Such information shall mean that which (1) originated with or is otherwise within the knowledge of one company and not others, (2) currently is protected against unrestricted disclosure to others, and (3) pertains directly or indirectly to the project the parties are working on. With respect to information made available by you to our company, the obligations of this agreement shall extend only to information in any specifications, drawings, reports, or other writings existing prior to the date of this agreement, as your company has specifically identified by listing the same on Exhibit A attached hereto.

Duration

For a period of _____ from the date hereof, both of our companies will refrain from knowingly using proprietary information received from the other party in connection with manufacture or sale of products or services, and to prevent dissemination to third parties, each party will exercise the same degree of care as it employs for protection of its own proprietary information.

Public Information

No obligation will exist under this agreement with respect to any item of information (1) known to the recipient prior to receipt from the other party, or (2) after substantially the same information is published or becomes available to third parties without restriction through no act or failure to act on the part of the recipient, or (3) after substantially the same information becomes available to the recipient from a third party having no obligation to hold such information in confidence.

Manner of Disclosure

Proprietary information made available in written form by one party to the other will be conspicuously marked with an appropriate legend. No sheet or page of any written material will be so labeled which is not, in good faith, believed to contain proprietary information. A recipient of information hereunder will have no obligation with respect to (1) any portion of any written material which is not so labeled, or (2) any information received orally unless a written summary of such oral communication specifically identifying the items of proprietary information is furnished to the recipient within 15 days.

Additional Rights

No rights or obligations other than those expressly recited herein are to be implied from this Agreement. No license is hereby granted, directly or indirectly, under any patent.

Letter Form Consulting Agreement

Here is an example of a "letter form" consulting agreement. It would be appropriate for only the simplest of situations, but it is a useful form. Note that many times legal documents do not need to be formal. You are often best served by documents like this, which sound friendly and informal, while effectively covering important legal issues

---

FORM 4. "LETTER FORM" CONSULTING AGREEMENT

Dear _____:

   [Company Name] ["the Company"] desires to retain you to discuss with Company personnel information relating to the field of_____ ("Field") under the following terms and conditions:

   1. Under this Agreement, you will perform certain services, including, but not limited to _____. Your services hereunder will be under the general supervision of _____.

   2. This Agreement will be in effect for_____ (_____) day(s) __(Date)__ .

   3. As full consideration for the services performed by you hereunder, the Company shall pay you _____ dollars. ($_____). In addition, you will be reimbursed for all reasonable out-of-pocket expenses incurred by you at the Company's prior request and approval.

   4. You agree to be available for discussions with Company personnel at Company's facilities, or other mutually agreed upon location(s), on the day(s) referred to in Paragraph 2.

   5. During the term of this Agreement and for a period of five (5) years thereafter, you will exercise due care to prevent the unauthorized disclosure of Confidential Information. Confidential Information shall include all information concerning the company and the Field disclosed to you by the Company or developed as a result of your services under this Agreement, except any portion thereof which: (a) is known to you before receipt thereof under this Agreement, as evidenced by your written records; (b) is disclosed to you after acceptance of this Agreement by a third party who has a right to make such disclosure; or (c) is or becomes part of the public domain through no fault of yours. Further, during the term of this Agreement and for said five (5) year period, you shall not use Confidential information for any purpose without the Company's prior written approval.

   6. Any information, inventions, or discoveries (whether or not patentable), innovations, suggestions, ideas and reports, conceived, reduced to practice, made or developed by you as a result of your services under this Agreement shall be promptly disclosed to the Company and shall be the sole property of the Company. You agree, upon the Company's request and at its expense, to execute such documents and to take such other actions as the Company deems necessary to obtain patents in the Company's name covering any of the foregoing.

You hereby agree that any copyrightable materials that you may create for us will be a "work made for hire" under the copyright laws and shall belong to the Company. To the extant that such items do not qualify as works made for hire, you hereby assign all copyrights to them, and agree to execute such additional documents as the Company may request to complete such assignment.

7. You agree that you will not knowingly disclose to the Company any information which is secret, confidential, or proprietary to any third party.

8. You warrant and represent that you are permitted to enter into this Agreement and that the terms of this Agreement are not inconsistent with any other contractual obligations, expressed or implied, that you may have with any third party.

9. Your status under this Agreement shall be that of an independent contractor, and you shall not have the authority to bind or act as agent for the Company or its employees for any purpose whatsoever.

10. This Agreement shall be governed and construed in accordance with the laws of the State of _____.

If these terms are acceptable to you, please sign and date both copies of this letter in the space provided below and return one copy to the Company.

Very truly yours,   Accepted:

[The Company]   [Name]

_____   _____

Date:_____   Date:_____

14

Your Lawyer and Your Insurance

All small businesses should have a competent insurance advisor. On the other hand, the reason you need insurance is to protect against risk, and what we usually mean here is legal risk. You want to protect yourself against someone suing you. That means that your insurance program ought to be discussed with your lawyer so that you know what your realistic exposures are and what kind of insurance you need. Following are some things that any insurance advisor will tell you. You do not even need to discuss them with your lawyer.

We all know that the automobile is the source of a lot of potential liability. Not only must you have your own cars insured, but you must be sure that anyone driving a car on company business—even if it is his or her own car—has adequate insurance also. Be sure to discuss this with your employees and your insurance advisor. It is possible that you can obtain a blanket coverage so that even if your employees do not have enough coverage, your insurance will respond. However, you must clearly identify this problem and make sure you know what kind of coverage you have or do not have. *If you do not have some kind of overriding blanket coverage, you must make sure that no employee does anything for you unless that employee has demonstrated to you that he or she has adequate insurance.* If you send an employee to the post office and the employee runs somebody over, and it turns out that the employee does not have adequate insurance, you are going to be liable. That employee is performing duties for you in the course and scope of his or her employment, and the law will clearly impose a secondary obligation on you. Of course, the primary obligation is on the employee, but that does not do you much good if the employee has little insurance and not much money. Automobiles, then, are such a frequent source of difficulty that you must be absolutely sure that any automobile used in your business is adequately protected.

Of course, you need the normal array of insurance on your premises to protect against liabilities for slips and falls, etc. You should be protected against fire, vandalism, theft, etc., in whatever amounts seem appropriate under the circumstances.

The second level of coverage is those risks which are peculiar to your business. You should discuss these with your lawyer and insurance agent together. These are the areas where the insurance agent will tell you that a particular type of policy is available and ask you if you want it. The decision as to whether you want that coverage will, in part, depend upon your realistic legal exposure. For example, in our little business it would be possible to obtain a policy of "publisher's errors and omissions coverage" which would protect us if we should libel someone or if we should be incorrect in some statement of law and someone were to rely on that to his or her detriment. I have elected not to procure such insurance, because I do not think that is a realistic exposure. The kinds of legal things that I write about simply do not lend themselves to libel claims. Anything I say about a named individual or a company is something which is already reported in a public document, such as a court case, legislative history, or a federal regulation. There is simply no realistic exposure to a libel suit.

Another example of how legal risks and insurance interact is liability for incorrect information in a publication. This, of course, is from my own experience and I offer it to you simply for illustrative purposes. Some cases hold that a publisher who publishes incorrect information is responsible to a user who uses that incorrect information and is then injured. Some lawsuits may involve, for example, a publisher of a chemistry book that improperly sets forth a formula. When the student mixes the chemicals as instructed in the book, there is a violate reaction and the student is injured. The textbook publisher may be sued in a case like that. Another group of cases involve allegations that investors have been damaged by inaccurate information in financial newsletters that advocated either buying or selling specific securities.

It is possible to buy insurance for this exposure but the insurance is costly.

On the other hand, virtually all the cases addressing this issue in the context of economic losses say that, if the publication disclaims any responsibility for the accuracy of the data, the disclaimer is effective and someone relying on the data, even if it is incorrect, cannot recover. Therefore, instead of paying for expensive insurance on the remote possibility that some lawyer might act on the basis of information contained in any of our publications, we simply put a disclaimer to the general effect that the information is not necessarily accurate and the reader should be sure to check the primary or original sources. In other words, by the simple expedient of putting a disclaimer in our publications we believe we avoided the necessity to pay for expensive insurance coverage on this point. You may find that in your own business similar tradeoffs are possible. You can usually buy insurance coverage for just about any kind of exposure. On the other hand, some of those exposures can be reduced by legal means—usually the effective use of documents and contracts—to the point that expensive insurance may not be necessary.

Similarly, I could procure a valuable paper insurance policy that would protect manuscripts for books such as this and for all the other writing that we do. If all of those papers were in one place and if we had a fire, we would indeed be out of business, and this kind of insurance would be an absolute necessity. But there is a rather simple way to deal with this problem: Make sure that you have copies of things at various different locations. In my own situation, for example, my mother keeps a complete copy of our list of subscribers and everything we write at her house. There is also a complete copy in our home as well as in our editorial offices in downtown Cleveland. The possibility of all three of these places burning down all at once is remote. I have also elected, then, to forgo this kind of coverage.

Each situation, of course, will be somewhat different, but these illustrate the general approach you should take. First, understand clearly what your legal risks are and whether insurance is available and, if so, at what cost. These are the kinds of situations that you should discuss jointly with your lawyer and insurance agent. Second, whenever insurance is proposed to cover a catastrophe ask yourself if there is some other way to cover that same catastrophe in a more efficient and economical manner. Perhaps something as simple as keeping a duplicate set of records off-premises could save you a lot of money in insurance premiums.

Generally, it is not necessary—and I would think it would be inappropriate—to have your lawyer review your insurance contracts. Frankly, if you cannot trust your insurance agent to review these for you, I think you need a new insurance agent. Insurance agents are generally compensated by commission, and they should do the job for you without any extra out-of-pocket expenses on your part. Your lawyer should be used to identify and quantify risks but not to pour over insurance documents and make sure that they say what the insurance agent said they said.

A final thought about insurance: You probably should have the same insurance advisor for both your individual and your corporate insurance. The reason is that these can be so interconnected. Disability, health, and life insurance are prime examples. I think it is obvious that in today's world we all need adequate disability and health insurance, and also a certain amount of life insurance. On the other hand, there are a number of ways for the owner of a small business to obtain this coverage. It can be done through a corporate policy or policies, individual policies, or a combination of the two. The key thing is to make sure you understand exactly what insurance you have, how much it is costing you, what you are protected against, what you are not protected against, and the tax treatment of the premiums.

This last point raises the ever-present tax dragon and points out the necessity of having your tax advisor familiar with your insurance picture. If your corporation buys some of this insurance, it may have tax consequences to you. For example, a corporation can provide all of its employees with $50,000 worth of group term life insurance without any tax consequences to the employees. The corporation can deduct the premium, and there is no requirement that the employees report this premium on their income tax return. On the other hand, if the insurance is greater than $50,000, there is a requirement that the employees pay a tax on the premium attributable to the difference. Similarly, if a corporation provides you with disability or health insurance, that may or may not be taxable to you, depending upon exactly how it is done. A recent change in the tax law beginning in 1980 did take away one of the available perks for the owners of a small business. It is no longer possible to have your corporation directly pay any excess medical expenses which are not covered by the corporate insurance plans. Before 1980 it was possible to establish a special plan whereby certain key officers or directors would have a reimbursement program. The company would pay any medical expenses which might not be covered by insurance. Now, however, that is no longer possible unless you do it for everybody in the company.

The interaction between insurance and taxes is complex. The point I want to stress here is simply that your tax advisor may have some useful ideas for you if you make sure that he or she is aware of all the insurance that you have personally and that the corporation provides you.

One exception to my general feeling that you do not need a lawyer involved in your insurance program other than to assess the kinds of risks you face and help you quantify them would be where you have to fill out a rather elaborate application for insurance and where the facts seem a little complicated. Keep in mind that an application for insurance really is a set of promises and warranties. If you say something incorrect on that application, and if it is important, the insurance company can seize upon that misstatement to get off the hook on the basic policy. In such situations I recommend that you go over the actual insurance application that you are going to submit to the company with your insurance advisor, and, if it seems at all appropriate, it might be worth a few dollars of your lawyer's time also. If you should want product liability insurance, you would probably have to submit a rather detailed application, and it might be worth a legal review.

Directors and officers' liability insurance is available to large companies to safeguard the directors and officers against personal claims of mismanagement or improper business decisions. Generally, it is not available to small companies.

Insurance against environmental problems is also a difficult subject. The bottom line is that you probably cannot get any meaningful insurance protection. Almost all general liability policies have a "pollution exclusion clause" which is fairly broad. Nevertheless, if you do have exposure to environmental matters it may be worth discussing with both your lawyer and your insurance agent.

To summarize the legal advice I would give on insurance matters:

1. Any insurance agent can provide you with insurance coverage on just about any possible calamity that you can think of except your own mismanagement. A first-rate insurance advisor can think of additional possible calamities that you never thought of and suggest insurance policies for those, too. You may find it in your best interest to discuss your realistic legal exposure with your lawyer before spending money on some of these policies.

2. Insurance often has tax implications.

3. Special kinds of insurance (e.g., product liability, environmental, officers and directors' liability) may require a fairly elaborate application. A legal review of the application to make sure there is nothing the insurance company can use to get off the coverage hook may be worthwhile.

4. Legal involvement in your insurance program should be extremely modest. If you and the insurance advisor do your homework and present a suggested program to your lawyer, a couple of hours of your lawyer's time to get his or her advice is all that would be required.

Recent Developments: Suing
Your Insurance Company

One of the important developments of the 1980s was a tremendous increase in the amount of litigation between the insurance company and its policy holders on many of the subjects covered in this book, but principally environmental laws and employment discrimination laws. Many times corporations will find that, at least arguably, their comprehensive general liability policy will cover exposures they may have under our environmental laws or liabilities that they may have incurred under antidiscrimination laws.

This very technical area of the law is very difficult to describe because of two important variables. First, state law is very different from one state to the next. Indeed, if you feel that you might want to make a claim against one of your insurance carriers for this type of exposure, the first thing most lawyers will do is research the appropriate state law to find a state with favorable laws, and then try to find justification for suing the insurance company in that jurisdiction. The second variable is the insurance contract itself. Insurance contracts are just that—contracts—and the interpretation of what they cover and do not cover often depends on a very detailed analysis of the exact wording of that contract.

Any time you face an exposure of any type, particularly under the environmental or discrimination laws, you should gather up all your insurance contracts—especially your comprehensive general liabilities policies—and be sure that you discuss the situation with your lawyer. It may be that you should at least notify the insurance carrier of the existence of the claim. Note that this must often be done very promptly or any claim that you may have under the policy will be waived. Immediately upon learning of any potential environmental or employment discrimination claims, you should discuss your insurance coverage with your legal counsel, not later on after you have tried to figure out exactly what the claims are about and what your exposure might be.

Note. Most comprehensive general liability policies are so-called occurrence-based policies, which means that the policy in effect at the time of the event giving rise to liability is the one that should respond. For example, if you have an environmental exposure caused by a shipment of waste you sent someplace 20 years ago, it can often be argued that the policy in effect 20 years ago covers the exposure. This means at least two things.

1. You should never destroy any insurance policies.
2. You should, at your earliest convenience, be sure that you gather all

prior insurance policies that you have ever had and keep them in a safe place. This simple precaution may save you a lot of money down the road. Insurance companies have gotten a lot smarter in recent years and have done a fairly good job of excluding some of these environmental and employment law problems. Remember, however, its not the recent policy that may govern; it may be one a dozen or more years old. That policy may not have the current exclusions in it, and you may be in a much better position arguing for coverage under those older policies than under the newer ones.

In summary, one of the more important insurance law developments of the past decade has been a marked increase in the number of suits by the insured against their insurance company alleging that the insurance company is responsible for any exposures they may have for environmental or employment discrimination problems. Obviously, in that kind of adversary relationship you're better off getting advice on the legal meaning of your insurance contracts from your lawyer then from the insurance company representatives.

15
Miscellaneous Calamities That Can Send You to Jail (White Collar Crime)

I have reserved this chapter of the book for a very brief discussion of miscellaneous calamities that can really bring the wrath of the federal government or state enforcement officials down upon you. These are things to avoid at all costs. There is no cost-benefit analysis, no risk weighing, no mitigating circumstances, and no excuse for getting tangled up in any of these matters.

I speak not from a moral standpoint. I speak only from a practical business point of view. The reason is simple. If you happen to get involved in one of these matters in a serious way, you are very likely to end up losing your bank account to the lawyers and losing your business due to diversion of your own attention to these matters rather than to your business. Adverse physical and psychological consequences are also a distinct possibility—these are traumatic experiences.

Tax

I have spoken briefly in this book about tax planning. I have suggested an *agressive point of view*. Wherever there is a doubt, resolve it in your favor. If there is an opportunity to structure any business deal to minimize taxes, I am all for it. However, there is a line between tax avoidance, which I and all other business counselors strongly advocate, and tax evasion, which is where you go to jail. The following things are likely to cause a serious risk of criminal prosecution, assuming substantial amounts of money are involved. "Substantial" probably means a couple of thousand dollars of tax for each of two or more tax years.

1. Deliberately not reporting substantial amounts of income, and taking steps to hide the unreported income.
2. Knowingly putting substantially erroneous information on your tax return.
3. Claiming deductions for nonexistent expenses, such as people on the payroll who do not exist, or payments to fictitious organizations.
4. Using corporate money for your own personal expenses and then attempting to camouflage this fact so you do not have to pay taxes on it.
5. Keeping off-the-book accounts.

If you own all the stock of a corporation, you can do almost anything you want with the money. There is no law against having the corporation pay for your mortgage or automobile payments, or for that matter even the food on your table. On the other hand, those kinds of things are taxable income to you, and you have to report them as such. It is just as if the corporation paid you a salary and you used it for those purposes. If instead you try to camouflage this by fictitious accounting so that the corporation pays the expense and you do not report the income, the Internal Revenue Service is going to get very mad.

The IRS is currently concerned about tax shelters. They feel that some of these border on fraudulent activities. In the majority of situations, the IRS will bring any criminal action against the lawyers, accountants, and principals involved in the tax-shelter scheme itself. If they feel the program is not legitimate and the investors have taken deductions to which they are not properly entitled, they will only assess deficiencies against the individual investor. On the other hand, this assumes that the investor does not deliberately participate in organizing or structuring the fraudulent tax shelter. The best protection here is simply to avoid tax shelters which look too good to be true or which are not sponsored by reputable people.

Antitrust

Antitrust is a vast and complex body of law, but the portions that give rise to criminal liability are simple and straightforward. Criminal liability under the antitrust laws will arise when *competitors* get together and agree, or attempt to agree, on prices, territories, or customers. The portions of the antitrust laws which deal with price discrimination, distributorship arrangements, termination of distributors, unfair competition, deceptive advertising, mergers, and the myriad of other things that you read about in the newspapers all give rise to civil, not criminal liability. Further, these kinds of matters usually come up in normal business operations and there is time to discuss them with your lawyer. On the other hand, when you are meeting with competitors at business or social arrangements, your lawyer is not going to be around, and you are going to have to keep the antitrust principles firmly in mind.

Under no circumstances should you discuss prices, territories, or customers with any competitor in any setting—business or social. This includes trade associations. In fact, if there is a single common denominator to criminal price-fixing conspiracies, it is that those arrangements were either initiated or furthered at some trade association meeting. Government enforcement officials are highly suspicious of trade association meetings and will subpoena trade association records and the records of the people who attended trade association meetings in the course of any criminal investigation. In short, price fixing is a criminal no-no, and if you engage in it you are being foolish.

For antitrust purposes, prices are considered to be any aspect of the deal. They include, for example, whether or not you give credit, whether you give trading stamps, or what kind of formula you use to base freight charges.

Resale price maintenance can also be a criminal violation, and local antitrust officials and perhaps even the federal government may prosecute it. Resale price maintenance is an arrangement between you and your customer to fix the price at which your customer sells the product. A few years ago, this was legal. It was an exception to the antitrust laws and was referred to as "fair trade" in states which authorized such resale price agreements. However, the federal law has been amended to remove this exception, and what used to be "fair trade" is now "illegal resale price maintenance." You must remember that your customer—even if it is a distributor of yours—is an independent businessperson, and you cannot tell your customer at what price "your" products have to be sold. That is his or her judgment.

There is an unfortunate misconception in the minds of some business people about exactly what an agreement or conspiracy is. They feel that there must be some kind of *express* agreement. This is definitely not true.

ANTITRUST IS THE ONLY AREA OF LAW I KNOW ABOUT WHERE IT IS VERY POSSIBLE TO BLUNDER YOUR WAY INTO A CRIMINAL PROBLEM WITHOUT ACTUALLY KNOWING WHAT YOU ARE DOING.

Example

You are at a trade association meeting, and a group of competitors consisting of six people from your city go out to dinner. During the dinner discussion, one of the people at the table says that he is no longer going to give trading stamps (or give discounts for cash, or whatever). Everyone else at the table says nothing. Later that month, the person who spoke stops giving trading stamps, and during the second month the other five people stop also.

That is enough to give rise to a criminal indictment. There would be enough evidence for the government to ask a jury to determine whether the six people at that table agreed—admittedly implicitly—to stop giving trading stamps. Of course, once you get a case this far most of the damage is already done. You have been indicted for a criminal violation, there has been much anxiety, attorneys' fees, etc., and the decision of the jury is completely subjective and impossible to predict.

The Securities Laws

Federal and state securities laws can give rise to criminal liability, but the possibility is fairly remote. The only time you will run into criminal problems under the securities laws is if you engage in some kind of deliberate fraud. For example, if you were to create a fictitious balance sheet and sell securities in a company representing that company to be financially solvent when in fact it was not, it is likely that you would violate the securities laws during this kind of scheme. If it was deliberate, the violation could be criminal. We are talking about some fairly deliberate con games here. I am not speaking about selling securities in a company when, in retrospect, it turns out that you forgot to disclose something which the court feels is material. Those are very serious problems because they could give rise to extremely large civil lawsuits.

On the other hand, criminal prosecutions under the securities laws are reserved for deliberate fraud, the bogus balance sheet, the empty salad oil drums, the land which turns out to be underwater, etc.

Another prohibition in our securities laws that can give rise to criminal exposure is insider trading. *Insider trading*, as its name implies, is simply buying or selling securities on the basis of information that you have but that has not been disclosed to the public. Most cases involve people who find out about buy-out offers about to be made at a high premium. These people then purchase the shares just before the announcement and often make a great deal of money when the announcement is made and the shares go up in value. That is a criminal violation of our criminal securities laws and, if detected, will be severely prosecuted. It is also a civil violation so that anyone trading on the basis of insider information would be libel to disgorge all of the profits they made plus substantial penalties.

While almost all insider trading cases involve publicly held companies, the rules also apply to a privately held company. In one case, for example, the owner of a closely held company received an offer to purchase the company at a very high price. Without telling his other shareholders he simply bought their shareholdings and then sold out at the higher price. That is just as much a violation of the federal insider trading laws as buying or selling stock in a publicly held company on the basis of inside information. In the insider trading or fraud area there is no requirement for a certain dollar amount or for a certain number of shares. In other words even a very small company is governed by the federal insider trading rules.

Insider trading has always been a criminal activity. In recent years, however, it has become much more serious. Several laws have been passed greatly increasing the penalties, and the interest of the government in prosecuting insider trading cases is quite high. There is also an increase in sophistication on the market exchanges for detecting unusual trades. For example, many of the insider trading cases are brought when an individual, in the habit of buying or selling one or two hundred shares of stock every once in a while, suddenly buys a thousand or more deep out-of-the-money calls. This change in pattern is often a tip-off to the enforcement authorities. If the underlying stock suddenly appreciates so that the investor makes a lot of money, you can expect that the FCC will want to know why the investor placed the order at that time. In fact many people believe that the emergence of heavy trading and puts in calls has been one of the factors that has contributed to a possible increase in insider trading. Using puts and calls, it is possible to make a tremendous amount of money with the investment of only a very small amount.

Example

A stock is currently trading at $40 per share. You could probably purchase a right to call that stock at $45 a share for very little money. If the stock promptly went up to $50, you could make a very large profit for hardly any investment. Since some tender offers of the late 1980s involved premiums of 10 or 20 points on the price of the stock, that type of transaction proved almost irresistible to someone who got advance word of the tender offer.

Caution. The enforcement authorities have gotten quite sophisticated, and it is not only very high visibility transactions that are questioned. Indeed, some rather small insider trading cases involving trading that was not particularly out of the ordinary have been prosecuted.

Political Contributions

Federal law *absolutely* prohibits *any* political contribution from *any* corporation in connection with a federal election. This is true no matter how small the corporation and no matter how few shareholders. If you incorporate your one-person business operation, you cannot use corporate funds to make a political contribution. To do so is a criminal violation, and there is a separate federal agency — the Federal Election Commission — which is charged with the responsibility for ferreting out such illegal contributions and causing them to be prosecuted. At this time, this is a highly sensitive area, and it is extremely unlikely that you can get away with making any political contribution out of your corporate till.

The only way that a corporation can become involved directly in the political process is through a "political action committee," which is a separate, segregated fund consisting of voluntary contributions from the employees of the corporation. These funds are legal and highly desirable. Most large companies have them. Most small companies do not because it is easier for the shareholders to simply make whatever political contributions they desire directly.

State law on the use of corporate funds for political contributions varies. In some states, it is illegal; in others, it is not. Consequently, if you are thinking about making a political contribution to a state candidate — as opposed to a federal one — I recommend you specifically ask the question and get a letter from the candidate or the candidate's political committee (or counsel) stating that a corporate contribution would be legal. You can, of course, check with your own lawyer also. On the other hand, political candidates are certainly aware of the election laws — both state and federal — and it seems senseless to me for you to spend your own money on legal fees to separate out all these complex rules. Place the burden on the political candidate, his or her campaign committee, and his or her own lawyer. If you receive a letter from any of these people on their stationery stating that corporate contributions are legal under the laws of that state, it does not seem to me that you have anything to worry about.

Environmental Laws

Environmental laws are giving rise to increased criminal prosecution. Virtually all of the federal environmental laws — and most state environmental laws — contain provisions which impose criminal sanctions. Thus, if your business operation discharges harmful materials into the air or water or disposes of them by a landfill, it is incumbent upon you to understand at least the basic environmental rules which are applicable and to make sure that you do not engage in deliberate violations. Again, this is a politically sensitive area. Environmental protection agencies — at both the state and the federal level — are literally looking for targets for criminal enforcement actions. The biggest risk under environmental laws comes about through falsifying information or submitting false information to the government. This is discussed below.

Occupational Safety and Health

The Occupational Safety and Health Act contains a criminal provision which says that if there is a willful violation of the act which results in a death, the responsible corporate people can be criminally indicted. There have only been a few such indictments, but again, this is a politically sensitive area, and it is growing. The key here is "willful" violation which results in a death. For this purpose, the government would probably have to show that you knew about a hazardous situation and refused to correct it.

In a large company, the issue of who goes to jail if there is a criminal violation of environmental or OSHA laws is important. The enforcement officials want to prosecute the highest possible corporate officials — but they have to show something that the corporate official did in order to get a conviction. In most situations, this revolves around the question "What did the corporate official know?" If he or she knew of the environmental or OSHA violation and did nothing — thereby condoning the acts of the subordinates which actually constituted the violation — the government will likely prosecute the corporate official rather than the employees lower down the ladder.

However, in a small company this problem factors out. You as the owner are going to be the one the government prosecutes unless there are clear and convincing arguments showing that someone else in the company took the actions without your knowledge or consent. In a small company, that is unlikely. Many of the criminal prosecutions under environmental and OSHA laws are against the owners of small businesses for this reason. There is no bureaucracy for the government to cut through to find out who in the corporation was responsible.

Bribery

Bribing foreign government officials was made a crime under the Foreign Corrupt Practices Act. This is a controversial area because the bribery provisions of the act deal only with foreign government officials, and there are a host of problems in terms of United States laws imposing their own standards of ethics and morals on other countries where historically the practices have been different. The Foreign Corrupt Practices Act is essentially a compromise. It says that grease payments are not prohibited, but bribes are. The line between a grease payment and a bribe is hard to draw. This is a difficult and sensitive area. If you do business in foreign countries (particularly the less developed ones, and most particularly the middle east) you need legal counsel on the possible implications of this law.

Commercial bribery in this country may be and probably is subject to criminal prosecution under one or more of the ancillary criminal laws which are mentioned below. Some states have direct laws making it a crime. Of course, bribery of any government official — state or federal — is a criminal offense. There are many ways to handle government investigations or audits, but bribing the government representative is definitely not one of them. That is the quickest way I know to make a small problem into a big one.

Ancillary Criminal Laws

A large portion of criminal prosecutions are brought under what I call ancillary criminal laws rather than for a specific offense. The most important ancillary criminal laws cover the following areas:

1. Conspiracy

2. Making false statements to the government

3. Aiding and abetting

4. Obstruction of justice

5. The currency laws

For example, before the Foreign Corrupt Practices Act was passed, almost all of the improper payment prosecutions were based not on the illegal bribe, but on the fact that someone took currency out of the United States without filing the appropriate customs forms. Similarly, in many environmental criminal prosecutions, the case is based not upon the technical violation of the environmental laws, but upon some report or false statement that the person submitted. The prosecution is based upon the statute which makes it a criminal act to make any false statement to the government rather than upon the discharge of the harmful matter into the air or water.

Federal laws make it a criminal offense to conspire with another person to commit a crime. There is no requirement that the crime actually be committed. Prosecutions under the conspiracy statute are, therefore, much easier for the government to bring than prosecutions under the substantive laws. Similarly, federal criminal laws prohibit aiding and abetting someone else in a commission of a crime or obstruction of justice. The obstruction of justice statute is used in conjunction with the prohibition against making false statements to the government when people try to cover up some activity which in itself probably would not be too bad. For example, if your plant discharges material into the water in violation of your permit under the Clean Water Act, that is extremely unlikely to give rise to a criminal prosecution. On the other hand, if after this violation is discovered, you attempt to cover it up by means of falsifying documents, lying to environmental protection agency inspectors, or submitting false reports to the government, that can cause what would normally be a serious but civil matter to change into a criminal matter.

Similarly, if, during the course of a tax audit, the government finds items of income which you failed to report, that will usually give rise only to the assessment of more tax. On the other hand, if after the government finds these things, you continue to hamper their efforts to collect the tax by lying to them or submitting documents or letters which are at best misleading and possibly false, there is ample authority under these ancillary laws for the government to prosecute you — and they do not have to use the tax law which requires them to prove that you received income which you did not report. All they have to do is prove that you submitted a false statement to them.

Perjury is another of the ancillary criminal laws which can arise if you are called before a grand jury or if you testify in a case. Any testimony under oath which is false is a violation of the perjury laws, and you can rest assured that the government will give serious consideration to bringing a criminal prosecution.

The bottom line of this whole discussion is that, unless you deliberately engage in conduct which any reasonably intelligent businessperson would know to be criminal, you are probably not going to be subject to criminal prosecution for any of the substantive laws mentioned above. The one exception is antitrust—you must keep on your toes there. On the other hand, it *is rather easy to get trapped into a violation of the ancillary criminal laws*. It is only human nature to try to "defend" yourself or your company if you get into trouble on the basis of the antitrust, securities, environmental, or other laws. This is where most of the white-collar problems have arisen. The prosecution results not because the person violated the substantive law but because he or she violated one of these ancillary laws during the course of the government's investigation. Ever since Watergate, our society condemns any form of cover-up. This is reflected in an extremely high desire on the part of federal enforcement agencies to bring these kinds of white-collar cases.

Conclusion

The logical conclusion is that *any* government investigation should be discussed with counsel at the very earliest stages. If you go it alone, you are running what I believe to be an unacceptably high risk of criminal prosecution. Once the government begins any investigation in which you become involved, you have two exposures. One of them is the matter that the government is investigating, but the other, which I believe is the more serious, are these ancillary federal criminal laws which can trap even sophisticated corporate lawyers.

If you think that the government enforcement officials are there to help you, to learn the truth, and to prosecute only those people who are guilty of serious violations of the law, I am afraid that you are naive. The government prosecutors are there to prosecute. In my judgment, they start an investigation only when they feel there is a legitimate reason to do so. Further, I believe that they usually exercise an extremely high degree of discretion in favor of the public, and in fact refrain from prosecuting a lot of cases where they might be able to secure convictions. *On the other hand, once they do decide to start an investigation, they sweep with an extremely broad brush.* They do not limit themselves to the basic violations of the substantive laws.

If you get a subpoena to appear before a grand jury, you need a good criminal lawyer fast. Do nothing at all until you have spoken with your own lawyer. Further, make sure you have gotten a good criminal lawyer. Your corporate counsel is not the right person. Corporate lawyers may be able to suggest criminal lawyers who will help you, but the overwhelming majority of corporate counsel representing small companies do not know any more about criminal laws—let alone the federal criminal laws—than you do. In fact, if you have studied this chapter carefully, you may be ahead of some of them. Most corporate counsel do, however, have competent partners, associates, or friends to whom they refer criminal cases.

On the other hand, you should not conclude that any time any government official knocks at the door and asks for your records, that signifies an " investigation" which necessarily means you should start running up legal fees. This has to be a matter of judgment. I would not, however, endorse the feeling that if you have not done anything wrong, you do not need a lawyer. I am afraid that is way too naive.

16

International Buying and Selling

A key development in international business transactions since the first edition is the globalization of many markets. This chapter, therefore, presents a brief discussion of international transactions in this second edition, beginning with international sales and then providing a few comments on buying from abroad. The basic focus of this discussion is to highlight the things that may be a little different when you buy or sell internationally from when you make comparable transactions in the United States.

Help from the Government

The United States government has, as a matter of economic policy, decided to spend considerable resources on helping our export trade. You can therefore obtain much more help for international sales than for domestic sales. In mid-1987 the Department of Commerce established a system called the Commercial Information Management System (CIMS). This computerized system provides access to the Department of Commerce's storehouse of information on export opportunities in any country. You can look at this information simply by going into one of the Department of Commerce local offices (offices exist in approximately 67 cities throughout the United States). The information is very helpful and often very specific, including information as to which goods are being successfully sold in which countries, how they are being sold, and who markets them. The Department will try to match buyers and sellers. Without technically operating as a broker, it tries to act in a very similar function.

In addition to these various specific one-on-one areas of help, the Department of Commerce also offers other general information via publications, seminars, and conventions in this country and abroad. The programs are intended to assist U.S. companies in exporting and to assist foreign companies in buying U.S. products.

Therefore, the very first thing you should do if you are thinking about trying to market your products internationally is investigate the help that may be available from the government, principally the Department of Commerce.

Selling Abroad Through Agents or Distributors

A U.S. exporter will often find it advantageous to use a representative in a foreign country to handle export sales. This person could be an *agent*, who merely finds the foreign buyer and acts as an intermediary without accepting delivery or taking title to the goods. Agents receive commissions for their services. *Distributors*, on the other hand, buy the goods and resell them at a higher price. The margin becomes the distributors' profit. An important difference for agents and distributors under foreign law is protective legislation. Protective legislation precludes termination of an agency or distributor relationship except for cause and may require the payment of substantial compensation.

The general U.S. rule is that allowing someone to sell your goods as an agent or a representative (and paying a commission for the sales) does not involve an ongoing commitment to continue the relationship. Similarly, selling goods to a distributor and allowing that distributor to resell them does not, absent a specific contractual provision, obligate you to continue the relationship indefinitely. In foreign countries, however, there is almost always protective legislation which gives the opposite result. Foreign agents or distributors are said to have an independent ownership interest in the right to market your products. The theory is that they have devoted a substantial amount of time and effort to make your product known in the foreign market. Because they have created the market for your product, you should not be able to pull the rug from under them by discontinuing the relationship.

The technicalities of foreign protective laws differ from country to country. Some laws protect only agents, some protect only distributors, and some protect both. Further, some are more onerous than others. The key, however, is to remember that the United States is in a distinct minority in having a general legal principle that says that agents and distributors serve "at will." In most foreign countries, the law is that the agent or distributor obtains an independent interest in the relationship, which is enforceable in court.

It is therefore extremely unwise to enter into these relationships lightly. First, it is much easier to appoint an agent or distributor than it is to terminate one. Second, if you do a poor job on the legal documentation, the end result will be problems. You will have an implied contract under the local law, with all of the adverse provisions in the local law protecting the local agent or distributor. Most foreign laws allow at least some flexibility in limiting the adverse features of the protective legislation. To take advantage of the allowance, however, you must have a written contract with the agent or distributor spelling out the terms of your deal, the most important provision of which is how and when it terminates.

Unfortunately, history and experience teach us that exporters (particularly novice and first-time exporters) fail to appreciate this problem. Exporters will find a local representative and write a letter saying, "We are happy to appoint you as agent or distributor for our products. We look forward to a long and mutually profitable relationship." This places the exporter in the most legally adverse relationship because it creates an implied contract under the local protective law.

Your lawyers can minimize this risk, but it requires advance consultation, advance planning, and a clearly drawn written contract with the local representative. This is the single most important difference between selling domestically and selling abroad. It is also the most prevalent area of litigation and dispute.

A Foreign Direct Sale

Sometimes a foreign party will trigger the export sale by asking about the availability of your products. In other words, the transaction would be a direct one between the U.S. seller and the foreign buyer. If you sell directly, you must again be concerned with local laws. Two specific areas of local law present the most problems. The first consists of local laws protecting a local industry; the second of exchange control laws. Sometimes they work in tandem, but often they do not. Indeed, it is possible for a local buyer to obtain government approval to import a certain product but fail to get government approval to pay for the product in U.S. dollars.

Example

> In many countries, local laws protect a certain industry, such as the local automobile industry. The law would prohibit you from selling automobiles or automobile parts into that country unless the sale is approved by the foreign government.

Example

> Many countries have exchange control regulations requiring government approval in order to pay U.S. dollars out of the country. In our automobile example, a separate government approval would be necessary to pay an exporter in U.S. dollars for the automobiles even though the country will allow them to be imported.

Obviously, both laws are tremendously important, but history teaches us that they have operated as stumbling blocks for export sales. The biggest problem seems to be that U.S. sellers assume the foreign buyers know about all of these rules and will take whatever actions are necessary to obtain the required foreign approvals. Often, however, it turns out that the foreign buyer knows even less about the local laws than does the exporter. Those foreign buyers who are sophisticated about their local legislation may use the knowledge to their advantage (and to your disadvantage) in the negotiation process.

The typical pattern is that the parties negotiate a reasonable deal, but the foreign buyer later requires renegotiation of the deal because the government approvals cannot be granted on the original transaction.

Arbitration

Domestically, it is possible to have an arbitration clause in a sales contract, but it is the exception rather than the rule. In export sales, however, it is much more prevalent. While there are differing views on the desirability of arbitration clauses even in an international context, the bottom line appears to be that such a clause deserves more thought in an export deal. According to some counselors, it is almost a requirement. Much depends on the country. However, even in the case of our European trading partners, many counselors feel that an arbitration clause is highly desirable. When selling into a country that does not have as good a legal system as the United States and its European trading partners, an arbitration clause can become a necessity.

The Price—U.S. Dollars

In a domestic contract, the currency of account and the currency of payment is the U.S. dollar. In an international context, however, you have U.S. dollars and the foreign currency. It is very important to specify both the currency of account and the currency of payment in your contract. A contract stating merely that you will sell an item for $100 is ambiguous. You have not spelled out whether the $100 is merely the measure of value (the currency of account) or whether you expect payment in U.S. dollars (the currency of payment). Because of international exchange controls, this can be a very important consideration. It has generated substantial disputes in the past.

The Method of Payment

In domestic transactions, we often buy and sell on an open account basis. In export transactions, we often want a more secure basis, but the foreign buyer is unlikely to agree to payment in advance. The traditional compromise is a letter of credit, also known as a banker's acceptance. A *letter of credit* is simply a document issued by a bank that substitutes the credit of the bank for the credit of the buyer. For example, you may get a letter of credit from an English bank saying that if you present certain documents, the bank will pay a certain amount of money to you. You do not have to worry about the buyer being willing or able to pay; it is the bank's obligation as soon as you submit the documents.

The key is the submission of the documents. The contract must be very clear on exactly what documents must be submitted for payment to be made. Remember that the interest of the bank is often different from yours. The interest of the bank, usually dealt with by a clerical person, is in paying out the bank's money only when it is certain that the payment is required. Thus, the bank will require strict compliance with all the terms of the letter of credit. In an export sale, you are well advised to pay more attention to the method of payment and the documentation involved than you would in a domestic transaction. Letters of credit have proven to be troublesome and subject to quite a bit of litigation. One way to minimize dispute is to be very specific about the letter of credit. You may want to attach to the contract a draft of the letter of credit, which shows exactly what the credit will look like and exactly what documents must be submitted to obtain payment. Do not assume that letters of credit are some type of mysterious documents issued by the bank. They are not; they are a very important part of the commercial transaction and everyone must fully understand all of their terms.

The Commercial Rules

When we sell in the United States, the commercial rules are generally contained in Article 2 of the Uniform Commercial Code (UCC). (Article 2 has been adopted in 49 states and there is a similar law in the one remaining state.) Article 2, entitled "Sale of Goods," spells out the commercial rules of the game. In an export sale, we have to contend with the laws of the other country. In general, however, the commercial laws of most countries are very similar. In addition, the United States and at least some of its trading partners have agreed to a set of rules called the Convention on Contracts for the International Sale of Goods. The Convention essentially parallels the U.S. law. When you deal internationally, you can assume that, while there may be certain minor differences which may be very important in an individual case, the rules of the contract road are pretty much the same as they are in a domestic deal.

One rule, which is almost universal, is that a contract means what it says. In other words, whatever the general legal principles—be they ours or those of a foreign country—the parties are free within very wide boundaries to agree to their own terms and conditions. It is therefore important for us to pay attention to our international sales contracts. They will generally mean precisely what they say.

Another important thing to remember is that the Convention and many foreign laws contain essentially the same type of warranty provisions as does the UCC. It is therefore equally important for us as sellers to disclaim warranties of merchantability and fitness for particular purpose and to limit any express warranties to something fairly specific. We should also limit the buyer's remedies to repair or replacement or to some other manageable amount. Unless we take these steps, the commercial laws will provide for very broad warranties and/or extensive "make whole" remedies should our product not live up to expectations.

Preshipment Inspection

Another difference between a domestic and an international sale is that some countries, particularly the lesser developed countries, require preshipment inspection. This means that the foreign government will not allow you to export goods into that country until they have been inspected by representatives of that country in the U.S. The inspection serves two purposes. First, the foreign government wants to be assured that the goods are of good quality and conform to the contract. Second, it wants to be certain that the price is a reasonable one.

This second aspect of the inspection—a renegotiation of the price—has caused U.S. exporters some degree of difficulty. The key is to be prepared to justify the export price as being fair and reasonable. Should you have difficulty, the Department of Commerce may be able to be of some assistance. It has tried to address this problem and to make the procedures fair and equitable.

The Sales Entity

One who starts exporting must consider whether or not to establish a separate entity, either a statutory entity or perhaps another corporation. The statutory entity, an export trading company, allows some exemptions from the antitrust laws. You may find this helpful if you are engaging in export operations in conjunction with other competitors. Activities with our competitors in the United States might raise antitrust concerns, and, absent specific legislation, these activities would raise the same concerns in export sales. Luckily, the laws are a little more liberal on the export front. First, the antitrust laws require that a plaintiff show that any effect on U.S. commerce was substantial and foreseeable. Perhaps more important, by taking advantage of the provisions of the Export Trading Company Act, you can get an advance approval from the government on your specific activity.

On the tax front, there are also separate entities that may be beneficial. They require the formation of another corporation, not because the Export Trading Company Act requires them, but simply to take advantage of a statutory provision. When we export our goods we may be able to reduce or defer some of our taxes on the profit of those international sales by using special corporate entities authorized by the Internal Revenue Code. If you are able to take advantage of the tax saving devices, they will facilitate export operations rather than make them more complicated or costly. The bottom line is generally around 15 percent savings on the taxes. In some cases you can get even greater savings. Considerable technicalities are involved in foreign sales corporations (FSCs), but remember that an FSC is always a plus. All you have to do is have your tax and accounting people investigate all of the possibilities and the administrative and professional fees in complying with the tax law to see if it is worthwhile. An

FSC is not mandatory. You can elect to sell the goods directly into the foreign country, pay the tax just as you would on a domestic sale, and let it go at that.

The Antiboycott Rules

U.S. law has provisions prohibiting U.S. companies from participating or cooperating with the Arab boycott of Israel. The laws are very technical. In addition to prohibiting actual conduct, they require reporting of boycott-related requests. In other words, even if you never intend to do anything resembling participation in or cooperation with the Arab boycott, you may still get documents containing boycott-related requests. You have a legal obligation to report them to the DOC. Failures to report boycott-related requests have given rise to substantial fines. Requests tend to appear in routine documents such as shipping documents and letters of credit. If your employees are not alert to the requests, the company can commit repeated violations of the law, generating many dollars of fines. The conclusion is that if you are going to export, particularly into the Arab countries, you have to factor in extra costs for antiboycott compliance education. It is not a big deal, provided you tell counsel in advance that you will be exporting. The attorney must then obtain the necessary forms and establish procedures and educational programs on the reporting process.

The Foreign Corrupt Practices Act

In a domestic sale, it is illegal to bribe purchasing agents and to engage in other similar activity. It is, however, a rather rare occurrence and not something that we have as a high priority item on a sales checklist. The minute we start exporting, however, we have to be concerned with the Foreign Corrupt Practices Act. It says that we cannot bribe foreign government officials or pay money to any foreign agent where the circumstances tend to show that the foreign agent is using the money for a bribe. If you are going to export through an agent, particularly to Middle Eastern or African countries, you have to pay particular attention to the contract and the relationship you have with the agent. You must make sure that the agent is reputable and will sell your products on the basis of price, quality, and service, rather than by bribing local government officials. Failure to pay attention to this law can result in criminal sanctions.

Protection of Intellectual Property

Intellectual property refers to patents, trademarks, trade secrets and copyrights. In the United States, intellectual property protection is fairly effective both in a legal and a practical sense.

Exporting, however, poses increased risks. The legal protection in foreign countries for our intellectual property is less than it is in the United States. In any export sale, we have to accept the possibility of losing of some of our intellectual property rights.

There are two legal dimensions.

1. First is whether we can prohibit people from counterfeiting and sending the counterfeit goods into the United States. The answer is that we can, albeit with a qualification. If you have a particularly attractive and easily counterfeited product, some counterfeit products may enter the U.S. market over the short term. Overall, however, the United States does have good laws and provisions to enforce them.

2. The second dimension relates to foreign markets. Do you have the legal ability to prevent others from manufacturing your goods and selling them in non-U.S. countries? For example, can you legally prevent a French company from selling copied goods in competition with you in England? The answer is mixed. If you are talking about our major European trading partners, the answer is generally favorable. If you touch all the legal bases, the protection is similar to that in the United States. In countries other than our major trading partners, however, you may find that the foreign legal system is simply inadequate to protect your intellectual property. Further, even if the laws are on the books, they may not be enforced.

Outright counterfeiting is big business today. Assuming you have legally enforceable rights and the country in question is one that diligently tries to protect them, you may still find that your goods are being counterfeited by a back alley shop. If pressure is put on the operation, it simply closes and moves elsewhere.

To export goods, you have to look at your intellectual property situation. By sending your goods abroad, you incur increased risk. You must determine whether your potential profit is worth interesting foreign companies in possible counterfeiting or competition. Again legal counsels can do many things to minimize the risk, but they cannot entirely eliminate it.

Export Controls

Perhaps the biggest difference between selling products domestically and exporting them is that exporting requires a government license. This is a universal rule. There is no inherent right to export a product, and every export must be governed by some type of license. The rules do, however, contain statutory or automatic licenses that may mean that this requirement is very easy to satisfy. Therefore, one of the first things we should do when we decide to export is to find out whether we can do so under one of these general licenses, or whether we will need to get a specific one. In general, our export control laws focus on

1. Exports of militarily significant items
2. Exports to unfriendly countries

If we export items having no military application to our major trading partners in Europe, we will have little problem on the export control front. If we export items that have or might have a military application, and/or if the export is to a country other than our major European trading partners, the export control problems can be severe. Many problems arise in connection with the so-called dual use items. *Dual use* items are not intended to have a military application, but could be so used, such as computers and certain electronic parts. The key to dealing with these problems is to know about them in advance so that you can factor the costs and delays into the contract.

International Sourcing

International sourcing raises some of the same issues as international selling with one obvious addition—our customs laws.

U.S. customs laws say, in essence, that anything imported into this country must go through Customs and, unless there is some exemption, an appropriate duty must be paid. This means that for anything that you want to buy from abroad you have to arrange for appropriate entry through Customs. As a practical matter, almost everyone does this by hiring a Customs broker. We understand that 95 percent of all goods coming into this country are handled through a broker who in turn handles all of these technical requirements. Basically, the goods that you buy must be classified in accordance with the classification schedule and then a certain customs rate will be applied to the classification. The classification and the rate, multiplied by the value of the shipment, will tell you the amount that you have to pay as a Customs duty. The problems are:

> The classification system is far from scientific. Many things could be classified under one or two separate headings resulting in different duties. You can often get an advance ruling from the Customs Department as to how things should be classified, and this is often a useful exercise.

> The value of the transaction is usually stated to be the actual purchase price of the goods, but there are a host of exceptions and qualifications to the rule.

> All goods coming into this country must be appropriately labeled with the county of origin. If this problem hasn't been addressed, you may find your goods held up at the port of entry because they are not properly labeled.

U.S. Government Regulation

Another problem that arises once in a while in international sourcing is that the foreign manufacturers are unaware of the details of U.S. government regulations. For example, our toys are governed by standards issued by the Consumer Product Safety Act. In some cases people have imported toys that do not conform to these standards and problems have resulted. When we are buying things domestically, we can assume that the domestic manufacturer has at least a reasonably good knowledge of these kinds of U.S. requirements. When we buy things abroad, however, we cannot make that assumption.

Summary and Conclusions

If you decide to expand your marketing or buying horizons by doing business overseas, you should keep in mind a few legal implications. There are, however, only a few; we have hit most of them in this brief chapter. It is safe to say that it will be a very rare case where there is any substantial legal impediment to either buying or selling overseas. In almost all cases all we are talking about is legally dotting a few *i*'s and crossing a few *t* 's. Further, the government can be of substantial assistance.

The biggest help your lawyer is likely to give you is in facilitating your use of foreign counsel. This is particularly true if you're going to export. We have alluded to the problems resulting from an overly hasty appointment of an agent or a distributor. Your U.S. lawyer, however, is likely to know only that, as a general proposition, foreign laws contain this possible trap for the unwary. To deal with the foreign local laws, your U.S. attorney will probably have to rely on foreign counsel. In some cases, however, you may be able to obtain enough help from government agencies to at least satisfy yourself that you can go ahead on a preliminary basis without running too much of a legal risk.

Today, the statistics we read seem to say that exporting is still the province of the larger companies but that smaller companies are getting more and more involved. That is why we included this chapter in the book. As you can see, the legal problems are rather minor, and if you feel that your product will sell overseas, it is certainly worthwhile to investigate that possibility.

Economically, the biggest problem seems to be currency fluctuation, so you will want to be sure to price your product to allow for reasonable variations.

Index

About the Author

William A. Hancock is a lawyer and small business owner.
His firm, Business Laws, Inc., publishes information on all
aspects of federal business law. He first practiced law as
associate and later partner of a small Cleveland law firm,
and subsequently joined the legal staff of TRW, Inc., where
he was promoted to senior counsel. Hancock holds J. D. and
LL.M. degrees from Case Western Reserve University,
where he graduated first in his law school class.